TRUE CRIME

REAL-LIFE STORIES OF GRAVE-ROBBING, IDENTITY THEFT, ABDUCTION, ADDICTION, OBSESSION, MURDER, AND MORE

Edited by
LEE GUTKIND

InFACT
BOOKS
Pittsburgh

CONTENTS

CONTENTS

INTRODUCTION:
BAD MEN DO WHAT GOOD MEN DREAM?

Lee Gutkind

When I was a teenager, I had two friends—Glick and Girson—who committed murder while robbing a mom-and-pop grocery store. This took place in Squirrel Hill, the well-to-do Pittsburgh neighborhood where I grew up, near the lovely, sprawling Frick Park and a short walk from the high school from which all three of us had recently graduated. The two old people who ran the store, Mr. and Mrs. Cua, were notoriously cranky, which made kids visit their store more often than necessary just to aggravate them, asking stupid questions or haggling over the price of a package of cigarettes or a can of Coke. The store was dirty and dusty, and the shelves were rather bare. No way could the Cuas have made enough to live on from that store—and in fact, there were constant and unsubstantiated rumors that they were hoarding mounds of cash in their living quarters in back of the store. I never talked with anyone who knew where the rumors had started. It was just something we high school kids—freshmen to seniors—were always speculating about.

Probably the supposed hidden fortune was a joke. I mean, why would anyone live in such filth if they had the means to bask in luxury—or, at the very least, hire someone to dust their shelves? It seemed kind of senseless to me. I dreamed daily about owning a Harley Sportster and a Corvette Sting Ray, and if I'd had the cash I'd have gone hog wild spending it. Not that I envisioned the Cuas revving a souped-up engine or screeching around corners with abandon. But they could have had a Cadillac—and a mansion on Nob Hill, wherever that was.

Glick and Girson must have thought they would find the stash—or, frankly, in retrospect, who knows what they thought? They obviously didn't think things out too clearly or carefully. I wouldn't have imagined that they were, together or individually, capable enough to plan and execute a robbery—or any organized project or event. I knew Girson as kind of a bully, mean and moody, and Glick was a victim in high school. Not that he was pushed around or pummeled; let's just say he was not highly respected. His grades were poor, his attendance record in high school worse, and he seemed to always be in dutch with his family.

Anyway, it wasn't a very successful robbery: As I recall, their "take" was less than $20—quite disappointing. Which is maybe why Girson—he was supposedly the guy with the gun—shot Mr. Cua to death.

I haven't seen either of those guys since they were arrested, but I think about them nearly every time I pass the site of the murder. Glick, I am told, committed suicide, and the last I heard, Girson is still in prison. I don't know if either of those stories is true. I've done a bit of Googling, unsuccessfully.

Why do I remember this event—while so many of my high school memories have faded? Any murder is shocking, of course, but for me there's a mystery to it—so many unanswered questions. These guys came from comfortable, respectable middle class families, not unlike mine. Girson's dad was a merchant, as was my father. Our moms were typical 1950s/1960s housewives, stay at home moms. Glick's parents were divorced, I think, though I don't remember for sure. But they both lived in a good neighborhood, and were—I think everyone would have said—"good kids." We all were. Maybe not so popular or perfect, by any means; we did a lot of things wrong—but we knew what was right. What on earth were they thinking? What went through their minds that prompted them to get a gun and shoot down an old man for the sake of a few dollars?

It was crazy—though also not entirely. Maybe not out of the realm of possibility, at all, especially for young and rebellious boys.

Having been, myself, a fairly rebellious boy, I frequently wonder how close I came to doing something similarly destructive— something awful that I would forever regret. In high school and the few years afterward, before I went into the military and finally to the university, I was all about taking chances with weapons and illegal substances, and setting off on illogical adventures—just because I wanted to do something different and also, I guess, because I wanted to call attention to myself.

So the story of Glick and Girson is, for me, I think, a sort of worry stone: something to turn over again and again, and examine from various angles. Am I capable of such an act? Could I be that stupid—so ruinous to my life? Or in the reverse, could I be a victim?

As I read through this collection recently, I thought about those long-ago murders, and about why true crime stories have such a strong appeal for so many of us.

There's no doubting our fascination: Just talk with magazine or book editors, or librarians, about the popularity of true crime stories. Better yet, turn on your TV. It's nearly impossible to escape crime programs—whether fiction or nonfiction. In prime time and rerun, there are the many popular ripped-from-the-headlines dramas like "Law & Order" (and its numerous spin-offs), "Criminal Minds," NCIS, and CSI. The selection in true crime is equally rich. Two popular long running network shows—"Dateline NBC" and "48 Hours"—are devoted to true crime. There's also an entire true crime cable channel, Investigation Discovery, which, according to the New York Times, grew 69 percent in total viewership from mid 2010 to mid 2011. They've got some rather raunchy-sounding crime series programs, like "Blood, Lies and Alibis," "Sins and Secrets," and my personal favorite, "Happily Never After"—and some recognizable personalities anchoring these shows, like "On the Case," with the former popular CNN anchor Paula Zahn.

People can't get enough of these stories—but why? I think true crime stories fascinate because they make us more aware of how vulnerable we are not only as potential victims but also, perhaps, to a certain extent, as perpetrators. I remember something a character on one of the Law & Order series programs—Detective Goren, played by Vincent Donofrio—observed in one episode: "Bad men do what good men dream."

• • •

One day recently I sat down and read the stories in this collection one after another. It's not that I hadn't read them before—to the contrary, I have read and reread each repeatedly as editor, but never all in one great burst. Originally, I had intended to read the entire manuscript over the course of a couple of days, but one story seemed to flow and feed into the next . . . I was hooked. Even during two brief coffee breaks at Starbucks that day and evening, I couldn't quite disconnect myself. I was caught up in the stories, imagining myself as victim, perpetrator, bystander.

But there was something else about these pieces, in particular, that kept me riveted and reading, story after story, on that day. That's the personalities, the voices, the motivations and emotions of the writers telling the stories. These writers—among them are criminals, law enforcement officers, and victims—elevate the substance of the gritty crime, leading the reader far beyond the surface and the hype. They transform the stories they are dramatizing into rich, high-powered literature in which characterization and motivation are as important, perhaps even more important, than the stories themselves. I should say that I believe that the literary quality of these nonfiction stories sets them apart from the run-of-the-mill crime fare. They dig deeper than the average sensationalist fare on television. There's great tone and style in each piece included here—but also substance to ponder and discuss.

And that, after all, is the challenge and the mission of the creative nonfiction writer: to take a true story, gather the details from every conceivable source and angle, and employ literary techniques— dialogue, description, inner thoughts and points of view—to make the characters, the locations, and the stories themselves as vivid and cinematic as possible.

It goes without saying that such a task is difficult—but the stories in this collection demonstrate how effective such approaches are when done well. Who could resist getting caught up in the story of AC Fraser, confronted by a prison guard who seems to know more about her than she knows about herself? Or Lacy M. Johnson's mind-boggling story of being kidnapped by her ex-boyfriend, or Steven Church's unconventional meditation on ears and savagery, which takes on everything from Mike Tyson to Travis the Chimp, and David Lynch to Van Gogh. Included also in this book are stories about gang violence in the suburbs; women police officers in physical combat with criminals; and a fascinating deconstruction of the origin of a murder, which traces the perpetrator back in time, examining the circumstances that helped to determine his life and that may have propelled him directly into the act of killing.

Two of the stories included in this collection are especially important to mention—for both are taken from a seemingly unlikely source: your daily newspaper. Many journalists, critics, and pundits like to say, these days, that long form narrative can no longer exist in newsprint—that newspapers, not to mention the art of reporting, are dying. The stories here put the lie to that contention: For "The Lynching of Claude Neal," Ben Montgomery of the Tampa Bay Times conducted dozens of interviews over a two-year period with historians, residents of Jackson County, Alabama, and relatives of 23-year-old Claude Neal, lynched in 1934—a crime for which no one has ever been punished. Montgomery's story is a riveting reminder of an era that will forever haunt and taint our national legacy. The other newspaper piece, from The Arizona Republic, is equally captivating: Shaun McKinnon's reconstruction of the days and hours leading up to the Gabrielle Giffords shooting. The detail of McKinnon's reporting and his crisp, hard, Hemingwayesque prose, which tells the story from the points of view of the shooter and many of the victims and bystanders, create a unique and compelling profile of a crime the country will never forget.

Finally, the collection ends with an in-depth interview with a master of the true crime genre, Erik Larson, author of books including *The Devil in the White City* and, most recently, *In the Garden of Beasts*. In an interview conducted by *Booklist* critic and essayist Donna Seaman, Larson explained how he begins his work by reading broad histories and, as he puts it, "circling in," looking for his main characters. Then, he heads into the depths of archives such as the Library of Congress, devoting years to capturing the minute and compelling details of the characters and events, and gradually moving out into the field to immerse himself in the locations where the events took place. He becomes fully engaged in all aspects of the story before sitting down to write, explain, and recreate it.

"If the story doesn't come alive for you, it's not going to come alive for your readers," Larson says, and I think that says a lot about the appeal of true crime nonfiction. The stories here, I think you will find, gnaw away at you, piquing curiosity and feeding the hunger to understand more about human nature—why we do the things we do, how we can end up in previously unimaginable situations, and also what we are afraid of. Our lives can change in an instant: seemingly normal, nondescript teenage boys, for example, can become murderers; citizens waiting in line to meet their congresswoman can be massacred; a car accident can begin a chain of tragic events that unfolds over decades.

And the thing is, you can never know how you will react to these events should they happen to you or near you. You can't know how you will react to someone who threatens you, hurts you, or just confuses you. Will hunger for money and adventure—or boredom, or stored-up frustration and anxiety, or something else entirely—push you over the edge into a world from which there is no return? I don't know. We can't know, until it happens to us. But reading this book, true story after true story . . . you have to wonder.

ORIGAMI
& THE ART OF IDENTITY FOLDING

AC Fraser

"Fraser. Get Up."

A stream of bright light smacked my eyes. I groaned and rolled over to bury my face in a cool spot on my pillow.

"Now." The tone of the guard's voice made it clear that she would brook no dissent. "Sheriffs will be here to get you in half an hour." As she spoke, the beam of her flashlight continued to dance along the side of my head.

This wasn't right. My early morning fog of confusion transformed into a cloud of annoyance. "You've got the wrong person," I mumbled, not bothering to move. "I have video court here in the afternoon. Go find the sucker who actually does have to get up now."

"I have found her," insisted the voice. "The papers say *Fraser*. And what the papers say goes. Get up." The guard rattled the omnipotent papers as she turned from the doorway and disappeared back into the unit.

I lay there and listened to the squeak of rubber-soled shoes and the clatter of keys fade into the distance.

Quiet engulfed the room. Silence was a rare commodity in jail, harder to find than a toothpick-sized joint of contraband pot. Day in and day out, the prison was filled with the sounds of women—inmates and guards alike—playing out the pageant of institutional existence. Shouts and laughter competed with television and radio noise. Buzzers and beeps and clicks of electronic locks percussed. Walkie-talkies crackled, and overhead speakers hissed. The voice of Control rode roughshod over the cacophony, directing the show. Yet, in my cell, hours before dawn, the only sounds were the ragged breathing of my roommate Sara and a soft purring from the ventilation system.

I tossed back the thin cotton blanket. Cold air hit my skin and shocked me fully awake. I dressed quickly, slipping into the Alouette Correctional Centre for Women's uniform of gray sweats. Wrenched from the freedom of dreams and swathed in fleece, I was again just another inmate: Number 05073507.

In a way, I enjoyed the sense of community. This wasn't my first trip to jail, and being back felt like returning to the neighborhood bar where everyone knows your name. In prison, we were all the same. Dealers, fraud artists, car thieves and robbers alike were smoothed out and refolded identically: We were a thousand paper cranes, our gray wings incapable of flight.

My bed made and my body dressed, I ventured out into the unit in search of the insistent guard. Under dimmed lights, the dusky violet modular seating and pea-green walls looked especially nonstimulating. *Just the effect the decorators were going for*, I thought.

The guard was exactly where I knew she would be, waiting in the glassed-in office by the unit's front door. Though the regular cadence of institutional life drove some crazy, most inmates were creatures of habit. I, especially, found the predictability reassuring.

True, on the outside, you got to hang out with Freedom. Freedom was a cool chick—totally outside the box. She had a penchant for all-night dancing, ice cream for breakfast and black platform boots. The problem with Freedom was the questionable company she kept.

Freedom rolled with her junkie friend, Chaos. Chaos had no idea who you were, nor did she care. She was an instigator par excellence. Just when you started having fun, Chaos broke a window, smoked the rent money, and got into a fistfight with your boyfriend. Midnight moves were her trademark, and she always waved to you as the police hauled your ass off to jail.

Nope, I didn't miss either one of those crazy bitches.

Life at ACCW was a series of scheduled guarantees: wake, dress, eat, work, eat, lockdown, work, eat, TV, lockdown, sleep and repeat. Within this framework, I was at ease, firmly rooted in time and space.

The guard escorted me across the grassy quad, still dark in the predawn hours. I took a last breath of fresh air before I was loaded into the back of the British Columbia Sheriff Service's modified Chevy transport van. The metal interior of the van was cool, but its decor was luxurious compared to our destination. The driver fired up the engine, and the rocking of the van lulled me back to sleep.

We arrived at 222 Main Street within the hour. Vancouver's criminal courthouse, a brick bastion in the heart of the city's infamous Downtown Eastside, was surrounded by a seething landscape of poverty, drug abuse and degradation. As if in empathy, the city cells, located deep within the bowels of the courthouse, were similarly barren and filthy.

The sheriff removed my shackles and ushered me into a cell that could have doubled as a walk-in refrigerator. Two long plastic benches were riveted to the cinder block walls. A small metal sink and toilet were partially screened from view by a three-foot privacy wall. Unblinking, a security camera monitored the entire area. I sat on one of the benches and folded my body into a tiny ball. I leaned my head back on the wall. The bricks, once white, were covered in the grime of a thousand faces. They looked vaguely organic. I closed my eyes and settled into a fitful sleep.

"Fraser," shouted a male voice.

I woke with a start, unsure of how long I had been asleep. It felt far too early for court, and yet, there was a man standing at the door of my cell. He was dressed in the navy-blue uniform of BC Corrections.

The officer was in no mood for pleasantries. "What's your address?" he demanded, placing his meaty hands on his hips.

I paused for a moment, held back by a deeply ingrained suspicion of anyone in a uniform.

"What's your address?" he asked again. Irritation leaked all over his words like urine from a stopped-up cell toilet.

"My address?" I was loath to give away any more information than necessary. "Are you serious, buds? I think you know perfectly well where I'm living." I laughed, attempting to smooth over my noncompliance, and gave him the address for ACCW.

The officer's brow tightened. "Your real address, smartass."

I considered the situation. The officer was clearly determined to get the answer he wanted. *Well, it's not as if he can't just look it up in the computer*, I thought. I sighed and gave him my last known address.

The disclosure seemed to bolster the officer's indignation, and he settled into the mood as if reclining into his favorite La-Z-Boy. He rocked back on his heels and folded his arms across his chest. "That's what I thought," he replied, "but I didn't recognize you out of your nurse's uniform." A smug look danced across his countenance. It was the look of a man who knows something you don't. I hated that type of look. It made me nervous. The officer gave a final smirk and left.

Nurse's uniform?

Since I had nothing but time, I tried to tease out some sense from the encounter. I didn't recognize the officer's face. In fact, nothing about him was distinguishing. He looked as unique as one bowl of oatmeal from the next. Officer Porridge—the thought brought a smile to my face.

He knew who I was; that much was certain. But I was used to that by now.

Police, court, corrections—all were in the business of knowing about people like me. Over the years, irrefutable facts had been compiled about my person. I became a "KNOWN OFFENDER." My race, place and date of birth were recorded. My fingerprints and mug shots were indelibly inserted into the digital record. The system meticulously documented our encounters with colored labels: SUSPECT, CHARGED, SUSPICIOUS PERSONS, FRAUD, FALSIFY, THEFT, POSSESSION, IMPERSONATION, PROHIBITED. The police knew where I was supposed to be and what I wasn't supposed to be doing. All these bits of data were bundled together in a single file and preserved for posterity within the Canadian Police Information Centre.

Yet, even the system appeared to understand the transitory nature of identity. CPIC listed my physical statistics as "EYES BLUE, WAS 173 CM (5 FT 08 IN) 054 KG (119 LBS) IN 2005-10," as if at some point between then and now, I may have grown to new heights of depravity.

It wasn't just physical details that were slippery and transmutable. Names were just a series of letters, easily rearranged into something unrecognizable. Various aliases, like loose bits of yarn, had to be carefully wrapped around the tangled ball of information.

The real trouble seemed to arise when the system sought to nail down more ephemeral aspects of character. Inexplicably, my CPIC file warned, "<<CAUTION>> VIOLENT." How had they come up with that characterization? Was there a look in my eyes that even I had missed in the mirror? Were police officers trained, like their canine counterparts, to sniff out the most primal of human emotions?

Still, I can't fault the system for its shortfalls. How could they be expected to know who I was when I no longer knew myself?

There was a time when my identity had been held in place by the web of relationships that was my life. I was the person I thought my family, friends, co-workers and schoolmates wanted me to be. I was considered a success in the eyes of others. I was miserable.

The change came both in the blink of an eye and so slowly that I didn't notice until well past the point of no return. I discovered crystal meth and fell instantly in love. From the first inhalation, I knew I had found an answer. I became the person I had always wanted to be: I was creative, funny, outgoing, ambitious, and full of energy.

As for the rest of it, "magna est vis consuetudinis"—great is the power of habit. Daily drug use begat daily crime. This alchemic combination of drugs and crime reshaped my concept of identity. Speed and sleep deprivation blurred the already thin veil between reality and fantasy. The first time I slipped into another person's identity, I felt as if I had been given the keys to the universe.

Whereas I could envision myself in only one shape before, now I could see hundreds of possibilities. Had I moved closer to my true essence, or was I now so radically removed I could no longer tell who I was meant to be? As cold leached from the walls of the cell and permeated the thin layer of my sweatsuit, I wondered if I would ever know the answer.

"Hey. Get up and move over. You've got friends in here with you now." Officer Porridge was back. He shepherded three inmates from Surrey Pretrial Services Centre into my cell. So much for first come, first served. I pulled myself up into a seated position and cleared half a bench for the new arrivals.

A woman as broad as she was tall sat down on the bench beside me. There was a piece of what I hoped was breakfast stuck to the front of her sweatshirt. She ran a hand through her black hair, lank and greasy, and started in on introductions.

"I'm Guno. This is Billy," she said, nodding across the cell at a pretty, young native woman, who was so thin I could see her collarbones jutting from beneath her sweatshirt. Guno pointed to the woman on Billy's left. "That one can't talk. Don't know her name. She's new. But she seems OK." The mute woman had thin grey hair and looked elderly, although you could never really tell in jail. I'd seen plenty of women prematurely aged by the combination of drugs and hard living. The last woman smiled, revealing a large black gap where her two front teeth should have been.

During the time I'd been asleep, the city cells had come to life. The neighboring cells were packed with men. Despite the thick metal doors, crude conversational snippets were hurled in our direction. Billy, Guno and I joined in the fun, hollering back insults and encouragement. Soon, the hallway sounded like a drunken frat party.

Within minutes, heavy footsteps rounded the corner. My new friend from BC Corrections had returned. He ignored the sounds of baritone and bass, and instead walked directly up to our cell. With his not-thin, not-fat face pressed against the small window in the door, he looked directly at me. "Fraser! What's all the yelling about? This is your last warning. Knock it off!"

"What's that asshole's problem?" asked Guno, once he was gone.

"No kidding. He's riding you pretty hard," agreed Billy, while our fourth companion nodded emphatically.

"I don't know," I said. I settled back into my corner. Paranoia flitted at the back of my mind like a wasp trapped inside a car on a hot summer day.

My name was called for court within the hour. I was guided into the small pen at the side of the courtroom reserved for prisoners in custody. After the stark interior of cells, the wood and carpeting of the courtroom felt opulent. I stared at the various faces in the gallery as the lawyers went through their pro forma motions.

The prosecutor ran through a litany of my current charges. As he summarized his case, I felt as though he were talking about someone else. But there was no way around it; he was talking about me. The prosecutor was handing the judge still pictures taken from security camera footage. The pictures clearly showed my boyfriend, my dog and me carrying boxes of car audio systems out the doors of Audio Video Unlimited. (To be fair, the dog was simply along for the ride.)

Early in my criminal career, I took care to avoid detection, concealing my identity with various disguises. Recently, though, a more nihilistic mood had taken root. I no longer bothered with wigs or costumes. I simply walked in as my own tired, strung-out self. This was a mask well known to Vancouver's Identity Theft Task Force. Arrests ensued.

My carelessness was a sign of a deeper malaise. I felt like a piece of origami paper that had been folded and refolded into a hundred different shapes. All that was left of me was a two-dimensional sheet, marked with the lines of past contortions. I felt weakened to breaking along those creases. I didn't want to be myself, and I no longer had the energy to be anyone else.

I'd had grand illusions when I got into the game. Everyone does. There isn't a dealer on Hastings who doesn't think he's going to make it to kingpin; every two-bit teenage gangster from the suburbs sees himself as a potential Hell's Angel. I had envisioned myself starring in a modern day remake of the exuberant con-man classic "Catch Me If You Can"—complete with international intrigue, haute couture and stacks of credit cards that never maxed out. The reality, as realities tend to be, was far smaller. My crimes, as I heard them read out loud in open court, sounded downright pathetic.

There was no glamour in the prisoner's box. The names being read by the prosecutor weren't just pieces of information on paper. They were people who were victims of crime. My crimes. And what had been the point?

I wasn't amassing luxury goods or having exciting adventures. I was barely enthusiastic enough about life to get out of bed. My drug addiction was a money pit. Even paying the rent was a monthly struggle. I was practicing subsistence fraud—a third-world farmer clinging to a minuscule plot of land in hopes of wringing out an existence from the rocky soil. My crops were meager and wilted, regularly wiped out by drought and flood cast down upon me by the police and my own stupidity.

"Fraser, get up. You're being moved."

I opened my eyes and was not surprised to see the blurry white face at the door.

I was placed in a small, triangular cell. Even more barren than the last, this cell was devoid of everything but floor, walls and a ceiling. I was the sole occupant. No camera hung above the door.

Officer Porridge followed me into the cell and swung the door towards shut. Only an inch of space separated the two of us from the outside world. "Do you know who I am?" he asked. His cheeks pinkened like cherries dropped into a bowl of oatmeal.

My heart raced. I didn't like being backed into an unmonitored cell with no witnesses and one very pissed-off corrections officer.

"No," I spat back. "Why don't you tell me who you think you are?"

The cherries smeared into a layer of jam that seeped down Officer Porridge's neck and disappeared beneath the navy collar of his uniform. "Do you know why you're here?" he asked. He clipped each word as if biting it off with his rounded, white teeth.

"That depends on your definition of *here*," I countered. "Do you mean this particular cell or jail in general? Or . . . are we talking existentially?" I laughed and stared into his eyes. "Probably not that last one, eh?"

"Quit talking," he growled. He moved toward me, jabbing his finger in my direction. "You messed with the wrong people. I've personally passed your picture around to every sheriff and every corrections officer. They all know who you are and what you did. And they all hate your guts." The officer paced the small expanse of the cell with the frustration of a tiger trapped for years inside a zoo enclosure. The decibel level of his voice ratcheted up with every sentence.

As he screamed, I ransacked my pockmarked memory. I still didn't recognize him. Not in the slightest.

There is a reason identity theft is called the faceless crime. For the perpetrators, it is impersonal and cold. People's lives are reduced to a series of numbers: addresses, birth dates, card limits, overdraft amounts, credit scores. The victim never sees the face of the person who ran up the credit card bill and trashed the credit rating. Even something as violent as robbery or assault has more of a human component.

I never met the rightful owners of the identities I stole. I never had to look into their eyes and answer for what I had done. To me, they were simply information shells to be slipped on and discarded after use.

And yet, right here in my face was a victim demanding a response.

The officer's cheeks and neck turned deeper shades of red and purple. "Have you ripped off so many people that you don't even recognize me?" He crossed his arms over his chest and stood glaring, starched uniform heaving under his self-embrace. He took one last look at me and spoke so quietly I almost missed what he was saying. "I think you know exactly who I am." And then he was gone.

Alone in the cell, I could hear my heart beating furiously. I lay down on the cool concrete floor. Steadied by the hard surface, I closed my eyes and tried to remember.

Like smoke rising from a meth pipe, a memory wafted up from the depths. The Nurse. I remembered a nurse. I grasped for her name but failed. All I could remember were the scrubs. The scrubs and the fear.

The fear was always present, to one degree or another. It lurked, herpetic, beneath the surface of my existence. No amount of dope or desperation could ever eradicate it.

In its most benign form, the fear manifested as extreme procrastination. I had spent weeks getting to know the Nurse. I memorized her address, birth date and Social Insurance Number. I knew which hospital she worked at, what her shifts were and how much she got paid. I learned where she liked to shop and what type of birth control she was on. I studied her banking habits. I digested information bit by bit until I felt like I inhabited her life.

Once I had convinced myself, I set about compiling the items I would need to convince others. I smoked cigarette after cigarette while my Fargo card printer screeched layer after layer of color onto plain white cards. Finally, I had a set of ID I was happy with: a fake Alberta driver's license and BC Care Card with her name and my face. Everything was in place. And still I waited. Days passed without me leaving my house.

Time was running out. The rent was late. Very late. If our landlord didn't receive the money by sundown, eviction was imminent.

At 4:30 P.M., the fear stirred. Tiny ripples of anxiety floated through my stomach, belying the fear's true size. An hour and a half until the bank closed.

"Get dressed," I commanded myself. "You can at least get dressed." I slid the scrubs I had bought at Value Village over my bare skin. The cotton felt cold and rough. I had passed over patterns of laughing frogs and balloon bouquets in favor of a plain blue pair. Now, I found myself wishing for those cheerful, lighthearted patterns.

By the time I tightened the drawstring around my waist, my hands were shaking. My hipbones were sharp under the cloth. I worried the bank teller would wonder why a nurse was so skinny.

An hour and a half. "Just do it and get it over with," I thought. "Hurry now, before the fear metastasizes."

I had picked a branch far from where the Nurse lived. This location of the Toronto Dominion Bank was housed in a small strip mall off the Fraser Highway in Aldergrove. The neighborhood was rural; I hoped for a trusting, corn-fed teller with milky, innocent eyes.

I hitched a ride on the back of my boyfriend's old Honda motorcycle. As we rode, I felt the scrubs snapping against my legs in the wind. When we arrived at the bank, I stood staring at the glass-front windows, wondering what awaited me inside. I took a deep breath and crossed the parking lot.

Inside the bank, I was immersed in air-conditioned silence. A handful of customers were huddled in conversations with tellers, conducting their financial transactions with tactful discretion. One teller was free. A man, mid-50s. Not my favorite type by far, but it would look strange to hesitate. I arranged my face in a caregiver's expression, soft yet stoic. I forced my mouth into the smallest of smiles and walked toward his counter. My sensible, white sneakers, the type seen in hospital hallways everywhere, squeaked loudly with each step.

I wished I was anywhere but there.

I set my purse on the countertop and drew out a small wallet. The teller looked bored and a bit tired himself, as if he were eager to reach the end of the workday.

"I can't wait to get these shoes off," I said, smiling ruefully. "I've been listening to them squeak all day."

The teller chuckled. "I bet," he said, "My feet are killing me. If they could talk, they'd likely be a lot louder than your shoes. What can I do for you?"

I relaxed slightly. So far, so good. Now go for the kill.

"I need to take some money out of my savings account," I said, "But I can't find my bank card for the life of me. Here's my Alberta DL. Oh, and my Care Card." I slid the identification across the expanse between our hands.

The teller looked at the cards. He began typing information into his computer. I was committed now. Sweat prickled against my blue cotton scrubs. Time slowed to a crawl.

Finally, the teller looked up. "How much can I get for you?"

"$1,500," I replied. Enough to get the landlord off my back with a bit to spare, but not enough to be suspicious. "I'll take that in hundreds, please. And in an envelope if you've got one laying around."

The teller handed me the envelope, and I walked out of the bank, the squeak of my shoes slow and steady.

Safely back on the Honda, I exhaled. Now that I had money in hand and the bank was disappearing over my shoulder, fear faded into the exhilaration that always kept me coming back for more.

The door to the tiny cell opened. Two sheriffs had arrived to take me back to Alouette. As they snapped the shackles in place around my wrists and ankles, I looked around for the corrections officer. He was nowhere to be seen.

The sheriff's van rocketed through the night. I thought about the officer and his nurse. Maybe she was his sister or his wife; maybe he didn't even know her. In the end, I supposed, it didn't matter. Whoever that officer was, he felt he was a victim. What I believed he truly wanted from me wasn't a pound of flesh or a public hanging, but recognition that harm had been done and that I had been the one to do it.

A small corner of my soul, folded and refolded to the point of breaking, disintegrated as I realized I didn't want to give him even that.

AC Fraser is a writer and yoga instructor from Vancouver, British Columbia. Her work has appeared in *The Incarcerated Inkwell*, *Contemporary Verse 2*, *ditch*, and *carte blanche*. She is currently enrolled in law school.

"Origami & the Art of Identity Folding" was the winner of the *Creative Nonfiction* True Crime Essay Contest, awarded by the editors of *Creative Nonfiction*.

LEVIATHAN

David McGlynn

For two hours each morning and two hours each night, Jeremy Woodley and I swam together in the moldy, six-lane pool appended to the back of the high school. We carpooled to and from workout—or, rather, since we were freshmen and not old enough to drive, our mothers carpooled, and Jeremy and I climbed into whichever car waited outside the pool to take us home. During the school day, we had four classes together, plus lunch. I won't say we were best friends, for the phrase suggests a romanticized loyalty we didn't enjoy. We were on the same team, but we spent most of our time competing against each other. I stood behind the blocks during the relays, watching the clock and subtracting out the splits, unconcerned about beating the opposing team so long as I beat *him*, even if only by one one-hundredth of a second. The other team would board the bus and go home after the meet, but Jeremy I had to see every day. He was a lean, handsome boy; a favorite among his teachers; and not above ribbing me for my slower split in the relay, my double chin, my flat-footed run. He poked his finger in my stomach and giggled like the Pillsbury Doughboy. It made the girls on the team laugh, and I hated him for that.

All the same, we were friends. At 14, proximity was the sole requirement for friendship; we were stuck together, so we stuck together. We'd earned spots on the varsity squad, but our lockers were on the far side of the locker room with those of the other freshmen, who swam at a different time. Dressing after workouts, we heard the older boys howl and swear and punch one another in the arm, their voices distorted and tinny from the rows of crosshatched metal grating between us. When they remembered we were there, two freshmen alone in the corner, they drifted over to steal our deodorant or twist our tits or goad us into boxing.

If we stuck up our dukes, we got punched. If we didn't, we got punched anyway. We learned to dress quickly, keep our voices low and misbehave in secret.

Jeremy lived in a red brick house, as impenetrable as an army fort, on a quiet cul-de-sac tucked deep within a labyrinth of cul-de-sacs filled with red brick homes. Twenty miles northwest of Houston, his neighborhood was far larger than mine; nearly 75,000 people lived in it, and his street was so far out of the way that I sometimes got lost looking for it whenever I rode my bike to his house. Jeremy had an older sister with two children of her own, an older brother fresh from the University of Texas and living at home to save money before his wedding, and a younger sister, who swam with my sister Devin in the evenings on the club team. His parents both worked for big downtown petrochemical companies and exuded a calm that suggested perpetual financial and familial security. They slept in twin waterbeds in their expansive master bedroom. I thought it was weird at first, too Ward and June, until Jeremy explained that waterbeds were more comfortable when you flew solo. "Unless you're doing it," he said. "Then the wave is cushion for the pushin'." He had a waterbed, too, and showed me how the wave was made by kicking his heels against the foot of mattress, moaning, "Oh, baby, oh yes."

The sturdiness of Jeremy's house—the long afternoons we were allowed to linger on the living room floor in front of the television, his mother dancing with a beer in the kitchen on Friday nights—made it my preferred refuge from my own house. My father had decamped for California three years earlier with a former evangelical missionary, who, in my mother's estimation, had stolen my father from our family and turned him into a religious nutcase. My mother's own hasty re-entry into marriage had been less than smooth. My stepfather technically lived with us in Houston, but most of his business was in Dallas and Austin. He was gone for most of the week, and on the weekends, his son and daughter flew in from Dallas. My stepfather's temper rivaled my mother's; in their ire, they were equally yoked. When they wore out screaming at each other, they got on the phone and screamed at the Texas Child Support Division, at my father, at my stepfather's ex-wife.

They were most tender when they were hurt. The night my mother broke her wrist by lunging at my stepfather—he stuck up his arm to deflect her, and she fell backward on the bathroom tile—was one of their best. He carried her to the car and drove her to the hospital. She returned home with her arm in a sling and his arm around her waist. A period of quiet affection followed. My mother made tacos for dinner, and my stepfather decided to work from home for a few weeks so he could help more around the house. I prayed it would last even though I knew it would not. I prayed the next injury wouldn't be so severe even while I braced for the possibility of greater violence.

When the violence came, however, it came not to my house but to Jeremy's. One night at the end of September, the beginning of our sophomore year, two men arrived at his house. They tied Jeremy to his brother, Greg, with a nylon cord and forced them to kneel on the living room carpet, side by side, near the entryway. Jeremy's father sat on the fireplace with a gun to his head. There's reason to believe, given the forensics report about the order of the shootings and knowing Mr. Woodley, that he begged for his sons' lives, but, of course, there's no way to know for sure. Greg was shot first, three times, execution-style, in the back of the head. Jeremy watched his brother's murder before his own, with four bullets instead of three. His father was beaten with the handle of the gun, made to kneel beside his sons and shot six times. All three were shot with .22-caliber revolvers, which are quieter than other weapons and don't discard shell casings. None of the neighbors heard anything. The men—police speculate that, given the number of shots fired, there were two of them—let themselves out, closed the door behind them and disappeared.

According to the forensics report, the killers arrived between 8:30 and 8:40 P.M. and were inside the house for less than 10 minutes. Jeremy and I talked on the phone until 8:20 that night. His mother left the house a little before 8 to pick up the girls— his sister and mine—from swimming practice. It was her night in the carpool. Mrs. Woodley dropped off Devin right at 8:40. I was watching television in the living room when the lights of her Oldsmobile flashed through the slats of the blinds. Devin slammed the front door behind her when she came inside. I heard the car shift into gear, Jeremy's mother and sister drive away. It was five minutes from our house to theirs.

My mother was awake when the phone rang. I'd gone to bed a half hour earlier, but I wasn't asleep yet. I was drifting, hovering, thinking about the weekend. My father was in town from California, and I was imagining the downtown hotel where we would stay, the room with a view of the Houston skyline, oysters on the half shell at Pappas, a Coke with a cherry bobbing in the ice. I heard my mother's ankles crack as she moved down the hallway to answer the phone in the kitchen. The phone rang again, then once more, before she picked it up. I heard her say hello. "What?" she said. "Is this a joke?" Then I heard her call my name.

I ignored her at first. She and my stepfather often argued after I'd gone to bed; I'd grown accustomed to the sound of her screaming in the kitchen and had learned to block it out. She shouted again before I understood she was calling for me.

I threw back the covers, opened my bedroom door. I stood in the hallway in my underwear. "What?" I shouted back.

"The Woodleys are dead! Oh, my God, the Woodleys are dead!"

"What?" I said. "What did you say?"

"That was Trey Smith's mother." She paused, then disappeared around the corner. "Come quick. It's on the news."

I did not go quickly. I walked slowly, not yet comprehending what she was saying and, therefore, certain that when I reached the end of the hallway, I'd learn she had said something different than what I had heard her say. Whatever had incited this panic would prove benign, an overreaction. Or maybe my unconscious understood what my waking mind did not—the magnitude of what waited for me in the kitchen, the way it would reroute the course of my life— and so it moved me slowly to keep me from burning my energy too quickly. It was 10:20 on a Thursday night. I wouldn't sleep again until Saturday.

A reporter stood in a blue windbreaker in front of Jeremy's house. Yellow *Police Line: Do Not Cross* tape stretched across his front yard. Siren lights flashed in the windows. The wooden sign announcing Jeremy's membership on the swimming team was nailed to the pine tree: a white circle depicting the maroon silhouette of a swimmer rising out of the water, Jeremy's name clearly visible beneath. "The victims are Barry Woodley and his sons, Greg and Jeremy," the reporter said. "They were shot execution-style. It appears to be a professional hit."

Execution-style? A professional hit? Such phrases belonged in a spy novel, part of some elaborate, far-fetched plot set behind the Iron Curtain. Not in real life, not in my life. They didn't make sense.

"Why would anyone want to kill them?" my mother asked.

I was stuck on the "what" and hadn't yet moved on to "why" or "who."

The camera showed the front of the house again, this time without the news reporter standing in front of it, just the curved cement walkway leading to the front step, the open door a creamy glow in the center of the screen. The camera panned closer and zeroed in on the sheriff standing in the doorway with his hands on his belt, his beige Stetson pointed toward the ground. He stepped to the side, and I could see through the doorway to the foyer and, just beyond, in the living room, to the bodies lying facedown on the carpet. They were barely visible, but I could see them. Jeremy was at the end, his left arm by his side, his face turned toward his brother. I recognized his T-shirt.

Then coroners were wheeling the bodies down the driveway, each one covered in blue tarps and strapped to a gurney. An ambulance waited with its rear doors hanging open, its siren lights dark and still. The phone started ringing. The news went to commercial. I stood up, turned off the set.

• • •

School was in session the next day, but no work was getting done. Between bells, the students processed through the hallways, desanguinated and silent, as if circling a field where a plane had crashed, the wreckage too hot to approach, impotent to do anything but watch the fuselage smolder, the rubber and glass melt into the earth. Some cried when they saw me, and others simply stared. Jeremy and I had been seen together so often that once people figured out who he was, they figured me out, too.

The swimming team roamed the hallways in a pack, gathering in the cafeteria and, later, in a classroom. We sat on the floor, and our friends came to sit with us and cry. The girls on the team leaned their heads against my shoulders and cried until their tears soaked through my shirt and the moisture slid down into my armpit. I'd have given anything to cry—I would have loved nothing more than an hour of clean, uncomplicated grief—but I was unable to manage it. I dropped my head between my knees and stared at the carpet, hoping that gravity would help. But no tears came.

In the afternoon, we slipped back to the pool and piled into an old Buick station wagon. The upholstery was a washed-out midnight blue and reeked of old cigarettes. The felt batting drooped from the ceiling. We left the radio off and the windows rolled up, the dull sunlight magnifying through the glass. We sat with our shoulders together, sweating and staring out the windows. The lawns were brown, and haloes of parched needles surrounded every pine tree. Only a few people were outside, mostly mothers with small children, but also the UPS carrier in his brown shorts and a man in a white polo, standing on the sidewalk and scribbling on a clipboard. I searched for clues, as though there was a chance I'd see the killers return to survey the scene of last night's crimes. Trey Smith, riding shotgun, stared down at his fist, opening and tightening it as if adjusting his grip on a handful of sand.

We turned onto Jeremy's street. News vans lined the curb, their heavy-duty yellow power cords snaking along the ground to the cameras. At 2 o'clock in the afternoon, the sky was stagnant and white; nothing was happening, but the cameras were rolling. The police were parked across the street. The driver of our car rolled down the window and told the reporters to get the fuck out of there. An officer walked over and asked for our names. Some of the boys gave fake names, but I didn't. The cop walked away, and a minute later, a detective in a beige suit came out of the neighbor's house and asked me to come inside. He knew about the carpool, and he knew my name.

"Did you know they were selling their piano?" he asked me. "Did he mention someone coming over to see it?" He used only pronouns—"they," "he."

"No," I said. I didn't know, and Jeremy didn't say anything.

The piano sat against the wall, like a desk, with picture frames arranged on top. I never once heard it played. It made sense they'd sell it.

I told the detective that Jeremy and I had talked on the phone until 8:20 the night before.

The detective wrote this down on his notepad. "He didn't mention anything?" he asked. "Could you hear anything in the background?"

"He was in his room, I think. We talked about the football game."

The detective nodded into his pad, crossed and uncrossed his knee.

"Didn't anyone see anything?" I asked.

"We're talking to everyone," he said. "You're probably the last person to talk to him, you know that?"

I nodded.

The detective gave me his card and told me to call him if I remembered more. I went outside and got back in the car. We drove to the end of the street and stopped. I got out and yanked the power cord from one of the news vans. It sprang loose, and the cord rocketed into the sky, like an eel swimming for the ocean's surface. The cord coiled over the hood of the Buick, and the plug bounced against the windshield. We jumped back inside the car and sped away. I was 15 and the last person to talk to Jeremy alive. I needed to do something.

• • •

The impunity given to the swim team in the days immediately after the murders was given to me for longer. I skipped class whenever I pleased, and no one said a word. My quota of tragedy and horror had been met, and I felt certain my luck would hold, at least for a while. The day a fire drill emptied the school into the parking lot, I proposed to Vince, a teammate, and Carla, his girlfriend, that we take off. They hesitated, but I urged them on. It was a Wednesday in November, not yet 10 in the morning; sitting in school seemed pointless. In the car, however, none of us could think of any place in particular we wanted to go. We drove to the mall. It was nearly empty at that time of day. An elderly couple strode around in bulky white tennis shoes, and a gray-suited businessman talked on a pay phone while leafing through the pages of his day planner. The security guard glared at us from across the food court. I regretted leaving school, but I couldn't admit that. "Let's go to my house and watch a movie," Vince said.

We turned on "Ghost" and settled down on his brother's unmade bed, the sheets beneath us musky and unwashed. Before Patrick Swayze got shot, Vince and Carla got up and went into the next room. I heard them having sex, and I sat and watched the rest of the movie with my arms looped around my knees. The sun through the plastic blinds was the color of mustard, the walls were squeaking, and I felt, as I'd felt every day since my mother called me from bed, that time was a problem. I wasn't in the wrong place; I was just there at the wrong time. I shouldn't have been watching "Ghost" at 1 in the afternoon, just as I shouldn't have been watching the news at 11 that night back in September. I shouldn't have spoken with a detective inside a stranger's house at 2 in the afternoon. I shouldn't have been inside a church in the middle of the week. I shouldn't have been mowing Jeremy's lawn, looking through the rear windows into the living room, where the bodies had been found.

When the movie ended, we went back to school. Vince and Carla were hauled into the principal's office and given three days of detention. A week later, I was called to see the assistant principal.

Rising from my desk and walking to the front office, I was ready for whatever punishment they were going to hand out. I even looked forward to it. Jeremy had been dead for two months, and I understood no more about why he'd been murdered than I did the night it happened. I wanted some confirmation that actions had consequences.

When I arrived at the principal's office, a detective was waiting to talk to me. He was denim-clad—jacket and jeans—and heavyset, a different man than I had talked to in the neighbor's living room. He shifted in the metal chair and tried to look casual by leaning on an elbow. He wanted to know whether Jeremy was ever mixed up in any gangs.

"Gangs?" I asked. I laughed, though I didn't think the question was funny.

The assistant principal laced his fingers together and stared down at his desk. The detective flipped through his notebook, turning the spiral-bound pages as if searching for another question. No one knew anything about the murders and probably never would.

December came, and with it the dark season. I arrived at the pool before sunrise and left after the last of the light had drained from the sky. The swimming team began to fall apart. Curt Wood locked himself in his car outside the pool and stayed there for hours. I knocked on the window, but he wouldn't let me in. Allen Swift wrecked his Honda CR-X twice before the collision that sent his girlfriend through the windshield. Trey Smith, who'd clutched his fist so intently the day after the murders, became a skinhead. He was the team captain, with scholarship offers from the best swimming programs in the country, but he said he felt as though someone was stomping on his chest. He wore ox-blood-red Doc Martens boots that rose above the curve of his calves and carried a 6-inch steel lag bolt in his pocket. Thick enough to join bridge girders, encased from top to bottom in chromed hexagonal nuts, it made his fist twice as large and 10 times as heavy.

With Trey and two other boys, I ventured into Houston's decaying inner-city wards, neighborhoods without streetlamps or lighted store fronts, neighborhoods with police cameras mounted to telephone poles. We went to poorly lit, spartanly furnished clubs (if "clubs" is the right word): boxy spaces without tables or chairs or windows, with linoleum on the floor and walls, and peopled by an inexplicable mix of scalped young men and tattooed women; black men in groups of seven or eight; and grizzled gray-haired men, who, I learned from my friends, were the ones you approached if you wanted a beer or a joint or a hit of acid. No one checked IDs at the door; I was allowed in without question. The bands were all thrash-punk. The drummers pounded away with their eyes closed. The guitarists leaned forward to crank the strings as though drop-starting a chainsaw. The vocalists dripped sweat as they ran the length of the stage and screamed.

There was a song that started out with a low, tempered riff on the bass and the singer whispering "Hi" into the microphone. He said "Hi" three times in a row—the first like a greeting, the second time louder and like a question, and the third a full-lunged, desperate wail. At that instant, the rest of the band launched into its electric protest, and the crowd began to brawl. I learned to recognize the band and the song, and I felt my pulse leap up whenever the singer mumbled out the first "Hi." I imagined Jeremy saying "Hi" when he opened the front door to the men who would end his life: his first "Hi" trusting and unassuming, his final "Hi" his plea to live as the revolver pressed against his skull. Other times, I heard the words as my own, directed toward the killers, the singer's screams my screams when I let loose all my fear and rage. I stood beside the woofer, the bass thumping in my face until my ears began to ring. I ground my teeth. I banged my head.

The stage lights burned the rank air as they flashed from white to red to blue. Three security guards in yellow windbreakers sat on the edge of the stage, pushing back audience members who scrambled up to dive into the crowd. Some in the audience stood in place and punched at the air; others stomped in a circle, throwing shoulders. Trey Smith fought the hardest and emerged from the pit with his knuckles and elbows streaked with blood, his eyes swollen. I liked it, too: the shoving and slugging, the slamming bodies, the armpits and sweat-drenched hair and bare backs, bodies hurtling from the stage, the atavistic urge to climb up from the swarming hive and swim along the tops of heads and shoulders, the lightness of being held aloft by a hundred unknown hands. There had been days, roaming through the empty halls of my school, when the entire world felt empty, as though Jeremy's death was the spark of an apocalypse and soon everyone on Earth, all the good people of the world, would disappear. My father lived 1,500 miles away, and my closest friend was dead. I took comfort in the claustrophobic heat, the beery sweat and body odor, the thump and strobe. Twice, I took a fist in the eye, and after the second time, I grew cautious. In time, my interest in the music waned, as well.

One afternoon, I walked into the locker room at the back of the natatorium and discovered Curt Wood holding his ex-girlfriend pinned against the wall. The veins in his bicep were pulsing, and he was screaming. "Get out of here!" he yelled. He held her by the neck with one hand and pointed at me with the other. "Get the hell out of here! This doesn't concern you." The girl—a tiny, blonde freshman; 14 years old—yelped a weak little "help." It was the most terrified sound I'd ever heard.

I grabbed Curt's shoulder and pulled him back. I put myself between him and his ex-girlfriend, who quickly fled the locker room, with her hands covering her face. Curt stumbled back a step, then spun and pushed me. I pushed him back, as hard as I could. His back slapped against the lockers. His eyes widened, surprised. He was built more like a football player than a swimmer, with thick, round arms and a solid chest. If he chose to fight me, I would lose. All the same, I was willing. I wanted Curt to swing at me so I'd have a reason to ram my fist between his eyes. I'd never punched anyone in the face before, but now, I squared up with Curt's face, aimed for the top of his nose.

He came toward me with both fists raised. I bit down to brace my jaw. Curt's arm sailed past my ear. He hooked his elbow around my neck and pulled my head until our ears were pressed together. I tried to duck out of his grip, but he held on tight. He began to sob. He let go of me and sat down in a puddle outside the showers. "She wouldn't listen," he said. "I only wanted to talk."

Curt wasn't a bad boy. None of my friends were. They were once loyal, generous, large-hearted boys. But one of us was missing, for unexplained and unfathomable reasons, and in his place, the seeds of darkness took hold. Like a root in search of water, the darkness snaked into the hearts of every person I knew, souring every good intention.

"I just wanted to talk," Curt said again. He looked up at me. I could tell he wanted me to stay with him, that he was asking for my help, but my own good intentions had gone, too, and I left him sitting in the puddle, alone.

The August before the murders, I'd called my mother from California to tell her I wouldn't be coming back to Texas. She'd threatened to send the police if I didn't come home. In May, we struck a compromise: She'd allow me to spend the summer with my father, a full 10 weeks rather than the three decreed by the divorce settlement, so long as I promised to return in time for school to start.

My father and stepmother lived in Laguna Beach, in a little yellow bungalow hidden behind an overgrown hedge of oleander. My stepmother grew dill and mint in terracotta pots, brewed iced tea in glass jars along the railing and prepared her Bible study notes in her bathing suit. Since leaving Texas, she'd resumed her evangelical vocation and worked as a children's pastor at a church on the inland side of Laguna Canyon. Her daughter, my stepsister Stacie, worked in a ladies' clothing shop in downtown Laguna Beach, where surfers slept in the backs of Volkswagen buses or lay in the sand with their wetsuits peeled to their waists. Honeysuckle popped along the fences, and from the dining room, we could see the ocean between the eucalyptus trees. I swam in the ocean every day.

I had a hard time finding a job in California, so I filled in as best I could. I rolled posters and shrink-wrapped lithograph prints for a local artist. I dug out a long strip of hardened cheat grass from the backside of a carpenter's workshop. I went door to door with a bucket and sponge, offering to wash cars. I didn't have any friends, and I didn't mind. On days off, I rode with my father to his sales calls. His territory ranged from Sherman Oaks, north of Los Angeles, to Oceanside, north of San Diego, and I was happy to ride along wherever he went. I was happy just to be with him again.

My father kept the car radio tuned to AM talk radio. For as long as I could remember, he'd liked talk shows, liked banter and argument, liked talk, though back when he lived in Texas, the talk was mostly about strategies for selling and motivating corporate teams. During the divorce, he'd accepted Jesus as his Lord and Savior, and now, he listened to Rush Limbaugh and Dr. Laura and then punched over to the Christian station and listened to Chuck Smith and James Dobson. They all said more or less the same things: America had grown too liberal, and its traditional foundations were eroding. Soon, the well of grace would run dry. Nations that turned away from God would be turned away by him.

My father's Honda Prelude sat so low to the ground that I imagined him changing lanes by sliding the car between the tires of a semi-trailer and emerging on the other side. The cars ahead of us appeared to dissolve into the rippling gas vapors. He kept the radio loud to drown out the traffic noise. Now and then, my father would say, "True," or else point to the radio dial and look at me as if to say, "You hear that?" but most of the time, he simply listened and nodded.

Dr. Laura and Dr. Dobson railed against promiscuity, and promoted chastity and marital fidelity, no matter the circumstances. I couldn't help noticing the irony: Infidelity, a failing of chastity, had catapulted my father from Texas to California and landed him in this car, on this freeway, listening to this show, nodding and pointing. My awareness of this irony had, up till then, worked as an antidote to my father's faith, but I was beginning to think of my life as attached to forces other than ordinariness, to God's will rather than chance. Each afternoon, when my father and I snorkeled through the reef and I watched the sunlight beam through the kelp and the garibaldi drift among the anemone, I wondered if everything—not only my parents splitting up, but the murders, too—were part of a grand design I couldn't see.

The more I thought about the things I heard in my father's car, the more sense they made. "Rebellion," by definition, is a movement against established authorities or normative values, whatever they may be. It's always defined by its context. I couldn't think of anything that bucked the cultural tide more than if I vowed to preserve my virginity. It smacked of naiveté and brainwashing, of blindness to the realities of the modern world, but in the last year, I'd known too many realities. I'd seen more than I bargained for. Too much had been lost. I needed something to refuse. I needed something to save.

Even though Stacie would be attending a Christian college in the fall, my stepmother worried that higher education would threaten her faith. So, in July, Stacie spent two weeks at a summer camp in Colorado Springs, analyzing "major worldviews" through the lens of Christianity. The afternoon of her return, she sat on the floor of her bedroom, cutting her cassettes with a pair of orange-handled kitchen scissors. She pulled the tape from the spools in long strokes, extending her arm toward the ceiling, as if she was curling ribbon. The wastebasket overflowed with her discarded music. Her open suitcase sat on the bed, full of books about how Oliver North was a scapegoat in the Iran-Contra affair, how feminism derived from communism, and how bands like The Beatles and Prince and Quiet Riot were lascivious and satanic.

"I'll take those if you don't want them anymore," I said.

"That's not the point," she said. "They shouldn't be in the world. The music shouldn't even be heard."

"The devil's music," I said. I meant it as a joke.

"Exactly," Stacie said.

That night, we went to dinner at the Old Spaghetti Factory in Newport Beach. My father liked the restaurant because we could eat for $5 apiece, including salad and dessert. He ordered waters all around before anyone had a chance to ask for a Coke. When the waiter walked away, Stacie announced she'd awakened as a Christian. She promised she would no longer remain passive in her faith. It wasn't enough to believe, she said; she'd use her college degree to work for the kingdom. Most importantly, she had come to understand the importance of chastity, and she vowed to defend her purity until her wedding night. My stepmother began to cry, stood up from her chair, wrapped her arms around Stacie and kissed the top of her head. My father smiled. He'd come through a difficult time and was in a good place again.

I smiled, too. It was a Saturday night, and beyond the restaurant's windows, the sun was setting over the Newport pier and boardwalk and the entire blue horizon of the Pacific. The wind through the open doors smelled of salt and sunscreen, and I could hear the valet attendants shouting as they shuffled the cars. We all ordered the same pasta dish, and when our plates were taken away, the waiter brought out silver cups of spumoni. We were happy, and our happiness had been wrought by Jesus, the source of all things good and dependable. That could only mean that a life without Jesus meant a life of fear—a high-wire walk across a treacherous ravine during which a single misstep meant not just a fall into the hell that follows death, but the hell of an unprotected life. The hell of murder. The hell of impermanent family. The hell of loneliness. All those hells were at bay, and scraping the spoon against the side of my dish to catch the last of the ice cream, I felt safer than I had in months. I didn't hesitate to promise God my entire life. I'd take up his cross and deny my every want and desire to follow him. I'd remain celibate until my wedding night. I'd vote Republican in every election. It seemed to me a fair trade.

David McGlynn's books include the memoir *A Door in the Ocean* and a story collection, *The End of the Straight and Narrow*, which won the 2008 Utah Book Award for Fiction. His work has appeared in *Men's Health, Best American Sports Writing, The Missouri Review* and other publications. He teaches at Lawrence University in Wisconsin.

GABRIELLE GIFFORDS SHOOTING:
A FATAL CHAIN OF EVENTS UNFOLDS
Shaun McKinnon

It begins with a phone call.

Hi, this is Gabby Giffords . . .

Supporters will gather for a quick photo. A few worried voters have tough questions to ask.

Come to Safeway tomorrow . . .

A friend plans to drop by to offer a thank-you. A photographer will pack his cameras.

Tell me how we can make government work . . .

Friday turns into Saturday.

In the darkness, at the north edge of Tucson, a young man checks into the Motel 6 by the interstate.

A set of lives are on a collision course, hurtling toward morning.

Sometime after 2 P.M. Friday, Jan. 7, the phone rang at Bill Badger's house in Tucson's Catalina Foothills.

Badger had just finished a few chores in the yard. His day had been full so far: a two-mile walk through Pontatoc Wash with Kirra, a 4-year-old husky-Lab mix. A drive in the spotless 1973 Jaguar XKE. He put the solar cover on the swimming pool and went inside.

The phone call was a recorded invitation from Gabrielle Giffords, the Democrat who represented the foothills in Congress. Come meet me tomorrow at the Safeway down on Ina Road, the voice on the phone said. Giffords wanted to talk to the people in her hometown.

Badger, 74, had never met Giffords, but he knew she was a military spouse, married to a Navy pilot turned astronaut. She understood veterans like Badger, a retired Army colonel. He could ask her about the higher premiums on the medical plan he used.

The Safeway event would fit into Badger's plan the next day to see a friend at a car show at a mall a little farther up the hills. He put it on his schedule.

Later that afternoon, the phone rang at James Palka's house off Orange Grove Road.

The phone call brought back good memories for Palka, a 63-year-old freelance photographer who met Gabrielle Giffords at an Independence Day celebration in Oro Valley more than three years earlier. He had supported her election and decided to photograph her at the July 4 event. The pictures had turned out nice, and he sent her copies, no charge.

After listening to the invitation to Giffords' event, Palka knew almost instantly he would attend. I'd like to see her again, he thought. She's one of the good ones. He would take his cameras, get photos of her mingling with the crowd.

Around 5:30 P.M., the phone rang at Roger and Faith Salzgeber's house in a secluded foothills neighborhood.

The automated call was as good as a personal invitation for Roger, a retired nursery wholesaler and a guy who had developed a taste for politics. He tells people he's "a Democrat with a capital L," a liberal ranter and raver.

Giffords was more conservative, but she won him over with her support for the health-care overhaul—for Salzgeber, 61, it was a case of political love at first vote.

He signed up as a volunteer in her 2010 re-election campaign the day after someone vandalized her district office, an attack many suspected was tied to her vote on the health-care bill. He had not seen her since the week after the election.

"Faith, let's go down there," he said. "It'll be a social call."

Toward the end of the afternoon, the phone rang at Susan

Hileman's house, an angular structure at the edge of Tucson National Golf Club.

Hileman did not think of politics, not exactly. To her ear, the invitation sounded more casual, friendly: *Hi, this is Gabby Giffords. Come to Safeway tomorrow and tell me how we can make government work better for you.*

Government. She knew who was interested in the government: her friend Christina-Taylor Green. At 9, the little girl was already an elected official, even if the student council at Mesa Verde Elementary was a little less official than the U.S. House of Representatives. Surely, she would get a kick out of meeting Giffords in person.

Hileman, 58, hung up the phone and called the Greens, who live around a couple of winding corners in the comfortable neighborhood. She invited Roxanna Green and both her kids, but Roxanna and her young son were busy. Well then, she asked, was Christina-Taylor up for a Saturday morning outing with Susan? Was she ever! They could make it a girls' day out.

The date was set.

Friday afternoon turned cool as the sun slid down over Tucson, the chill desert air still beholden to January. It's too cold to ride bikes, Raoul Erickson fretted, but his friend disagreed and in the end, she won and the two suited up.

Gabrielle Giffords did that a lot, talking her way to what she wanted. The year before, she wanted a third term in Congress.

Giffords was a former Republican and she could never be described as a liberal. But she was a Democrat in a year when a "D" by your name—and especially "D-Ariz."—was a liability. To win, she would have to muscle her way through the crowd of incumbent-toppling contenders.

She was up for the campaign, but the overt hostility bothered her. The threats, the gun at a town-hall meeting, the shattered window at her Tucson office. The crosshairs over her district on a campaign map distributed by former Alaska Gov. Sarah Palin.

She kept talking, and she got her way. After the election, the vote-counting took a week, but she returned to Washington the winner.

Even then, the violent imagery tugged at her. She confided her fears in Mark Kelly, her husband. "I'm somewhat concerned that at some point, someone's going to shoot me," she told him.

On Jan. 5, Giffords stood in the House chamber on Capitol Hill, repeating the oath of an office she had fought so hard to keep. When the Republicans staged an opening-week reading of the Constitution aloud on the House floor, Giffords joined in and proudly read the First Amendment.

Now she was home, and she wanted to ride her bicycle.

Erickson had picked her up at the airport and had given her a lift to her central Tucson condominium. She and Raoul had been friends since the 1990s and, with him, the politics were set aside.

The next day, she would be at one of her favorite events, "Congress on Your Corner." If all was going as planned, her staff by then had sent out a press release and an e-mail newsletter, and had triggered hundreds of automated phone calls to people in the area.

Before Giffords and Erickson finished their 10 miles, she snapped their picture with her cellphone camera, a reminder of a lovely Tucson evening.

Night cloaked Soledad Avenue on Tucson's northwest side. No street lamps illuminated the neighborhood where Jared Loughner lived with his parents.

This is dark-sky country, where light-pollution ordinances favor astronomical observatories on the peaks.

As midnight passed, the streets grew quieter. The lights blinked out in windows.

But on Friday night, Jared Loughner wasn't home. While the suburbs slept, he was on the move.

At 11:35, he eased a faded Chevy Nova into the parking lot at the all-night Walgreens drugstore along Ina Road. Traffic had thinned as midnight approached.

Most nearby businesses had long closed, their windows dark. The big-box sporting-goods store. The big-box office-supply store. The chain pizza restaurant. The greasy smell of cooking burgers and fries from the 24-hour fast-food joint across the street mingled with the exhaust of passing cars.

Loughner climbed out of the Nova and entered the drugstore. He headed for the photo counter, passing a cashier who chirps a cheery "hello" to late-night customers. Loughner left a roll of 35mm film, with the store's promise that prints would be ready in about an hour.

He fired up the Nova and steered back into traffic, heading off on a circular path through the night.

About an hour later, he stopped at a Circle K convenience store off Ina Road near Interstate 10. The store buzzed, even at the late hour, drawing motorists from the freeway and night owls seeking soda, cigarettes and beer.

Loughner then guided the car across the street to a Motel 6.

The motel sits off the main drag, alongside the railroad tracks that follow Interstate 10. A room costs $43.71 a night plus tax. Internet service is $3, cash only.

In Room 411, the king-sized bed wore a spread festooned with seashells, flamingos, cityscapes and saguaros.

The room looked out on Miss Saigon, a Vietnamese restaurant, and logos for Jack in the Box and the Waffle House hoisted on signs easily visible from the freeway. A rhythmic rumble of diesel rigs on I-10 provided the bass line to a soundtrack of traffic and the braying horns of the freight trains.

Loughner wouldn't stay in the room for long. He was on the move, rambling up and down Ina Road, racing the dawn.

At 2 A.M., Loughner dialed Bryce Tierney, a friend he hadn't seen since March. The two started hanging out their freshman year in high school. They shared a taste for the same music and for weed.

In 2007, they were cited for possession of drug paraphernalia when a sheriff's deputy found pipes, rolling papers and marijuana in Tierney's van.

Both later went through a court-run drug-diversion program and had the charges wiped from their records.

Tierney didn't answer the phone, so Loughner left a message.

"Hey, it's Jared," he said. "We've had some good times. Peace out."

About 20 minutes later, Loughner returned to Walgreens and retrieved his photos. In some of them, he was wearing a thong.

Another 90 minutes passed. He logged onto his MySpace page and posted a message: "Goodbye," it said. And then, "Dear friends . . . please don't be mad at me."

A little after 6, with dawn still more than an hour away, Loughner stopped at a Walmart near the Foothills Mall, about 4 miles from the motel and deeper into the suburban neighborhoods. A sign at the sporting-goods counter informed customers that no one would be on duty until 7 A.M.

Loughner doubled back toward the freeway, stopping at another Circle K not far from his house. Then a little after 7, he drove back to the Walmart and asked to purchase ammunition. The clerk disappeared in the back for a moment. During the delay, Loughner vanished from the store.

Less than 30 minutes later, he arrived at another Walmart, in a newer power center west of I-10 on Cortaro Road in Marana. The shopping center was still quiet at that hour. A few people followed the smell of brewing coffee to a Starbucks. Other stores and eateries remained dark as the sun peeked over the Santa Catalina Mountains.

Inside the store, Loughner bought ammunition and a black diaper bag, the kind with straps to be worn like a backpack.

He already had a gun.

It was a 9mm Glock, the kind police carry. Small, light, reliable. He had bought it over the counter at a sporting-goods store a few months back.

Loughner turned onto Cortaro and headed east, under the freeway. An Arizona Game and Fish Department officer was at the same intersection and saw an old Nova roll through the red light about 7:30.

The infraction had nothing to do with game or fish, but the department's officers can make traffic stops when public safety is at risk. Running a red light was enough. The officer pulled the Nova to the shoulder.

The 22-year-old driver handed over his license and registration, and the officer ran the records. There were no warrants, no red flags. The officer gave the driver a warning. Loughner went on his way.

Eventually, he returned to Soledad Avenue and the home he shared with his parents. The slump-block house with a flat roof was almost hidden behind the scraggly mesquite tree and cholla cactus in the neatly kept front yard. The driveway was the usual spot for the Nova and a battered white pickup truck.

Loughner started to remove the items he bought, when his father emerged from the house. The two started arguing, and Loughner pulled his black bag from the car. His father would later say he could tell something was wrong.

Loughner muttered and then fled, crossing the street to the north until he reached a dry wash that runs through the neighborhood. His father tried to chase him down, on foot and then in a car, but couldn't catch him. Loughner made his way down the wash and disappeared into the desert.

Bill Badger arose early Saturday morning and took Kirra out for their morning stroll. The retired Army colonel and his wife, Sallie, adopted the animal more than three years ago when their son found her at a pound.

The dog was tough. She had come into the pound with three gunshot wounds, but she survived. A home in the foothills and a 2 1/2 mile romp through the wash were her daily rewards.

Back home, Badger ate a bowl of Oat Cluster Cheerios Crunch. The cereal was supposed to be good for his heart, and it didn't taste half bad. He told Sallie he was headed to La Encantada shopping center a couple of miles up Skyline Drive. His friend was displaying a 2011 Corvette at a car show.

Badger would take the family Toyota and not the Jag.

"Just tell me when you'll be back," Sallie said. "I want the car later."

Badger stayed at the car show for about 10 minutes, then turned the Toyota back down the hill toward the Safeway.

Roger and Faith Salzgeber arose around 6 A.M., with a full day ahead of them. The University of Arizona was playing Stanford at 4 P.M. A season-ticket holder for 28 years, Salzgeber had more than just a passing interest in Wildcats basketball.

The couple had coffee and breakfast, then leashed up Lola and Ripley, their Australian shepherds, for what turned into a long Saturday walk.

Roger had met many of the neighbors after canvassing the area for Giffords, so he waved often as they turned down one street and up another. The roadways rise and fall through shallow arroyos. Around the houses, thickets of cactus and palo verde trees envelop the homes.

With yard work yet to be done, Roger and Faith left home around 9:10 and turned into the Safeway parking lot almost half an hour before the event was to begin.

Susan Hileman pulled into the Greens' driveway about 9:45 A.M. She wore jeans, a cardigan, a long-sleeve white shirt and cowboy boots. Christina-Taylor bounded out of the house, oblivious to the morning chill. Her mother pointed her back inside for a sweatshirt.

Roxanna Green chatted with Hileman while they waited.

"Does she really want to go with me?" Hileman asked. "Is there something else she would rather be doing?"

She and Christina-Taylor had become fast friends, working in the garden, going on outings. Sometimes they played pickup sticks. The little girl would distract Hileman and then move game pieces. They both knew about the subterfuge, and they both ignored it.

Roxanna smiled. "Anyplace she goes with you, she's happy."

James Palka packed his cameras. Not everyone shows up at these events on time, he thought. She's going to be there for an hour and a half. The best pictures will show her interacting with people and people standing in line chatting with each other.

There was no point in getting there early. Palka decided to wait. He would time his arrival for 10:30.

Jared Loughner waited at a Circle K on Cortaro Farms Road as the sun rose higher in the sky. He was on foot now.

He had left the Nova at the house, where his father had confronted him. He ran into the desert and hiked north and a little east. Along the way, he dropped the black bag, ammunition rattling inside.

At the Circle K, he called a cab. The car rolled up at 9:40, and Loughner got inside.

The route from the convenience store to the Safeway passes Pima Community College's northwest campus, backdrop for Loughner's recent past.

For four years, he had taken an array of classes. Algebra, business management, yoga.

In 2007, he even met his congresswoman there.

She was holding an event on campus. He submitted a question for her on a card, a question odd enough that a friend of his would remember it years later: "What is government if words have no meaning?" Giffords struggled to offer an answer. Still, her office later sent him a form letter, thanking him for attending. He kept it at home, in a locked box.

Later, his behavior grew more erratic. His outbursts scared some instructors enough that they began reporting incidents to campus police. Five times police went to classrooms because of him. In February 2010, he disrupted a class after another student read a poem about abortion. In May, he turned hostile when a Pilates teacher told him he would receive a B.

Loughner railed about ideas of free speech, about the meaning of words, then of numbers.

In June, a math teacher called campus police. She had used the number six in class. No, Loughner had insisted, bullying her. That number isn't called six. Call it 18.

Soon, he was waging his own private war with the school. He recorded a video tour of campus and posted it online.

"This is my genocide school," Loughner said after he received only partial credit on a late assignment. "And I haven't forgotten the teacher that gave me a B for freedom of speech."

After administrators saw the videos, and Loughner berated a biology teacher over an assignment, the college decided it was time for him to go. He would be removed from school until he had a mental-health screening.

Campus police delivered a letter of suspension to his house in September, reading it aloud in his garage. Loughner listened in silence.

But all that was months ago. Loughner had never returned to school.

Now he rode in a taxi, east into the foothills. A crescent moon was rising over the mountains, a thumbnail in the blue sky.

The drive to the Safeway took only a few minutes. At 9:54, the cab pulled into the parking lot at Ina and Oracle.

The fare was $14.25. Loughner had a twenty, so he told the cab driver he wanted to get change in the store. The driver accompanied him inside.

A few minutes later, Loughner emerged. A line of people stood in a walkway between the grocery store and the adjacent Walgreens, waiting to meet the congresswoman. A man walked alongside the line, asking people to sign a sheet of paper.

Loughner walked toward the front of the line and approached a young man sitting at a folding table.

"Is Giffords here?" he asked.

The shadows of the Santa Catalina Mountains had nearly retreated, giving in as they did every morning to the rising sun, when John Roll, the chief federal judge for Arizona, rounded the last curve on Valley View Road and parked outside St. Thomas the Apostle parish church.

The skies were clear, the air was brisk, the sounds of the city quieted by the mesquite and palo verde that clothed the desert landscape. The view, for those who sought it, stretched out for miles to the Tucson Mountains and the Santa Ritas, even as the creosote and acacia hemmed off the outside world.

Roll, 63, attended Mass here every morning. On weekdays, it prepared him for one of the hardest jobs on any bench, presiding over a district where the caseload had become overwhelming, worsened by judicial vacancies. In a letter to 9th Circuit Court judges, he had called the load a tsunami.

On Saturdays, the Mass typically preceded the day's chores, but today, Roll would mix business with pleasure, dropping in on Rep. Gabrielle Giffords at one of her "Congress on Your Corner" events to say hello and talk about her efforts to help the judges.

On this Saturday, the reading was from the fifth chapter of 1 John:

And we have this confidence in him, that if we ask anything according to his will, he hears us.

And if we know that he hears us in regard to whatever we ask, we know that what we have asked him for is ours.

From the church's hilly cloister, Sunrise Drive winds down out of the high foothills, curving gently, the sun providing encouragement from behind. Cyclists hug the edge of the road, slicing through traffic.

Sunrise turns into Skyline Drive. Apartments and businesses edge closer. Skyline turns into Ina Road, growing busier as it passes First Avenue and finally reaches Oracle Road. On the left is La Toscana Village shopping center—a Walgreens, some small shops, and the Safeway where the congresswoman would meet the neighbors.

Gabe Zimmerman was already unloading a pickup truck in front of the Safeway when Pam Simon pulled into the parking lot at 9 A.M. Zimmerman, Giffords' community-outreach director, had brought folding tables and blue-cushioned folding chairs, the good ones from the district office.

Simon pulled a stanchion from the truck bed. The short stands with retracting ropes helped keep people neatly in line.

She struggled with it. It was heavy.

"OK," she told Zimmerman with a laugh. "I'm doing chairs. You're doing stanchions."

Simon, 63, was an outreach coordinator in the district office. Technically, Zimmerman, 30, was her boss, but he wouldn't let her say so. "Pam, we work in a partnership," he would always say.

Together, they emptied the pickup, moving efficiently in the nippy shade of the building. Simon shivered. "I wish I'd brought some gloves," she said.

Zimmerman had also forgotten his gloves. Simon decided to find some cheap mittens in the Walgreens. "Do you want a pair?" she asked Zimmerman. No, he said, he was fine.

When Simon emerged from the drugstore, hands now hidden inside mittens, Zimmerman had more help. Sara Hummel Rajca, Giffords' constituent-services director and designated photographer, had arrived, as had Daniel Hernandez, the new intern, and Alex Villec, an intern who volunteered to help.

Zimmerman directed the setup. These events were practically his creation.

Giffords would greet constituents in a covered walkway on the north side of the Safeway entrance. Brick pillars, part of the architectural arches on the front of the building, helped create a sort of corridor. A folding table blocked the end closest to the glass Safeway doors. Visitors would enter from the Walgreens side and could stand or sit in a row of chairs.

An American flag and an Arizona flag provided a backdrop for photos. A round picnic table with benches, bolted to the concrete walkway, offered another place to sit and talk. The stanchions helped rope off the spaces between the pillars. Giffords liked to make sure she saw people in order as they arrived, so a line was vital.

A banner stretched between two poles read "Gabrielle Giffords, United States Congress," with the seal of the House of Representatives.

Zimmerman made sure an A-frame sign announcing the event was set up near the parking-lot entrance.

The interns laid out leaflets and issue papers on a second folding table. Sometimes the paperwork alone could answer people's questions. The staff would jump in as needed. Everything would be free-form, no speeches.

Simon liked that aspect of the events. People would show up and say, "I was Gabby's third-grade teacher." Or someone would spot Simon, a retired schoolteacher herself, and say, "Do you remember me, Mrs. Simon? I was in your class in 1985."

People started arriving for the event just after 9:30.

Simon sent Giffords a text. "It's chilly out here. Be sure to dress warm."

A few moments later, Giffords replied: "Too late. I'm on my way."

Simon turned to Zimmerman. "We're pretty much set up. I'm going to run in and get some hot cocoa for Sara and myself. Do you want anything?"

"No, I'm fine," Zimmerman said. He was focused on the event. "But ask Daniel." In the setup, she had almost forgotten the new intern.

Two more staffers arrived: Ron Barber, Giffords' district director, and Mark Kimble, a communications aide. About a dozen people were already in line.

A couple of minutes before 10, the congresswoman pulled up in her green Toyota 4Runner. She preferred to drive herself.

She parked and pulled out her iPad. At 9:58, her fingers tapped out a message: "My 1st Congress on Your Corner starts now. Please stop by to let me know what is on your mind or tweet me later."

Giffords walked briskly to the walkway. She wore a red jacket with red plastic beads around her neck and a short black skirt.

"Yea, you're here!" Simon said. Giffords greeted the staffers, then turned to her first constituent.

• • •

Roger and Faith Salzgeber had been up for hours and wanted to see Giffords and be on their way. They turned into the parking lot at 9:30.

They signed in with the new intern who was working the line, and chatted with the staffers Roger already knew from his work on the campaign. He had worked with Sara Hummel Rajca on solar-energy issues, and talked with her when he put solar panels on the house.

Susan Hileman found a parking spot a little before 10, Christina-Taylor Green bubbling beside her. On the short drive from their neighborhood, Hileman had quizzed her young friend about Congress and the government. Add it up, she would say. How many senators? How many representatives? Don't forget the president and vice president. And Christina-Taylor got it all right, so good with numbers in her head.

"Do you have your question?" Hileman asked. "Do you know what you're going to say?"

Christina-Taylor didn't know yet. She wanted to meet Giffords first.

Hileman gathered her things as she got out of the car. She was always forgetting things, leaving them behind. The young girl knew it was her job to check.

"Do you have the keys?" Christina-Taylor asked.

Hileman held up her hand, jingled the ring and flashed a grin at her friend.

Christina-Taylor left behind her pink sweatshirt, the one with the little peace sign on it. The sun was out. The two headed for the line in front of the store.

Bill Badger found open parking on the Walgreens side of the parking lot, though he noticed there were still not many cars in the lot. He looked at the walkway where the event had begun. He saw Giffords. He could see a young girl talking to a woman. About 10 feet from the line, an aide to Giffords stopped Badger and directed him to a sign-in sheet.

The line formed, ready for the event.

First up was Matthew Laos, a Giffords supporter who had come at the encouragement of Zimmerman. Laos wanted to chat about a piece of legislation and have a picture taken.

Dorwan and Mavy Stoddard, an older couple who lived just a few blocks away off Oracle, were second and third. They had long wanted to meet Giffords and stopped by early, with plans to go to breakfast afterward.

The Salzgebers were fourth and fifth.

Hileman and Christina-Taylor were next, holding hands and laughing as they waited.

Others began to gather. Patricia Maisch had stopped to pick up a few items at Safeway and wanted to meet Giffords and tell her about how the federal stimulus package had made a difference for the heating-and-cooling business she and her husband run.

Steve Rayle waited outside while his girlfriend ducked into the store. He watched Giffords, near the doorway, talking to an older couple.

Zimmerman stopped to chat with Roger Salzgeber about the John Deere ball cap he was wearing.

Pam Simon talked with the Stoddards. Would they like a picture with the congresswoman? That would be nice, they agreed.

A young man in a hooded sweatshirt and baggy pants emerged from the Safeway and walked over to the table where Villec was checking people in.

"Is Giffords here?" the man asked.

Villec nodded and told the young man he needed to sign in and wait in line. Twenty, twenty-five minutes at most. The young man turned away from the table. Villec watched him walk off, wondering if he'd lost interest. He turned his attention back to the others in line.

Joseph Zamudio was standing at the counter in Walgreens, waiting for his debit card to clear, when he heard the sound.

He had stopped for a pack of cigarettes before heading to work at his mother's art gallery. A quick stop. She would be waiting for him.

Then as he waited, he heard the first pop.

Zamudio, 24, knew about guns. He often carried his 9mm, had it with him that very moment. He knew what he was hearing.

Another pop. Then another.

Gunshots.

Another series of pops.

Zamudio's holster was at his side.

Pop.

He left the cigarettes on the counter and raced out the door.

The events in front of the grocery unfolded so quickly, those who were there barely understood what was happening before it was over.

The sequence can be found only among shattered memories and the limited angles of surveillance cameras.

At 10:10 A.M., a gunman walked up to U.S. Rep. Gabrielle Giffords, 40, and shot her in the head. She crumpled to the concrete.

Then the gunman turned to the line of people and squeezed the trigger 31 more times.

U.S. District Judge John Roll, 63, was shot after Giffords, possibly as he tried to push Ron Barber out of danger.

Roll fell to the ground.

He died at the scene.

Dorwan Stoddard, 76, who was talking with Giffords when the shooting began, tried to protect his wife, Mavanell Stoddard, 75. She was shot, but survived.

He died at the scene.

George Morris, 76, a retired Marine who had driven down from Oro Valley, tried to protect his wife, Dorothy, 76. He was shot twice but survived.

She died at the scene.

Phyllis Schneck, 79, who retired to Tucson with her husband seven years ago, stopped to see Giffords even though, according to her daughter, she wasn't very political. She was shot.

She died at the scene.

Gabe Zimmerman, 30, a social worker and Giffords' community-outreach director, was engaged to be married. He was shot.

He died at the scene.

Christina-Taylor Green, 9, who wanted to become the first female to play major-league baseball, was shot through the chest and died.

Susan Hileman, 58, tried to shield Christina-Taylor with her own body. Hileman was shot three times.

Ron Barber, 65, Giffords' district-office director, was shot and suffered wounds in the cheek and the leg.

Pam Simon, 63, who worked part time for Giffords as a community-outreach coordinator, was shot in the wrist and in the chest. The second bullet pierced her body and lodged in her hip.

Bill Badger, 74, the retired Army colonel, was injured by a gunshot that grazed his head.

Kenneth Dorushka, 63, was shot in the arm as he pushed his wife, Carol, away.

Eric Fuller, 63, was shot and wounded in the knee and in his back.

Randy Gardner, 60, was shot in his foot.

Mary Reed, 52, had gone to the store with her daughter, Emma McMahon, who worked for Giffords the previous summer as a page. Reed was shot three times as she shielded her daughter from the gunfire.

James Tucker, 58, described by his neighbors as a "gentle bear," was shot.

Kenneth Veeder, 75, a retired Vietnam veteran, was shot in the leg.

The people in line were gathered in an enclosed corridor, just a few feet wide along the front of the store. They were flanked by a brick wall on one side and large concrete pillars on the other. Tables, temporary barriers and a row of folding chairs hemmed them in. There was little room to run.

Alex Villec saw the gunman raise his arm.

"Get down! Get down!" Villec yelled.

Bill Badger heard the noise and jerked his head up. Was someone trying to harass Giffords with firecrackers? Then he saw the gunman, firing into the line of people. Badger dropped to the concrete and seconds later, felt a burning sensation on the back of his head.

Roger Salzgeber had the same thought: Firecrackers? Here? When he realized what was happening, he hit the ground toward the back of the line. His wife, Faith, dived into the row of chairs, trying to pull one over her.

Patricia Maisch knew she had two options: Run and risk becoming a target or hit the ground and risk being shot as the gunman neared. She hit the ground. The woman next to her was shot, and Maisch waited, wondering what it would feel like.

Then the shooting stopped. The gunman had run out of ammunition.

Salzgeber saw the gun, locked open, empty. He jumped up and, without thinking, hit the gunman. He almost collided with Badger, who was struggling to reach the gun. Badger grabbed the shooter's left wrist and pulled back.

The gunman went down on his right side, still holding the gun, fighting to reload. The gun hit the concrete and fell from the shooter's grasp.

"Get the gun!" someone yelled.

Maisch was on the left side and couldn't reach the gun, but she saw the shooter reach into his pocket for ammunition. If he could reload, he could start shooting again.

Maisch grabbed for the extra magazine. The shooter held on to it, then abruptly dropped it. Maisch lunged and scooped it up.

Between them, Badger and Salzgeber held the gunman down. Salzgeber pushed his knee into the shooter's neck and held his left arm back, pulling it. Hard.

Joseph Zamudio had reached the scene. A man had picked up the gun, and Zamudio moved toward him and grabbed the man's wrist.

"No, no, that's the wrong guy," someone else said.

Zamudio looked down and saw the two men holding the gunman. Maisch was sitting on his legs, clutching the second magazine. Zamudio, a former football player, dropped and took her place. Zamudio was aware of his handgun, which he had not drawn.

I just want to shoot him, he thought.

Steve Rayle edged around the corner of a pillar. He saw the gunman still squirming. A big man, at 6 feet 5 and 230 pounds,

Rayle crouched over the shooter and pushed his knees into the man's kidneys.

In the rush and panic, people were yelling, but no one would remember later who said what.

"I'll kill you! I'll kill you!" someone screamed at the shooter.

"I can't believe you!" a woman cried. "How could you do this?"

Salzgeber felt a rush of anger as he pushed harder on the shooter. The gunman was pinned.

"You're hurting my arm," the man said, as Salzgeber pulled.

Bill Badger finally caught his attention. "Don't you think he needs to breathe?" Badger asked.

The two men were eye to eye. Badger's blood trickled over Salzgeber's coat.

Zamudio tried to dial 911 on his cellphone, but the emergency system was already overloaded with calls.

Rayle, a former emergency-room physician, rose from his knees and surveyed the scene.

A line of wounded people stretched back from where the shooter was pinned.

Several people, he could see, were already dead.

At the front of the line, the congresswoman moved on the ground. Near her, a young girl lay motionless.

With no one directing them, no one telling them what to do, the uninjured rose to their feet and began tending to the wounded. They strained to hear the sound of sirens. They needed help, a lot of help.

But in the air, only silence. They were alone.

And everywhere, there was blood.

Stuart Rodeffer climbed out of his pickup at Mountain View High School in Marana and checked in with the crew of the fire engine that had rolled out for the call. Nothing too much to worry about; another situation under control.

That was Saturday so far for Rodeffer, a battalion chief for the Northwest Fire/Rescue District in Tucson: everything under control. He had clocked in at 7 that morning, reveling in the small weekend luxury of wearing a T-shirt to work. He would work a 24-hour shift, then catch four days off.

Rodeffer celebrated his 46th birthday on Friday with a punishing kettlebell workout and dinner at Red Lobster with his parents and Maggie, his wife of 18 years.

Saturday, Jan. 8, was slow so far. A patient with chest pains; a minor bike accident, the cyclist skinned up and bruised. Rodeffer dispatched himself to both calls and handled them. Under control.

At 10:14, a call came across the radio: first-alarm medical. Severe emergency. An address about 7 miles to the south and east. Ina and Oracle roads.

Rodeffer jumped in his truck and headed there.

As Rodeffer sped through the sparse Saturday-morning traffic, radio chatter turned frantic. More units dispatched. Injuries. Multiple injuries.

He called Lane Spalla, another battalion chief.

"Lane, this is sounding like a deal," Rodeffer said. "What are you thinking?"

Spalla was already there—a shopping center with a Safeway. Rodeffer pulled up, but everyone was being held back. Police were still securing the scene.

Finally, medical responders were cleared. Rodeffer parked his truck on the west edge of the lot and walked quickly toward the store. A banner sharpened into focus: Gabrielle Giffords, in red letters, United States Congress in blue.

The banner didn't register in Rodeffer's mind. Instead, he saw only the scene in front of it.

In his years as a Marine, in a decade of emergency service, he had never seen this.

Bystanders were swarming the firetrucks, tugging desperately at firefighters, reaching for medical equipment. "People are dying here!" someone cried. "We need your help!"

• • •

Two miles away, the alarms sounded at Northwest Fire/Rescue District Station 30. The dispatcher's voice was measured, but the words conveyed the urgency: engine. Rescue. Battalion.

Firefighter and paramedic Tony Compagno reached for his fire gear and then heard the words: 10 people shot.

"At the fire?" Compagno asked his captain.

"There's no fire," the captain said. The radio buzzed. The units flew.

Compagno and his crew were among the first to arrive. They waited for police to let them through and found chaos. Bodies. So much blood.

Compagno was assigned triage: assess and count the victims and figure out who needed help first. No time to write it down. He had to keep it in his head.

I gotta get in there, he thought, gotta make the count.

He saw a man lying face down in a pool of blood and fixed on the image. His mind froze for an instant. So much blood.

Come on! he told himself. Come on!

He heard yelling, and one voice broke through.

"Congresswoman Giffords has been shot! Over here!"

Compagno ran to her. She was alive. He stood in the cramped walkway in front of the store and scanned the ground. He did the numbers. Four dead for sure. Seven people needed immediate attention. A little girl on the ground.

He heard another voice, from someone else in the crew.

"How many helicopters?"

"Launch all of them," Compagno said.

Then another voice. Engine 33 was on the scene.

"Who? Who's next?"

Who's next? he thought.

"Her," Compagno said, pointing to the little girl, bloodied, unconscious. "Her."

He knew her injuries were significant. Terrible. But the dad in him . . . he didn't want her to be dead.

The second crew was up. Compagno pointed them toward the woman in the red coat.

Colt Jackson bent down and took her hand. "Hi, I'm Paramedic Jackson," he said. "Can you hear me?"

She squeezed his hand.

He went through the basics, the ABCs: check her airway, breathing and circulation. He put her on oxygen. He turned to a young man at the patient's side, dark hair, glasses. The man hadn't budged, even with all the blood.

Hold her like this, Jackson told him. It will protect her back.

"This is Congresswoman Giffords," the young man said. "I'm staying."

Daniel Hernandez had been an intern for her office for exactly five days when he arrived for the meet-and-greet at the Safeway that morning.

When the shooting started, other staffers went down, hit. One of them, Ron Barber, turned to Hernandez. "Make sure you stay with Gabby," Barber said. "Make sure you help Gabby."

Hernandez had pressed his bare hand against her head to stop the bleeding until medics arrived.

Now, he walked alongside the stretcher, holding her hand.

The ambulance doors opened. He climbed inside.

As the ambulances rolled out, headed south toward University Medical Center, Compagno continued directing the help at the scene. More paramedics flooded in as helicopters droned. But that wasn't what Compagno noticed.

All around the victims were bystanders, family, friends—just regular people, comforting them, giving them CPR. One man used his belt as a tourniquet.

They're not alone, he thought. None of them is alone.

James Palka left his house a few minutes before 10:30.

He had packed two cameras he used for event photography, the lenses set up for the meet-and-greet. He left the house where he ran his freelance business and turned on to Ina Road, heading east.

He was really just going out of personal interest, to photograph U.S. Rep. Gabrielle Giffords at her "Congress on Your Corner" event.

About a mile away from the Safeway, a speeding paramedic truck passed. Then another. A firetruck. He wondered if there had been an accident.

As he neared the shopping center, traffic slowed and sirens wailed again.

His stomach seized as the thought hit him. What if someone had tried to kill the congresswoman?

He reached Oracle Road and saw firetrucks and emergency vehicles and one . . . two . . . three . . . four ambulances.

Palka eased through the intersection. Most of the entrances had been blocked by wooden sawhorses and police tape, but he spotted a side driveway still open. He pulled in and parked. He got out of his car and somehow remembered to bring his camera.

He stood for a moment.

A scruffy-looking man stood near him behind the police line.

"What happened?" Palka asked.

"Someone shot the congresswoman," the man said.

Palka felt weak. Why her? he asked himself. She's one of the good ones.

For several minutes, Palka watched as a bystander, as a person.

He took pictures of parties, fundraisers. His work as a photographer hadn't prepared him for this.

Then he remembered his camera. No one else was taking pictures, he realized, not even with a cellphone camera. He was carrying his 70-300mm telephoto and could see the scene from the police line.

He raised the camera and started taking pictures:

Emergency workers treating the wounded, lifting people onto gurneys.

Medical helicopters landing in the parking lot.

Police officers talking to witnesses.

Bloodied men and women comforting one another.

He heard voices rise, then saw paramedics pushing a gurney toward an ambulance. A young man stayed alongside, his hand on hers. The patient was clearly hurt badly, her head bloodied.

It was her. It was Giffords.

Palka snapped a series of photos as she was put in the ambulance.

It was 10:41 A.M. A half-hour had passed since the first shots were fired.

Anna Ballis crouched on the sidewalk in front of the Safeway, applying pressure to the upper leg of Giffords' district director. Ron Barber had been a total stranger only moments before. She propped his head on a jacket to make him more comfortable.

Ballis had stopped at the grocery store to buy beef broth for a roast she intended to put in a slow cooker. She saw Giffords' event and thought about stopping, but the line looked too long.

Then a man with a white beard stepped out and encouraged her to come by after she'd finished. Giffords would still be here, he said.

Moments later, the shooting started. Ballis reacted instinctively, ducking behind a pillar, then under a table.

When the shooting stopped, she regained her bearings. Then she saw the man with the white beard, bleeding badly. She ran to his side and put pressure on his wound.

Barber seemed more concerned about everyone else than himself, and Ballis had to reassure him that Giffords and the others were being cared for. He squeezed her hand. "Thank you," he said.

Steve Rayle sat on the gunman until sheriff's deputies arrived. Then his medical training took over. A hospice doctor who had worked in emergency rooms, Rayle surveyed the scene. He moved from victim to victim, offering advice, encouragement, comfort. He administered CPR to one man.

But he couldn't provide what the victims needed most.

Blood. They were losing too much blood. Someone brought clean rags and aprons from Safeway's butcher shop. Rayle and others grabbed them, pressing down on the bleeding wounds.

Bill Badger could feel the stinging in his head, where a bullet had grazed him. Faith Salzgeber had found something from inside Walgreens to sop up the blood.

As paramedics treated his injury, Badger still held his mobile phone in his left hand. With his left thumb, he dialed home. His wife, Sallie, answered.

"I've been hit," he said, his own words difficult to believe. "But I'm OK."

Across the parking lot, in a Pima County sheriff's vehicle, a young man sat in handcuffs. He wore a dark hooded sweatshirt. His face was bleeding and swollen.

Jared Loughner said almost nothing.

Roger Salzgeber began to tremble as the rush of adrenaline subsided and the chill morning air wrapped around him. He shook as he watched the emergency workers, watched his wife helping.

As paramedics ushered the uninjured away from the shooting scene, Roger and Faith began to settle in with the uneasy reality of what had happened.

The rage he had felt as he pinned the gunman began to give way to the truth.

Everyone around me, he thought, is either injured or dead.

The first ambulances were allowed on the scene at 10:19. More arrived over the next half-hour.

Rodeffer, the battalion chief, pushed crews to move quickly.

"Let's get 'em in ambulances and get 'em on the road," he said.

Thirteen people went to hospitals. One man drove himself. Five people died at the scene. Several others were in grave condition.

As the ambulances sped away and helicopters flew some of the wounded to UMC, the news began to break upon a stunned city and then a horrified nation. Another mass shooting.

Except this time, the shooting was at a congresswoman's event.

Some of the earliest reports surfaced on National Public Radio.

The Internet blasted bulletins. Twitter feeds caught fire.

A brief mention on CNN grew into non-stop coverage.

The facts were scarce at first. Even as victims were rushed to hospitals, news crews could barely sketch out what had happened. How many shot? How many killed?

Then, soon, came the unthinkable. A dispatch presented with a question mark at first.

A report said it was true. Soon, other reports cited the first report.

The news caught up to anxious friends and relatives seeking word from hospitals. It caught up to worried onlookers.

It caught up to a private jet streaking from Houston toward Tucson, carrying a Navy pilot-turned-astronaut, racing to be with his congresswoman wife.

The word flashed across the Internet, then the airwaves.

Gabrielle Giffords was dead.

A few minutes past 10 on Saturday, Jan. 8, Randall Friese sat in his office at University Medical Center in central Tucson, catching up on paperwork.

Friese, a trauma surgeon, had been on call since the morning before and had just finished handing off to the next team coming on duty. The incoming and outgoing teams overlapped at 9 A.M.

By 10, Friese was done. Narong Kulvatunyou—Dr. K—took over.

Instead of cutting out, Friese went back to his office to pass some time. He was set to meet his trainer at noon at a private studio a couple of miles north. He knew if he went home first, he'd probably end up skipping the workout.

A short text message flashed on his pager and his mobile phone: Multiple gunshot-wound victims.

Friese had seen the same sort of page plenty of times. Usually it meant two, three, maybe four victims.

He tapped out a text to Dr. K. I'm still in my office, he said. Let me know if you need anything.

Less than 10 minutes later, the pager came to life again. Friese stared at the message: There were now 10 shooting victims.

Ten was a lot. It was possible only one or two needed serious attention, but there was no way of knowing from here. Friese headed for the emergency room.

On the way, he pulled out his mobile phone and called Peter Rhee, UMC's trauma medical director and the surgeon on backup call.

"Ten people have been shot and they're coming in," Friese told him.

"I know," Rhee said. "I'm on my way."

Friese pushed through the doors into the bright lights of the trauma unit. The hallways buzzed, the anticipation palpable as the staff from around the hospital arrived and prepared for the first victims. Two trauma surgeons, several ER doctors and nurses were there already.

The trauma center is a place on wheels: equipment tables, medical scanners, video monitors, even storage lockers filled with syringes, gauze and IV drip bags. When crews need something, it rolls in; when it no longer serves a purpose, it rolls out. In an emergency, everything is in constant motion.

In the middle of the trauma center, seven treatment rooms open onto a central hallway lined with glass walls and sliding doors. With all the glowing light and glass, there are no windows.

Quickly, the unit devised its strategy.

Friese knew each of the seven rooms would soon be full. Teams started splitting up to cover each one. The wounded would be assigned to a room based on their conditions. Rooms 4 and 5 were for the worst injuries. They were closest to the entrance, larger and offered quick access to blood for transfusions.

As he helped prep the unit, Friese learned that the shooting had occurred at a shopping center in the foothills, at Ina and Oracle roads.

That doesn't sound right, he thought. Gunshot victims from that part of town? Then another thought caught up to him.

His wife.

She was supposed to be at work that morning at a literacy program, closer to downtown, not near their foothills home. But what if she had stopped at the store? What if?

He picked up the phone and called her office number.

Another staffer answered. His wife: Was she there? Yes, he was told, she's in giving her lecture right now.

Friese hung up the phone. He didn't have to talk to her. He just had to know.

An ambulance pulled to a halt outside the trauma unit, where red columns flanked the covered entryway.

The stretcher clattered in through the glass door and across the sand-colored patchwork of the linoleum floor. Paramedics were performing CPR as it rolled.

Friese saw the patient. A little girl.

The crew went straight to Room 4.

Ross Zimmerman was puttering around his Tucson home Saturday morning when the phone rang. On the other end was a frantic Kelly O'Brien, his son Gabe's fiancée. He listened in shock as she blurted out the news.

Gabrielle Giffords, the congresswoman, Gabe's boss, had been shot. Gabe had been at the scene, a Safeway store in the foothills, but Kelly didn't know where he was now. She was with Gabe's mother, Emily Nottingham, and they were headed to UMC to see if they could get any information.

Ross and his wife, Pam, sped to the hospital. Gabe loved his job with Giffords, loved helping people. Ross remembered when he first met Giffords, how much she wanted to connect with the people she served. It was as if the job was meant to be.

At the hospital, the waiting rooms were filling. Some of Giffords' staff and friends gathered in the cafeteria. Ross, Kelly, Emily and Pam could only wait.

At the Safeway, Roger and Faith Salzgeber waited to give statements to deputies.

They had started with a simple plan for the morning: Roger, a former campaign volunteer, wanted to stop by Giffords' meet-and-greet event to say hello. Then the quiet Saturday shattered, as a gunman approached the gathering and opened fire.

They hadn't told anyone else where they were going, but as news broke, friends and relatives knew immediately. Roger was such an admirer. There was no way he wasn't there.

Their daughters started calling, frantic. First the home phone— no answer. Then Faith's cellphone—nothing. Faith would later realize it had disappeared in the chaos.

With their older daughter near hysteria, the younger daughter did the only thing she could think of. She started searching the Internet for news coverage, to find their parents' names, a photo, something. Anything.

In Houston, Mark Kelly was talking to his daughters about their text-messaging habits. His phone rang.

It was Pia Carusone, his wife Gabby's congressional chief of staff.

I don't know how to tell you this, she said, but Gabby's been shot. There's not much more information yet.

Kelly had been on the phone with his wife barely half an hour ago. He listened in disbelief. When he hung up, he looked at the phone's call history to make sure he hadn't imagined the conversation. Then he called Carusone back.

"What did you say?" he asked.

He told the girls and then called Giffords' parents and his. Then he had to go.

He called Tilman Fertitta, a good friend and the CEO of Landry's Restaurants.

"Hey, I need to get to Tucson ASAP. I can't wait for the commercial flights," he told Fertitta, explaining the situation. Fertitta offered his private jet. Kelly was in the air 45 minutes later.

As the jet raced west, Kelly watched the news coverage on TV. Then the bulletin flashed.

Gabrielle Giffords had died of her injuries.

Randall Friese swept his eyes across the patient in Room 4. A young girl. He would later learn her name: Christina-Taylor Green. She was 9. He focused on her as surgeon.

Injuries: apparent gunshot wound to the chest.

Condition: unconscious. Breathing tube.

Paramedics had been giving her CPR when she was wheeled into the trauma unit. Friese knew minutes—seconds—counted. If he was going to help her, he had to operate. There was no time to get to the ER. He would have to do it right there in Room 4.

The room was crowded with equipment. Video monitors, data display screens, trays on telescoping arms, all on wheels, moving in and out as doctors and nurses moved around the gurney.

The emergency-room doctors checked the tube to make sure it was in place. Another doctor tried to insert an intravenous line, but struggled to find a vein. She had lost so much blood.

Friese cut into her chest. He would perform a thoracotomy. It is surgery, aggressive surgery. Friese wanted to check the heart cavity for bleeding, look at the heart to see if it needed sutures. See if the heart was full or empty. Massage the heart to get it to beat.

Her heart was empty and still. Friese looked and saw almost no blood. She must have suffered huge losses at the shooting scene.

He focused again, aware that he was operating on a 9-year-old girl. But he knew he couldn't let that affect him. He was human, but to save her, he needed to push his emotions aside.

Her heart wasn't injured. But it wouldn't beat. He inserted an IV line straight into it, trying to fill it with blood. He put his hand around the heart and squeezed. Again. And again. Nothing.

Time pressed down on Friese. He feared the girl's chances were not good . . . but a child often responds better to trauma, so he kept at it. At least nine other victims were on their way . . . but no one else had arrived yet. There was still time.

And she was 9. Only 9. That had to mean something.

Friese worked desperately. Minutes passed. Three. Four. Five. Seven minutes. He poured more blood into her heart, but it wouldn't pump, wouldn't refill her body.

Someone brought word to Room 4: Another patient had arrived. A woman. Severe injuries. She was going into Room 5. Another critical case.

Friese made his decision. He knew he was done. But as he left, he gave instructions to the chief resident. Fill her heart one more time, he said. Try one more time.

He walked into Room 5 and began to evaluate the patient. A horrific injury to her head. Others were preparing equipment, wheeling monitors and carts into the room. She would need anesthesia, a breathing machine, if she was going to live. He took her hand and squeezed it.

"Ms. Giffords," he said, "you are in the hospital. We are going to care for you."

Hello, I'm Martin Savidge, CNN Center in Atlanta. We are following breaking news coming out of Tucson, Arizona. We understand that Congresswoman Gabrielle Giffords is among 12 people shot at a grocery store just hours ago. That is according to a Democratic source. There are unconfirmed reports that there are fatalities and I should tell you, and it's disturbing news, that NPR is now reporting that the congresswoman, Congresswoman Gabrielle Giffords, has in fact died.

The report of Giffords' death broke on CNN at 12:20 Tucson time. Reports had dribbled out like rationed water for more than an hour. Sometimes it seemed as if even the news anchors on TV and radio couldn't quite believe that an American congresswoman could be the victim of a shooting attack. It would be hours before someone dared use the word assassination.

For a while, the news came in 140-character bursts on Twitter. Rumors spread. The number of people shot fluctuated wildly. Twitter posters grew frustrated. Why had no one in the mainstream media reported the news?

In the first hour, the large news organizations played it safe. Local TV stations, working with skeleton weekend crews, struggled to confirm any details.

CNN finally interrupted its weekend programs with longer reports. An anchor interviewed an employee at a cellphone store in the Safeway shopping center. He claimed to know someone in

Tucson law enforcement and he was one of the first witnesses to describe multiple victims. Ten, maybe 12, even 15 people shot.

Then NPR, citing sources and a witness at the scene, announced that Giffords had died.

All the national networks were on the air with non-stop coverage.

Not every outlet posted the dispatch. The Associated Press had not sent a bulletin. But the *New York Times*, with a report on its website, seemed to give the news a finality: Giffords had died.

As she walked through crowded waiting rooms and the hospital's cafeteria in the hours after shooting victims began arriving, Michelle Ziemba, University Medical Center's director of trauma and emergency services, could see distinct groups forming: relatives, friends and what she thought of as professional family— aides to Giffords, other elected officials.

All of them wanted news of their loved ones. But with so many victims coming in from such a chaotic scene, most had been admitted without names. The hospital used its own system of initials and code words to keep track of the patients, but in many cases, there was no ID.

Doctors and nurses had to ask family members to describe the people they sought. Age. Sex. Appearance. Anything that could help identify them.

Giffords' close friends and aides gathered in the cafeteria, situated along an outside wall of UMC, past the information desk, past the waiting room, past a big blue wall. Windows looked out on a courtyard with concrete tables bolted to the ground, but the courtyard was small, the walls around it high. Little light made it into the cafeteria itself.

The room was all hard edges. Speckled plastic benches offered utilitarian seating. No one got comfortable.

Rooms were opened off to the side, but most people gravitated to one spot in the main room—the television, chattering with non-stop coverage of the shooting. The room grew quiet when

President Barack Obama delivered his statement.

Rep. Jeff Flake, one of Giffords' colleagues in Congress and a friend, drove from Phoenix to Tucson after hearing the news. He was passing through Casa Grande when he heard the report of Giffords' death. When he arrived at UMC, he found a small group of current and former state lawmakers. They all made their way to the cafeteria to await the official word.

Daniel Hernandez was covered in blood when he climbed out of the ambulance with Giffords, his boss of five days. The young intern waited for his family to bring him a change of clothes.

As he passed by a television, he heard the reports that Giffords had died. The news began to filter through the hospital.

Ziemba, too, heard the rumors. She began receiving text messages from people about the death. Her frustration grew. Why were these reports surfacing? As far as she knew, Giffords was still in surgery. She made her way toward the operating room.

"Somebody go into that room," she said, "and verify that she is alive."

Five people died at the scene of the Safeway shooting that Saturday morning, Jan. 8. Fourteen were treated at one of three Tucson hospitals.

One, Christina-Taylor Green, 9, died of her wounds at University Medical Center, despite the extensive efforts to revive her.

Phyllis Schneck, 79, died at the scene.

Kenneth Veeder, 75, a retired Vietnam veteran, survived a gunshot wound to the leg.

James Tucker, 58, was among the first to arrive at UMC with gunshot wounds and survived.

Mary Reed, 52, survived three gunshot wounds suffered as she protected her daughter from injury.

Randy Gardner, 60, survived a gunshot wound to the foot.

Eric Fuller, 63, drove himself to Northwest Medical Center and survived a gunshot wound to the knee.

Kenneth Dorushka, 63, survived a gunshot wound to his arm as he pushed his wife, Carol, away.

Bill Badger, 74, a retired Army colonel, was grazed in the head by a bullet. After first resisting efforts to take him to an emergency room, he agreed and was taken to St. Mary's Hospital. He survived.

Pam Simon, 63, an aide to Giffords, was taken to UMC. She survived two gunshot wounds.

Ron Barber, 65, Giffords' district director, survived two gunshot wounds.

Next to him, U.S. District Judge John Roll, 63, was shot and died at the scene.

Mavanell Stoddard, 75, survived a gunshot wound as her husband, Dorwan, fought to shield her. He died.

George Morris, 76, survived a gunshot wound as he tried to protect his wife, Dorothy. She died.

Susan Hileman, 58, survived three gunshot wounds as she tried to protect her friend, Christina-Taylor Green. Doctors performed urgent surgery on Hileman, and kept her heavily sedated as she recovered.

A little after 2 P.M., UMC surgeon Peter Rhee appeared at a news conference carried live on national television.

Rhee spoke in front of a white movie screen that remained blank. A line of photographers stood in back amid elected officials who had made their way to the hospital. Reporters sat in folding chairs, making and taking calls on mobile phones, adjusting recorders. The room never went silent, even as Rhee spoke, the sounds of electronic equipment and whispers adding a humming background noise.

But outside the room, the country was hanging on every word.

The hospital had treated 10 gunshot victims from the attack at Safeway, he said. Five remained in critical condition.

Rep. Gabrielle Giffords, he said, was alive. Under anesthesia. In intensive care.

Before the news conference, reporters had retreated from the earlier news, confirming that Giffords had survived the shooting.

Now, with Rhee's word, networks and websites scrambled to correct the reports.

Waiting in the hospital, Daniel Hernandez was elated.

On a private jet approaching Tucson, the pilot got word from the plane's owner, Tilman Fertitta.

"Let me talk to Mark," he said. The news reports were wrong, he told Kelly. Gabby is alive.

As physicians finished operating on patients, Rhee, the trauma medical director, circulated through the waiting room. He asked friends and relatives gathered there to describe their loved one. By process of elimination, he was able to identify them and deliver most of the news. By that time, much of it was good news.

Near the end of the process, one family still waited for any word at all.

Ross Zimmerman wanted to know what happened to his son, Gabe. No one seemed to know anything. When Rhee found his way to the family, they gave him Gabe's name.

No, Rhee said, he's not on any list I have. Maybe that means his injuries were so minor, he wasn't admitted.

Could it be true, the family wondered. Was Gabe all right?

Ross Zimmerman's wife, Pam, a physician, began calling other emergency rooms, talking to other triage nurses. Nothing. Gabe's name didn't show up anywhere.

As Pam ran out of places to call, Ross sank into a chair in the cafeteria. He felt worse than he had all day.

Then a sheriff's deputy took the family into another room, off the cafeteria. Finally, they knew.

Gabe had died at the scene.

Bill Badger, the retired Army colonel, had gone to ask Giffords about health-care reform. Instead, he helped wrestle a gunman to the ground.

After leaving the hospital about 4:30, he made his way back to the shopping center and persuaded someone there to let him take his Toyota home. The next morning, he and his wife would attend mass at St. Thomas the Apostle parish, where Judge John Roll began his final Saturday.

Photographer James Palka had packed his cameras that morning, planning to shoot a meet-and-greet. Instead, he found himself covering a national news story.

When he finally lowered his camera at the Safeway, he decided to go to the hospital, photograph the memorials and the vigils, see the day through. It was the only way he could make things better.

Roger Salzgeber, the campaign volunteer, wanted to stop quickly to say hello to Giffords; he had a basketball game to be at that night. Instead, he pinned a gunman to the ground.

Unhurt in the shootings, he and his wife, Faith, waited to be interviewed by investigators. A wire service photographer snapped a photo of them in the parking lot, ashen-faced, consoling each other. Their younger daughter found the photo online. They were alive.

Salzgeber talked to sheriff's deputies and the FBI. He drew them a diagram of what had happened. Then, he was free to go.

That afternoon, the University of Arizona postponed the game against Stanford.

When the Salzgebers arrived at their home, reporters were camped outside. But the couple couldn't talk. They passed the reporters quietly, walked inside and closed the door.

Susan Hileman had gone to Safeway so her 9-year-old friend could meet a congresswoman. Instead, she put herself in between the gunman and the little girl, trying to stop the bullets.

At University Medical Center, after surgery, staffers would slowly ease her back into consciousness. Her husband, Bill, was there. She looked into his eyes and asked one question.

"What about Christina?"

Crowds gathered around the Safeway. Well-wishers amassed outside Giffords' office, holding signs, crying. Outside the hospital, cards and flowers and stuffed animals began piling up.

After sunset came the vigil. Friends, strangers gathered in the winter evening.

The first candle was lit and flickered in the darkness.

Shaun McKinnon is a senior reporter for *The Arizona Republic* who has written about water, growth, and environmental issues since joining the newspaper in 1999. He has won awards from the Arizona Press Club, Best of the West and the American Society of Newspaper Editors. He has previously worked at newspapers in Las Vegas, Nevada, and Logan, Utah.

REGRET

Vance Voyles

If you were accusing my son, I wouldn't let him talk to you in a million years.

—A Sex Crimes detective, on talking to the police.

Spencer* stood as the judge asked the clerk to read the jury's findings. Dressed in light blue, with a clean shave of innocence, Spencer fingered the seam of his dark dress pants. His oxford dress shirt stuck to his back, damp from the steady stream of sweat that had run down his spine all morning. None of the jury members looked at him. He stared at them. Almost begging for a quick glance to tell him it would be okay. His lawyer stood next to him. He, too, looked for a sign. Throughout the day of witness testimony and breaks, Spencer mumbled the same mantra under his breath: "This can't be happening. This can't be happening." Nothing had changed in the ten months since I'd arrested him, since the day Nick had called me about the case.

"Sorry for waking you, Detective. This is Candy from the Comm Center. I have 150-A, Deputy Nick Kessler on the line, asking to speak to Sex Crimes."

My head is on my pillow, the phone stuck to my ear. I hope I heard her wrong. 150-A means midnights in Zone 50, home to the Disney Internship Program. Kids on their own for the first time, on vacation from Mom and Dad.

"Can I put him through, or do you need a minute?"

I breathe deeply through my nose and sit up reluctantly. I take another breath and stare at the wall, struggling to wake up. My wife stirs, and I make my way to the kitchen in the dark.

Some names have been changed.

"Detective?"

"I'm here. You can put him through." The line disconnects momentarily, and I lean against the counter. The light from the microwave blinks 3:17. Nick isn't a brand new deputy calling to tell me what he's got. He spent ten years in the Criminal Investigations Division. He finally got tired of the call-outs and the adverse effects that the constant triaging of cases had on his social life. For the last six months, he's been back on the road, taking a vacation from CID. So, if Nick is calling, I am going to be up for a while. He doesn't call for nothing.

"Go ahead, Detective—he's on the line."

"Good morning, Detective," Nick says, as if he's Ricardo Montalban on the welcoming dock of Fantasy Island—"Smiles, everyone! Smiles!"—except that he follows with "Living the dream, baby! Living the dream." This is his line whenever the day begins with overtime.

"Just tell me if I need to come out, Nick, because if you're just calling to let me know what you got, then I'm going to have to wait until noon, when you're sleeping, to call you back."

"Whoa. Don't shoot the messenger," he says, laughing. "My girl here was banging on dorm doors, crying for help, saying she was raped, and now her mom is on the phone from South Carolina screaming holy hell. Trust me. You're coming out."

"The mom is there?" I ask. The kitchen is brightening in the soft glow of numbers, clearing my sleep cobwebs. There is a commotion coming from the other end, somewhere behind Nick.

"No. She's been on the phone with her parents. They're threatening to sue Mickey Mouse. Hold on. Ma'am, please step—" Nick covers the phone and says something out of earshot. "Sorry, Vance. Your victim keeps calling me Andy Taylor. Earlier she was calling my partner Barney Fife."

"Is she drunk?"

"If she's not, she's got a good act. Anyway, she's not coming off the rape."

"Stupid cracker bi—" someone says before he covers the phone again.

"Who was that?" I ask. "Nick?"

The phone stays muffled. "Please, ma'am—"

"Who is that?"

"Sorry," Nick says into the phone.

"Who was that?" I ask again, but he ignores the question.

"We do have a scene. Liquor bottles, bed sheets, and a used tampon."

"A used tampon?" I feel like I'm still dreaming. I stifle a yawn and my ears plug, dampening the voice coming through the phone.

"In the bathroom garbage, and she can't remember how it got there. You want me to call forensics?"

"I'll send forensics to you. Did someone just call you a cracker bitch?" I ask, knowing full well that Nick does not let things like this sway him. Whatever a person says or does to undermine their account of the alleged crime, this is still just a case number to Nick—nothing personal, just business—and nothing will stop him from working it into the ground. He just makes sure to put it all in his report. If they stick with a bad story, it's still just another case number to him. He's not the one putting people in jail, the lawyers are.

"Are you going to come here, or do you want to meet her at the SATC?"

"It sounds like she'd do better to be removed from the area," I say, trudging toward the bathroom to get cleaned up. "I trust you can cover the scene, right?"

"You're not sending your secondary?"

Normally, I would send another detective to cover the crime scene with CSI, but why muddy the waters with another person to testify? "If it was any other deputy, Nick, I would; but since you're fully capable. . ."

"No, I got it," he says. I can see his jovial red face in my head. "Living the dream, baby!"

"Yeah," I say, flipping the receiver closed and reaching for my toothbrush.

• • •

Less than an hour later, I step into the interview room of the Sexual Assault Treatment Center and find Emily already seated in the overstuffed, blue vinyl chair. She looks small in the spartan room, like a twelve-year-old: baby-doll shoes, matching blue denim jeans and jacket, her hair swept back. I sit across from her, set my digital recorder next to me, and introduce myself.

"Nice to meet you," she says in a lilting southern accent, just above a whisper. There is no mention of Barney. No Andy. No "cracker" anything. Sitting here quietly, she's as sober as a nun.

I smile at her, explaining that I will be recording our conversation so she won't have to write down what happened. "I know this can be daunting, but I'm here to help, okay?"

Emily nods politely, but her body is tense and ramrod straight in her chair.

"Where are you from, Emily?" I ask, hoping to make her feel more at ease.

"South Carolina."

"Well, that explains the accent," I say, pressing the record button on the digital recorder. "This is Detective Vance Voyles, and I will be in the room with . . ." I motion to her.

"Emily Evans."

I tell the recorder the case number, the time of day, and where we are. "Emily, do you swear to tell the truth, the whole truth, and nothing but the truth?"

"I do."

"Can you tell me why we are here this morning?"

"Because Spence raped me?" she says, her eyebrows raised in uncertainty.

I try to smile to calm her nerves. "I'm sorry, Emily, are you asking me or telling me?"

"What?"

"I asked you to tell me why we're here, and you said you were raped. But you said it like a question. Like you're not sure."

"Well, to be honest, I'm not."

"Okay." This is not new. This should be easy to fix. I'll be home sooner than I thought. "What do you think happened?"

"Well, I was sleeping . . . in my room . . . and my roommate woke me up, crying, saying Spence raped me."

"You didn't know?"

"It was my first time drinking."

There is a knock on the door, and the deputy who drove Emily to the SATC pokes her head into the room.

"I'm sorry, Detective. Can I speak to you for a second?"

Does it look like it? I think. But Emily is calm, and my getting pissy with another deputy isn't good for our image, especially in this place of peace and tranquility. I turn off the recorder and excuse myself. In the hallway, I notice the victim advocate standing by the bathroom door, ready to pounce and give Emily a hug, if necessary. The treatment center is just an old house, remodeled after the hospital across the street went up. Old walls painted bright white over heavy spackle. It's supposed to be a safe environment in a troubling time. Posters of young girls just prior to victimization are taped haphazardly to the walls. Subliminal messages on boyfriends too good to be true, friends looking out for friends, and the perils of drinking too much. Propaganda and rhetoric about respect, abuse, and victim rights, expertly designed to get victims to press charges. It's a government building with feelings.

"These are the statements we collected on the scene. One is from the roommate, and another is from her boyfriend."

"Boyfriend? But I thought—" I say, tearing the pink carbon copies off. "Then who is the suspect?"

"Some guy she met at work," she says.

"But the boyfriend was there, too?"

"No. He came after."

I quickly read over the originals before handing them back. Everybody drinking. Too drunk to drive. Work guy sleeps it off in Emily's room. Roommate kicks work guy out after hearing noises. Boyfriend comes to the rescue.

"Thanks."

"You need anything else from me?" It's close to her quitting time.

"No, but if you want to sit in on the interview, you can," I say, smiling. I'll take any opportunity to train patrol deputies in the way we do things. "We might even get to do a controlled phone call."

When I enter the interview room at Central Operations two hours later, the sweet smell of malt has already filled the air. Upon my request, deputies made contact with Spencer at his dorm room. He answered the door on the third knock, his eyes glassy with sleep, and squinted at the deputies with a faint recognition. He didn't struggle as they put his hands behind his back and locked the handcuffs. Spencer now sits in the corner, still cuffed and still wearing the red-striped shirt that Emily described in her sworn statement.

"Morning, Spencer. My name is Detective Voyles." I set my case file on the chair opposite him. "Stand up for a second so I can get those cuffs off you."

"Can you tell me why I'm here?" Spencer says as he stands, turning away from me.

I step to his side and pull his arm upward. "The guy who put these cuffs on you locked them all backwards." I fumble with the key before unlocking him. "That's better. Have a seat." I move my file to the floor and sit down across from him. Reaching into my ID holder, I pull out a preprinted Miranda card. "Since you were put in handcuffs—something I didn't want done, mind you— technically, you're not free to leave."

"Well, no kidding," Spencer says, rubbing his wrists. "Are you going to tell me—"

I hold up my finger. "And since you are not free to leave, I have to read you your rights before we start talking about why you are here."

"Fine, but I can save you the time. I'm going to want to speak to my lawyer."

"Are you sure, Spencer? Because—"

"Why am I here?" he asks again.

"It's about Emily."

Spencer hangs his head and begins to shake it from side to side. He knew it as soon as he saw the police at his door. When I saw Emily in the SATC, she was cute. Halle Berry-esque. This guy is a mutt. Greasy hair. Flabby gut. Discount rack all the way. The only way she would have hooked up with him is if she'd been drunk. He needs to tell me this, tell me that she drank of her own accord. People do stupid things when they are drunk. Many a country song has been written about it.

"And I think that this is something you need to—should—talk to me about."

Spencer doesn't look up.

"But if you ask for a lawyer, then all I have is her word."

They tell us not to do this. He asked for a lawyer. Nothing he says from here on out will be used against him. But it can be used to help him. I have no hidden agenda.

"I'm not trying to trick you, Spencer. I just don't like having only one side of the story. I don't trust—"

Spencer looks up. "I'm sorry, Detective—what did you say your name was?"

"Voyles. Detective Voyles."

"Right. I'm sorry, Detective Voyles, but my father always told me not to talk to the police. No disrespect."

"None taken. After all, I was just about to read that you do indeed have that right." I stand up and grab the handcuffs again. "Can you turn around, please?"

"Wait. Why?"

"You want a lawyer, so there are no more questions, Spencer," I say as I lock the cuffs back in place.

"So I'm still under arrest?" I can hear the surprise in his voice. As if his mentioning an attorney was some get-out-of-jail-free card. It doesn't work that way. This isn't television.

"Yes, Spencer, for the sexual battery of Emily Evans."

"So you're taking me to jail now?"

"First, my desk. I have to write the charging affidavit. Then jail."

• • •

Minutes later, Spencer is sitting on the couch next to my desk, talking again.

"I'm sorry, Detective. I know you're trying to write, but sexual battery? That's rape, right?"

"Yes." Part of me laughs at this small talk. When I came into the interview room, he was polite, but holier than thou. It wasn't what he said; it was how he said it. *My father always told me not to talk to the police.* So busy not talking. So busy not listening.

"Emily says I raped her?"

"According to sworn, written statements. Emily isn't the only one. Some girl walked in on you."

"Melissa? She sent me a text after she kicked me out, but—"

"Listen, Spencer. I wanted to talk to you about this. I really did. But you asked for a lawyer. If you want to un-invoke your right to counsel, on tape, then we can discuss it."

"And if I do that, you'll un-arrest me?"

"No. Once you're arrested, the clock starts ticking."

"But I didn't rape her."

"I didn't say you did. She said that. You said you wanted a lawyer. That combination didn't give me much choice."

"Why didn't you tell me that before you arrested me?"

"I'm not allowed." I'm starting to feel the morning, and my lack of sleep is pissing me off. "It's called coercion, Spencer, and it would have violated your rights."

"So you just arrest me on her word?"

You, and the hundred that came before you, I think. If I had a dime for every guy caught up in a he said, she said. Case number such and such: Two girls on vacation with their families get caught sneaking in late after having a ménage à trois with this cute little seventeen-year-old surfer they met. What happens in Florida stays in Florida; that is, until they find their dads waiting for them at the beach condo. Then it's he raped us. We didn't want to do it. And now Dude Spicoli is up against two counts of sexual battery. That is all it takes to be a sexual predator. Two felony convictions. No more school. No good introductions to dads down the road. Nowhere to go but to the closet of your mother's house to hang yourself after bailing out of jail. We don't play in Florida. No sir.

"Her word, the statements, the phone call earlier this morning where you told her you guys had sex. All that." When the deputy and I walked back into the room with Emily, we scripted out what she needed to say. We prepared her for his answers and dialed his number for her. We made it easy, that awkward morning-after call. Almost as easy as swallowing the morning-after pill she was handed after her rape kit was completed.

"We were drunk. We were in bed, and one thing led to another. There was no rape."

I stare at Spencer in silence. He'd said all of this on the phone before I even met him.

"Get him talking, Emily. He'll apologize and admit the sex was a mistake." It was all too easy. Spencer did what every fly stuck in a spider's web does: he squirmed.

"What do you mean you don't remember? Of course we had sex. I thought you were into it. Are you kidding me? How could you not know we were having sex? We made out. We were drinking. Maybe it was a mistake. I hope this doesn't ruin our friendship."

And it's all recorded. Sometimes, I feel bad.

Sometimes.

What I wouldn't give for a magic megaphone, for the ability to scream into the ears of every young, horny guy on the planet. For this oh-so-valuable, sought-after friendship, sex must be the icing, not the cake.

If only he hadn't asked for a lawyer, hadn't laid that blanket of guilty conscience on himself when I asked him to talk about it. Had he given me his half of the he said, she said, I would have let him go home. Maybe I'd forget that he'd been in cuffs for a little while and apologize to the state attorney when the case packet arrived too late to pursue the matter. What's the saying? It's better to ask for forgiveness than for permission? Detectives are people too. But he didn't come at this right. Grown men shouldn't ask for their daddies.

"Then why did you ask for a lawyer, Spencer?"

Spencer looks confused. He sits back in the couch.

"If this is all such an innocent mistake, what do you need the lawyer for?"

Spencer doesn't answer. He just hangs his head and breathes deeply. I turn back around and start typing.

"So there's nothing I can do to stop this from happening?" he says to my back.

I swivel around and look him in the eyes. "Not today. At least, not right now. But your lawyer can. You also have the right to a speedy trial. So don't waive speedy. I'll write what you have told me, and maybe you'll get lucky and the state will dump it. Better yet, maybe Emily will change her mind. It happens all the time, Spencer. Eighty percent, usually."

I don't have to tell him this. But I heard the spitfire in Emily's voice while I was talking to Nick on the phone. She was supposed to be drunk, but in the interview room, there was nothing. No slurring. No bloodshot eyes. No telltale smell of the sickly sweet alcohol seeping out of her pores. She was acting out a role, just like me. I am the police. She is the victim. My hands are tied. I'm not supposed to feel this way. My job is to stand for the victim when she cannot stand for herself. She's not supposed to make a vitriolic rage rise up in my throat. I am supposed to feel compassion for her and wrath against him. It's what I was taught in the academy. It's what I grew up watching on television.

I want to rewind time and take them aside before they started to drink that night. I want to be Samuel Beckett from *Quantum Leap*. But however much I wish I could, I cannot travel back in time to put right what once went wrong. I can use this time, this moment, and I can give empty lectures. So far, there's no law against that.

•   •   •

The next day, Emily's boyfriend answers the phone as if he's in a hurry. "Student Center, may I help you?"

"Yes, may I speak to Joshua Williams?"

"This is Josh."

I introduce myself, tell him it's about Emily.

"Um, can I call you back in about two minutes? I'd prefer to take this outside."

When my phone rings, the recorder is on and Josh sounds confused.

"Am I catching you at a bad time, Josh?"

"No sir. It's just that I am surprised to hear from you. I mean, I wasn't part of what happened."

I lean into my desk, tracing my pen in circles as he talks. "According to Emily, she came banging on your door for help."

"Yes sir, but—"

"She also told me that you're her boyfriend."

"Well, we hang out, but I don't—" He pauses. "I'm surprised because I wasn't there that night. In her room, I mean."

"Yes, I understand that, but afterwards. After the incident, she came banging on your door."

"No sir. That was before."

"Before what?" I ask.

"Before she was raped. Sir."

This is not what I want to hear.

"So she came knocking on your door before she was raped, saying she was raped?"

"She was drunk. Flirting, kinda. . .asking me to help her before something bad happened. Then that guy Spence came up and helped her back to her room. They were all drinking a lot, sir."

"But you were there when we arrived."

"Only because Melissa came and got me. She told me what had happened and that Emily needed my help."

"Emily asked for you?"

"Well, I don't know. She had fallen back asleep by the time I got there."

And where was this information before I sat down with Emily? Did it come over the phone while I was sitting at home, too stuck in my sleep to hear it? Is this something I missed, or something that was left out?

"May I speak to Melissa, please?"

"Speaking."

I stare at the numbers on the phone with my finger poised over the mute button. I lower my voice to its police tenor, the one with authority. "Hi, Melissa. My name is Detective Voyles. I work for the Sheriff's Office, and I need to talk to you about Emily Evans." There is a silent recognition streaming through the phone. I peek over at my computer screen at Melissa's most recent driver's license photo. The voice doesn't sound right for the face. Too high. A bit whiny for the long, thick hair.

"Oh. Okay. Sure," she says, her voice softer now. More grave.

"Is this a bad time? Because if you want to come in—"

"No. This is fine. Um. . ." Her hair scratches the receiver. "Yes. Hold on a second," she says. There is shuffling in the background, and Melissa speaks to someone in a muffled tone. Over my cubicle, two other detectives laugh. I press the mute button and stand up.

"I'm taking a statement, guys." The look on my face tells them to quiet down. As I sit down, I hear my words come whining back from one of them, mocking me. This is nothing new.

"Detective? Are you there?"

I unmute the phone. "Yes. Sorry. Is this a bad time?"

"No, no. I'm at work, but this is better."

"That's what I was thinking. I'm sorry I didn't get to talk to you the night this happened. I was with Emily."

"Yes."

"And—well, I was able to read over a copy of your written statement that night, and I have some questions."

"Did I forget to put something down?"

"No, Melissa. I just find it easier to write what happened when I hear it from the witnesses themselves. From the horse's mouth, so to speak." I look at her long face in the photo and smile.

"Sure, I guess. Well, like I wrote in my statement, Emily—"

"Oh, I'm sorry, Melissa. Before you start, do you promise to tell the truth, the whole truth and nothing but?"

"Sure. Yes. I mean, I do."

"Perfect. You were saying?" I press the mute button so she can't hear the commotion on the other side of the cubicle.

"Well, like I wrote in my statement, I walked into Emily's room and saw she was passed out. And then I see Spence on top of her, raping her."

Unmute. "Do you two share a room?" Mute.

"No. She moved back to South Carolina with her parents. When they showed up—" She pauses for a second. "Well, they kind of insisted."

The joking from the other side subsides and I press the mute button again. I can hear my own breath back on the line. "No. I mean when this happened. Were you sharing a room with Emily?"

"No. Sir."

"Then why did you go into her room?"

"To make sure she was okay. She was really drunk—"

"Was she screaming for help?" I pick up my pen again, trace and retrace circles.

"No, but I heard moaning. And Spence was supposed to be sleeping it off, and this was the first time she ever had anything to drink and I was kind of watching over her."

"So you've said. But I'm curious—" I stab my pen in the beer stein mug I use for a pencil holder and flip through the file to find her statement. "Excuse me. I can't seem to get your statement in front of me. It must have slipped out of the file or something. Didn't you say something about Emily and Spencer kissing earlier?"

"On the couch, yes, but—"

"And you heard moaning coming from her room?" The statement is stuck to a stapled medical sheet. I pull it out to read as I talk.

"Yes, but—"

"Let me finish, Melissa, okay?"

"Yes sir."

"Okay, I've got it now. It says that you see the two of them kissing on the couch. Later, you hear moaning coming from her bedroom. And because you think it's a mistake, you decide to interrupt them?"

"Well—"

"You know he's in jail now, right? I arrested him."

"She was passed out."

"You said you heard moaning, right?"

"Yes."

"People who are passed out do not moan, Melissa." I wait for a response and get none. "I've also talked to Josh about this. It says here in your statement that they were dating?"

"Yes, that's what she told me."

"Would it surprise you to hear that Josh disagrees with that?"

White noise from the phone.

"He also told me that Emily told you that Spencer was fingering her earlier. Is that right, Melissa?"

"Yes." The answer is almost a whisper now.

"Okay. So, you saw them making out?"

"Yes."

"And she told you he was fingering her. Was this before or after you walked in on them in her room?"

"Before."

"Was she unconscious when she told you this?"

"No."

"And did she say she didn't want this to happen?"

"No, but—"

"Kind of sounds like she was hooking up with Spencer, wouldn't you say?"

"She was really drunk."

"So, after you kicked Spencer out and went to her, did she say she had been raped?"

"No."

"Did she ask you to go get Josh?"

"No. I thought—"

"Did you ever think that maybe she might be embarrassed?"

Melissa doesn't answer.

"Put yourself in her shoes. You're in the middle of a drunken hookup, and your roommate barges in, kicks the guy out, and calls another guy you've been dating off and on to come to the rescue."

Melissa breathes into the other end of the phone.

"Kinda embarrassing, huh?"

"Yes," she says, almost inaudibly.

"Spencer is in jail awaiting trial for sexual battery, Melissa. Rape," I say, punching through the phone.

Melissa doesn't answer.

"Does that seem fair to you, Melissa?"

"Well, not when you say it like that."

A year after Spencer had his day in court, I receive a plain white envelope in my inbox. The return address has his name printed in block letters at the top. He must have gotten my name from the original charging affidavit. I doubt he would have remembered it from our interview introductions.

I slip the letter into my laptop bag and carry it to my new desk in Homicide. I try not to think about Sex Crimes anymore. When I pull the envelope out of my bag, the return address catches my eye. Scribbled under Spencer's name, in what looks like an afterthought, is his prison inmate number.

I only saw Spencer once after his arrest, months later and in passing at the courthouse. I was there on another case. Surprisingly, I was never called to testify at his trial. When I called the state attorney, Scott, after the verdict, he told me that he'd wanted sworn testimony without any of my conflicted emotions. Nick never heard the full story, so he was the obvious choice.

"Your report told me how you felt, Detective," he said on the phone.

"I didn't write anything that wasn't true."

"But I know how you felt. You can't hide that from a jury."

"Five years, Scott," I said. "Over a he said, she doesn't remember?"

"She was a credible victim."

"She told me she was a virgin and she wasn't even sure—"

"And that's why I didn't call you to the stand," he said. "If it makes you feel better," he added before hanging up, "it wasn't you who put him there, Detective. He had an attorney."

Sure. He had the right to an attorney, and handcuffs were my answer to exercising that right. Emily's statement gave me probable cause to arrest him. It was weak, but not so weak that my boss wouldn't want answers if I let Spencer go on a hunch. If only he'd told me his side of the story. I could have used discretion. I could have explained Spencer's logic to my boss, presented the reasonable doubt. I could have taken my time preparing the case, waiting days or weeks before forwarding it to the state attorney for prosecution. Any defense attorney worth his retainer would have the case thrown out on a technicality.

"Your Honor, the fact that my client was placed in handcuffs at his apartment, transported in the back of a squad car by uniformed patrol to an interrogation room across town, and read his Miranda Rights clearly shows that he was under arrest. I would argue that speedy trial began at that moment, regardless of his subsequent release."

It wouldn't be the first time something like that happened. Wouldn't be the last, either. Chalk it up to detective error. I could have done that. But he had to go and ask for an attorney. The way I saw it, he might as well have stamped the word *guilty* on his forehead.

Legally speaking, when it comes to an allegation of a sex crime, all I need is the sworn testimony of one person to put a man in jail. Even newspapers need more than that to run a story. And she wasn't even sure. But I figured he'd spend a night in jail and never hook up drunk again. I thought I was teaching him a lesson and still giving him a second chance; two birds, one stone.

But that's just me rationalizing. I didn't have to arrest him. Nothing is ever black and white. Haven't I spent the majority of my detective life arguing the gray to one supervisor or another? I'm always preaching the spirit of the law and not the letter. So what happened this time? Is not arguing with a supervisor really worth five years of a man's life?

It wasn't you who put him there, Detective. He had an attorney.

With the tip of my letter opener, I let the razor cut a slit across the top of Spencer's envelope. On small, tablet-sized notepad paper, he asks for a transcript of Melissa's interview for his appeal. I staple my business card to the top of a signed copy and have it in the mail before lunch. I hope, for his sake, he's got a new attorney.

Vance Voyles works as a Major Case detective in central Florida. He received his MFA in creative writing at the University of Central Florida, and his nonfiction, poetry, and fiction have been featured in *J Journal*, *Rattle Magazine*, and *Burrow Press Review*, respectively. He is currently working on a memoir, *Waiving Miranda: Confessions of a Sex Crimes Detective*, about his time in law enforcement.

GRAVE ROBBER:
A LOVE STORY
Joyce Marcel

It was odd hearing his voice on the telephone after I'd seen him on television the night before. He was one of those "Antiques Roadshow" experts in a show out of Arizona, and he was evaluating a handsome red, white and black Navaho chief's blanket. I knew his name because he worked for an auction house in Boston, and I had made a phone appointment to talk to him in the morning about pre-Columbian artifacts.

Back in the 1970s, when I was in my early 30s, I ran away from home, my family and a crumbling marriage with the partially hatched idea of going to the Galapagos Islands. I landed in Guayaquil, Ecuador, a place I couldn't even pronounce back then. I couldn't speak Spanish. I was short, scared and wearing a T-shirt that showed too much cleavage for a Catholic country.

It was the age of Second Wave feminism, and our marching slogan was to become the man we wanted to marry; in other words, we would carve out our own lives, not live someone else's. How was I to know that the man I wanted to become was Jack Kerouac, and I'd be on the road for the next seven years?

Eventually, my adventure involved a bit of grave robbing. I'm not too proud of that now, but in 1976, I didn't believe in ghosts or national treasure. I just wanted to keep traveling.

I bought pre-Columbian ceramics, textiles, jewelry and artifacts from a secret village tucked away in the Atacama Desert, far outside of Lima, Peru; I wrapped the stuff in newspaper and brought it to the United States. I kept everything but the ceramics, which I dropped off at Sotheby's Parke-Bernet in New York. Back then, they didn't care about ghosts or national treasures, either. They auctioned everything I gave them and sent the checks to me in Lima, and I'd be back on the road again.

I kept the jewelry, textiles and artifacts because they were beautiful and because it thrilled me to hold in my hands things that had been made and used by people who lived thousands of years before I did. My collection contained fragile lace woven centuries before Europeans practiced the art; a fragment of cotton woven with a pattern of birds holding human skulls in their mouths; brightly colored tiny warriors marching at the edge of an ancient poncho; a coca bag with fringe; a metal knife in the shape of a monkey; a woven basket full of weaving implements; an emerald that someone had drilled a very long time ago by rubbing a pointed implement between their hands; and a mother-of-pearl bead in the shape of a pelican. I liked to imagine the people who last used each artifact—how they had lived and how they died.

Even after I stopped traveling—I never made it to the Galapagos—I treasured these things as a reminder of a time when I could hold magic in my hands, but eventually, they ended up in my attic in Vermont, just waiting to be loved. And by "loved," I mean sold to someone who would love them.

So I contacted the antique dealer to see if he would auction off my collection.

He wanted to know where I'd gotten these things. It brought back a lot of memories.

After about six months on the road, mostly in Ecuador, I was staying in the capital city of Quito. Chuck Lane picked me up one day at a fountain in the old part of town, where I was leafing through my copy of "South American Handbook." His line was that he knew his way around South America because he'd been thrown out of the Peace Corps for smuggling and was there anything he could help me with?

He was a good-looking guy, tall and big-boned, with sandy hair and an easy manner. I later found out that he was 24, 10 years younger than I was. There were a lot of these guys on the road; a few years later, I would recognize them as "my type"—tall, blond, tender, blue-eyed 24-year-olds. After a while, I started calling them "my B-24s." We'd have adventures together for a few days, make passionate love at night and then say goodbye—perfect love affairs, short and very sweet. Chuck, bless him, was my first.

Chuck was hot for me, for sure—I was a rarity, a young American woman traveling alone—but soon, I was hot for him, too. To him, I was a just silly tourist who would be leaving South America in a few weeks. So over dinner one night, he told me about his perfect scam.

There was this town in the Peruvian desert, he said, a few hours outside of Lima, where the natives, whenever they dug a hole to shit, uncovered a grave.

The graves dated back to the Chancay civilization, he told me. It had thrived between 1000 and 1450 A.D., before the rise of the Incas. Because it was in the desert, where for thousands of years rainfall has been so minimal as to be unmeasurable, the bodies in the graves were mummified, perfectly preserved. So were their clothes, jewels, ceramics, weaving equipment and the other things that were buried with them. It was spooky to think about.

The town was built on sand, Chuck said. It had no sidewalks, no roads, no running water and barely any electricity. The houses were made out of palm thatch woven into mats and roped together to make walls. The roofs were also thatch.

The natives were poor, living in the middle of nowhere in the desert, miles away from the Pacific. Dried fish provided their sole source of protein, he said. They weren't interested in historical preservation. They dug up the bodies, unwrapped the cloth, sewed the largest pieces they could cut away onto sheets of blue paper, rethreaded the beads on fishing line and sold it all.

Only five people knew the location of this tiny town, Chuck whispered dramatically, and for the past two years, he had been going there as often as he could. He'd been buying everything he could get his hands on, taking it back to the States and selling it. When the Peace Corps found out, they threw him out of the

Corps, but that didn't stop Chuck from returning again and again to South America.

Two weeks earlier, he said, he had been in a bar in San Francisco, talking about Peru with some guy who turned out to be an art dealer. He took one look at what Chuck was selling, gave him $3,000, bought him a ticket and sent him back down to Peru. On his way back, he stopped in Ecuador to visit some former Peace Corps friends, and that was how I got to spend a few days with him.

We went back to his hotel, and he showed me what he was carrying: pieces of lace and tie-dyed cotton, old and dusty but with some of the color and detail still fresh, and some of it stained brown from blood or maybe body juices. Many of the cloth pieces, even the lace, had cats' faces and crabs and pelicans woven into them; after he pointed them out, I could see them clearly. Hundreds of strands of gorgeous bead necklaces, some red, some rosy, some orangey, which he called "*corales*" or "*conchas*," were made from Pacific Ocean shells. Some of the necklaces had turquoise and quartz crystal beads mixed in, and they all had little objects dangling from the center. Chuck said these were drop weights from weaving spindles. He showed me little green metal devices that were really copper tweezers, which the ancients had used to pull out any stray beard hairs. He had pottery shards and some wonderful dolls made out of cloth from the graves. It was thrilling to touch the textiles, to run my fingers through the bags of cool shell beads, to see the wealth of a lost civilization spread before me on a sagging bed in a cheap hotel.

He bragged. I listened closely and made mental notes.

He told me how to find the town. It was a complicated story about finding a particular bus station in Lima, then changing buses in Chancay, getting a rickety little jitney into the middle of the desert and finally walking over a tiny bridge that consisted of two logs close together.

You had to be clever, he laughed, because sometimes the natives made fake necklaces. Some of the *corales* looked like macaroni bits, so when the natives got greedy, they dyed and strung pasta. If he had any doubts, he sucked on the necklace, he said. But it wasn't a big problem because most of the natives were open and honest, and there was so much of the stuff in that town that you could buy beads by the kilo.

"Isn't this illegal?" I asked.

It was illegal in Peru to buy and transport such material outside the country, Chuck said, but not to bring the stuff into the United States. According to Chuck, America had no national treasures treaty with Peru.

I worshipfully helped him fold the cloth and put the beads back in bags, and when the bed was clear, we made spooky grave love on it.

The sex between us was so good that he checked out of his hotel and into my *"residencial"* as my instant husband. There the sex progressed to Olympic quality, and orgasms fell off my body like stars.

The religious imagery of Ecuador was starting to seep into my subconscious, and with Chuck's large, warm body wrapped around me, this little Jewish girl started to have mystical visions. First, in a mountainous region that was clearly Ecuador but was the color of Judea, a many-armed Indian deity, made of mother-of-pearl, wheeled up through the mountains without using its arms or legs. It stopped in front of me with a message about loving people more, or lying about loving them less.

Then up wheeled a plaster statute of Jesus with his open, radiating heart. His head was bent lovingly, and he was surrounded by people and animals who loved him so deeply that to sustain this love, he didn't even have to appear but could be represented by a tacky plaster cast. I was standing outside the circle of worshipers, and the message was that I must find a way to love Jesus without asking him to do anything for me. Such power, beauty and love were transmitted to me that I woke up feeling blessed, graced, translucent.

I woke Chuck up and made love to him, opening myself to him, taking him lovingly in. I don't know if he could tell the difference between this clear, direct, loving openness and the usual screwing around.

Then Chuck went back to the States. I never saw him again. That's the way of the road: You share intense experiences with people who will soon disappear from your life. And that's the way you want it. You can be open and vulnerable precisely because they will never come back again.

I continued to travel. One night about six months later, in the Amazon jungle, the boat I was traveling on hit a log and sank. Rescued by a tugboat, I stood on the deck at midnight, watching my passport, my clothes and my money racing away down the Rio Putumayo. Then I remembered Chuck's story. It took four miserable months to hitchhike my way out of the jungle, but when I finally washed up in La Paz, beat and broke, I wired my parents for $400 and hopped on a bus to Lima.

The Peruvian currency had just been devalued, and people were angry. During one riot, I was chased across the main square of Lima by a tank. The beautiful Peruvian "*soles*"—copper coins embossed with graceful llamas—were suddenly worth more as metal than as currency. The Peruvians collected them and shipped them to Ecuador to be melted down. Within a few days, there were no coins in the city. It became impossible to buy anything that cost less than five *soles,* the smallest bill. Bus drivers gave Chiclets and sucking candy as change.

It was in this desperate economic climate that I followed Chuck's directions. I took a bus to Chancay and then a jitney into the desert. I stood in the bare scrub for a while, and then children appeared out of nowhere. Calling to me, they led me over a tiny bridge made of two logs and into a shantytown.

The children's cries alerted the adults. They came running, dangling what, to my eyes, appeared to be the wealth of Inca kings. It was the same kind of jewelry, ceramics and cloth I had seen in Chuck's bags—and in the Lima Gold Museum the day before. It was like meeting Atahualpa, the Inca king, face to face.

I bought necklaces, textiles and colorful dolls made from pre-Columbian textile scraps. I bought ancient ceramic whistles in the shape of people and animals. I bought ceramic bowls and statues. I bought pelican beads made out of mother-of-pearl, with inlaid coral and turquoise—so tiny that four of them could fit on my thumbnail, but each one with four holes for sewing it onto cloth. What kind of civilization had the ancients developed, I wondered, that allowed them time to practice this delicate craftsmanship?

I spent every cent I had. When the haggling was over—by then, I spoke market Spanish, and body language and gestures went a long way in the countryside—and there were smiles all around, the women told me that what they really wanted was American costume jewelry and underpants with the days of the week embroidered on them. And the men? American booze. They asked if I would bring this stuff back to them and trade for artifacts.

I took my treasures back to Lima and spent hours figuring out how to wrap the ceramics so they wouldn't break. Then I headed for Ecuador by bus to meet an old lover in Quito. As I came closer to the border, I grew more and more paranoid. I was smuggling archeological treasures. I also had changed all my money on the black market, thus violating the government's currency laws—and helping out the Peruvians, who needed the hard American cash.

At that point, I formulated "Joyce's Law": After you've decided to do something illegal or weird, give up on the worrying. No matter what nightmares you imagine, reality will be different. And anyway, it's out of your control.

At the border, nothing happened—except that the immigration man said, "I won't let you through; you're too pretty. I want you to stay with me."

Once back in New York, I took my treasures straight to Sotheby's, and I was in business. For the next five years, I had a routine. I flew from New York to Florida, where my parents were living in a retirement complex. I stopped at Kmart for costume jewelry and ladies underpants and scarves, picked up Scotch at the duty-free store in the airport, landed in Lima, stashed my purchases in a friendly hotel and hit the road. When, after six or seven months, I had spent all but $500 of Sotheby's money on travel and adventure, I went back to Lima, picked up my stuff and went to the desert.

It never failed—little children always materialized out of the sand and led me into town. Their parents and I would sit on logs while chickens moved among us, pecking. We traded earrings for beads, underwear for textiles and whiskey for ceramics.

Over time, I watched that little town grow: Woven huts were replaced by cement-block houses, paths in the sand by sidewalks, frond roofs by red tile. In time, ladies underwear from Kmart wasn't good enough; the women wanted Chanel. They were prospering. They were sending their kids to college to learn about pre-Columbian civilizations. They were serving as a clearinghouse for grave robbers from all over Peru—it was no longer just Chancay artifacts they were selling, but complex, colorful and ancient Tiahuanaco and Mochica pieces, as well.

And they weren't the only ones in the business. There were times when I could go to the back door of the Gold Museum in Lima after hours and buy ancient ceramics off the shelves. Peru was dirt poor. Everyone wanted dollars. Everyone had an angle.

The last time I visited that town, a young girl in the dunes told me, "You should see the cemetery. Holes, holes, holes. Only holes."

What put me out of business wasn't the holes. Or a conscience. It wasn't being priced out of the trade. It wasn't the competition from gringos who took the business much more seriously than I did. It was, as always, politics. The United States suddenly recognized Peru's national treasures act.

In 1980, instead of being passed through U.S. customs by bored inspectors, I was stopped. My luggage was searched, and I was taken into a small room and given a harsh lesson about the harm I was doing by robbing a country of its archeological treasures. I was such a small-time operator that they let me go with my last shipment intact. Later, when the big exporters came through, they were busted and their shipments confiscated. And when the really big operators arrived, customs not only confiscated their shipments but went to their homes and took their personal collections.

Not long after that, the Metropolitan Museum of Art featured a big pre-Columbian show—gold, ceramics, textiles, dolls, artifacts. I read in Time Magazine that the show had been curated from all the confiscated materials. By that time, I was living in Panama and teaching English as a second language to Japanese businessmen, but I happened to be visiting New York and caught the show. The artifacts were like old friends. Many on display were far more valuable than anything I had ever held in my hands. But there they were, behind glass, with little signs explaining them to visitors. When the exhibition was over, according to Time, the artifacts were sent back to Peru, where they belonged.

The auction guy listened to my story and rejected my collection. It turned out he'd recently accepted for auction another collection that was remarkably similar to mine: textile fragments sewed onto blue paper, dolls, beads, artifacts, weaving baskets chock-full of implements. He said there was a lot of this kind of material on the market.

Whispering, Chuck had told me that only five people in the world knew the location of that town. Of course, over time, I had watched the town grow and prosper as more and more antique dealers from Europe and the United States found it. But now, I see that from the beginning, instead of being on the hip, cutting edge of adventure, I was just one of many, many people who took that bus, changed to that jitney, went into that desert and met those smiling, waving children. They might as well have been running tour buses out there, because there's such a glut of this material on the market today. Even the auction guy had some of it. He told me that he and his wife had been in Peru in 1980, and they had brought back the same kinds of artifacts I was trying to auction off.

So it doesn't look as if I'm going to make any money in the near future selling my pre-Columbian artifacts. But I'll always have the memories of those trips into the desert, and they are far more precious to me than lace woven a thousand years ago in the deserts of Peru. Maybe I can sell them, instead.

Joyce Marcel has been an award-winning Vermont journalist for twenty-three years. This story is taken from an unpublished memoir, selected chapters of which are available online.

APOLOGY

John Nosco

"Your Honor, as you know, I have already pled guilty to the charges against me, but I appreciate this opportunity to provide some background for my actions, so that they may be judged within the fuller context I will here provide in explaining that on the night of April 24, after a long shift not selling cars at Ford West, a dealership in Bellflower, I drove home through a slight drizzle to San Pedro, stopping by The Port Hole, a small bar just up the street from this courthouse, where, between approximately midnight and 1 A.M., I consumed a gin and tonic, a bottle of Budweiser and a Kamikaze shot, and, deeming the day's sulk complete, exited to what had become a rather heavy downpour and walked toward my truck for the short drive to my apartment, along the way encountering a very wet African-American man, in his early 30s, asking for bus money to help him get to Torrance, to whom I responded, motivated simultaneously by benevolent empathy and a bluff-calling cynicism regarding his disposal of any funds presented, by offering a ride instead, a proposal that he, to my chagrin, accepted, so we took the Harbor Freeway northbound to Torrance, driving for the most part in silence through the steadily increasing rain, a quiet interrupted a few miles into our journey when I noticed my cell phone's absence from its customary place in the cup-holder of the truck's center console, reflected briefly on its possible whereabouts, determined my passenger the likely culprit and asked if he had taken it, an accusation vigorously denied, occasioning a conversational impasse repeated several times as we neared the Anaheim exit and I decided, in a glaring instance of panicked irrationality, that the best plan was to return to San Pedro and sort things out there, a course of action inauspiciously begun by my skidding over water pooled on the off-ramp, losing control, spinning completely around and crashing into a guardrail, after which, buoyed by an adrenaline-spiked cocktail of fear, anger, uncertainty and, one can reasonably assume, alcohol, I resumed driving, made a left on Anaheim, passed under the freeway and pulled onto the southbound on-ramp, a reversal that tipped the balance of panic toward my passenger, turning his indignation into desperate cries for release, to my lingering shame perfectly justified had he not stolen my phone, a (to my mind) unlikely scenario whose nevertheless legitimate possibility has provided much of the emotional impetus for my guilty plea, and as his appeals to be let out and my insistence that he first return the phone got louder, I again lost control of the truck, spun out and crashed into another guardrail, whereupon the engine died, my passenger exited and ran off into the night, and, after several failed ignition attempts, I walked to a nearby gas station, called 9-1-1, reported that I had wrecked my truck in the course of being robbed, requested a tow truck and returned to the scene to stand in the rain and await the highway patrol and tow service, both of which arrived within the time it took me to smoke a single, soggy cigarette, which the officers were kind enough to let me finish while explaining what had happened, an account quite similar to the one here provided, in response to which the officers administered a field sobriety test, an examination I feel I handled quite competently, although my assessment differs from that of the proctors, who decided to take me in for further testing, a turn of events I accepted cooperatively, to such an extent that the officers conferred and deemed me a suitable first arrest for Officer-in-Training Johnson, who then handcuffed me, read me my rights, helped me into the back of his patrol car and drove to the Harbor Division Station, where the breathalyzer registered my blood-alcohol content as .1 percent, just above California's legal limit of .08 percent, I congratulated Officer Johnson and wished him a successful and safe career, went through the remainder of the booking process, including the confiscation of my driver license, and spent the night in a communal cell, following which I was released to a long walk home and the realization that with my license suspended until the date of this court appearance, my tenure as a car salesman was effectively over, then a few hours later took a taxi to the impound lot, where the tow-truck driver, upon hearing my story, had a sudden inspiration, asked for my phone number, dialed it on his cell phone and by pretending to be a police officer investigating a murder committed by the phone's registered owner, a rather odd deceit perhaps itself illegal, ascertained that the man who answered "sounded black," was unwilling to identify himself or how he had come into possession of the phone and had no interest in returning it, hardly conclusive evidence that my suspicions were correct, and not nearly enough to assuage my conscience, but heartening news nonetheless, after which the tow-truck driver took me and my truck to an auto shop, where it was soon determined that the vehicle had suffered irreparable structural damage, and having spent all my money on the taxi, impound fees and tow truck, I began another long walk home and the month-long course of reflection that has filled my waking hours between that day and this, an honest, careful consideration of the past failures in judgment that ultimately brought me here, beginning with my excessive consumption of alcohol, which from now on I intend to moderate, and extending to the selfish and self-defeating choices I have childishly surrendered to under its influence—such as getting behind the wheel after drinking, such as magnifying the dangers of driving while intoxicated by inviting someone else to ride with me, such as leaping to conclusions and endangering the life of a stranger who may have simply been in the wrong place at the wrong time—and leading into the less important but still pressing calculations of how to pay for the graduate studies I am set to begin this September at the University of Chicago, an expense I planned to offset with my car sales earnings, but which presently seems quite daunting, particularly in light of the fees and fines associated with a conviction for driving under the influence, costs I humbly request your leniency in determining, and, finally, expanding to a broader contemplation of my future, the responsibilities I must embrace to become the kind of person I want to be, and how best to ensure that my decisions and actions always reflect the lessons I have learned from this experience, the sum of which I hope you will consider as you formulate your sentence."

Maybe that's what I would have said had the courthouse clerk found my name on the docket. She looked over my summons, then, after several phone calls, deduced that the officers hadn't filed charges with the District Attorney and told me I was free to go.

John Nosco lives in New York and is a student at Columbia Law School. "Apology" is the seventh chapter of "Damage," a collection of experimental autobiographical essays.

PARRISH, RAWLINGS, HOLLIS, AND FLYTHE, 2008

David McConnell

Randallstown, Maryland, is one of those well-maintained middle-class suburbs, like Gary, Indiana, that over the past decades, without any fuss, has become almost entirely African American—more than eighty percent at last count. Regulation plastic garbage cans are left atilt at the curb in front of modest single-family houses. The cars are mostly Toyotas, though there's an Infiniti in one driveway and the occasional beater or Harley. Unmowed lawns are rare. The air of conformity is standard-issue suburban.

Older people might mistake the town for an enclave of Polish autoworkers, because, frankly, it looks like the kind of place blue-collar racists tried to keep black people *out* of in the bad old days. Instead, no one has to think about integration here at all. As if bookending a whites-only past, nearly every face you see is brown—an even higher percentage of African Americans than in Baltimore next door.[*]

Many of the families in Randallstown came here to get out of crime-ridden Baltimore. Shrinking since 1950, Baltimore is now hardly more than a borough of the Boston-to-Washington megalopolis I-95 ties together. Thirty thousand old houses are abandoned and boarded up. The reputations of Edgar Allan Poe and Frederick Douglass have faded equally. The city's new mythology has come from the TV show *The Wire*. To a visiting New Yorker (me), the crime-consciousness feels like a throwback to the 1970s. The local, alternative, free *City Paper* runs a roundup column called "Murder Ink." A recent issue's headline tally was, "Murders This Week: 6;

---

[*] *Of major US cities, Baltimore has a higher percentage of African Americans than any but Detroit and New Orleans.*

This Year: 109."

Randallstown has little in common with *The Wire*'s gangsta paradise of Section 8 housing, trashed row houses, and hyperalert but stoned-acting loiterers giving the four-fingers-down signal of dope dealers. In Randallstown the kids are good, though they mostly go to the not-so-good Randallstown High School. That sprawling brick pile couldn't be more suburban, set amid acres of parking lots and tennis courts and basketball courts and playing fields. Almost hiding the entrance, a windowless, modernist Martello tower juts out toward a parking lot. Against the tower's mass of brick, a banner of the school's mascot ram is almost lost. A corner of the banner has come away and flutters briskly to the shouting of a thousand kids.

At the end of the school day the buses have lined up in front of the school. Most kids mill around waiting for their ride, but a lot walk home: a threesome of fat girls, an undersized, bespectacled loner with an oversized backpack, a knot of seniors with a student-comedian shuffling backward on the sidewalk in front of them telling jokes. Within an hour or so, like a wave into sand, the shrilling crowd disappears completely into the suddenly quiet suburb.

Sometimes Michelle Parrish, in every way an ordinary mother, would come to this school to pick up her son Steven and his best friend Steven Hollis. She'd drive them to her place and the two Stevens would have a sleepover. Or else the boys would walk from school several blocks to the Hollis home on Bengal Road, and they'd spend the night there. They were pretty much inseparable best friends.

Parrish was more handsome and gregarious. His nickname was "Scooby." Hollis's academic problems were somehow reflected in his face—he was an odd-looking kid. His nose, cheeks, and jaw jutted forward. The top part of his head was smaller and narrower. Attractive eyes receded under a strange, sharply V-shaped brow, a permanent frown that made him appear both uncomprehending and on the verge of anger. He'd had a blood disorder when he was born and was diagnosed with ADHD as a seven-year-old, but neither would account for that scarily tragic expression. Maybe it was why they called him "Loco."

In high school, a frustrated Loco discovered the one thing he excelled at, football. At six-one and 190 pounds, he was a good fit. Scooby encouraged him. As they got older the pair joined up with a whole band of school friends. Juan Flythe was "Woo." Jasiah Carroll was "Scrappie."

The boys found the Parrish place ideal for hanging out. Where the Hollises' small Bengal Road house—white with black shutters— was crowded in amongst other houses, the Parrishes' place was in Gwynn Oaks Landing, a vast rental project of two-story tan brick townhomes. The homes came in eight- or ten-unit blocks arranged in simple patterns on short dead-end streets off a stretch of Essex Lane. The streets had cute names like Strawbridge Court and Cedar Park Court and Mountbatten Court. The Parrishes lived at 21 Thornhurst Court. Though all rental, the complex looked like a well-maintained condo project. A parklike barrier of woods and artful boulders separated Essex Road from the townhomes and parking lots. Unseen, vigilant neighbors were everywhere.

But what made it such a good place for hanging out was that all those dead-end "Courts" and townhomes backed up against a dense patch of woods, heaven for kids to play in, to explore, to make out in, to get drunk or high in. 21 Thornhurst Court was all the way at the back where, right next to a garbage bin, a path opened into the woods.

The forest has a name only a mapmaker would know (Villa Nova Park), but it is just called "the woods." If you walk in past the garbage bin at the end of Thornhurst Court, you can go straight through brush down a steep ravine to Gwynns Falls Creek. Crossing the stream in a couple of hops, you can climb the even steeper far side of the ravine. Up there, trees and brush are suddenly replaced by lawns and gravestones, the more recent ones forlornly decorated with plastic flowers and burnt-out tea lights holding puddles of old rainwater like lachrymal vases. This is Woodlawn Cemetery, also a terrific place for a kid to play. Just the right mix of eeriness, emptiness, cranky groundskeepers, and a pond (a dammed stretch of the creek) almost too small for a huge, nearly tame flock of mallards. Idlers are always feeding them with crumbled bread.

If you turn sharply right from the garbage bin, you'll follow a path along the crest of the ravine's near side. This shortcut behind the townhomes of Gwynn Oaks Landing pops back out onto Essex Road where you can make a left on Windsor Mill Road. Down a hill is the area's main drag with a Royal Farms store (a local chain of gas stations/quickie marts) and the police station.

Idyll though all this appears for a boy whose family doesn't have a lot of money, when adolescence hits, and the shadow of Baltimore seems to inch closer, a boy's thoughts can turn to gangs, even in Randallstown. Even good kids give it some thought. The universal alarm that gang life inspires in places like Randallstown looks like power to a kid who's worried about disrespect. The all-diminishing mockery of high school can't touch gang members.

Still, compared to criminal Baltimore City types, these particular boys from surrounding Baltimore County might as well have been country bumpkins. How serious can a gang get in a suburb? Maybe it was more like a fraternity, an in-your-face version of the "Greek Life" some African Americans embrace in college. These guys, Loco, Woo, were on the football team, after all. What does this have to do with crime? Their interest in a gang had to be juvenile swagger, play. Unfortunately, the nature of play is always to mimic the real thing.

About to graduate from high school, the boys found part-time jobs. They had to. A storage center. A day labor agency. They were getting a glimpse of the life ahead of them. Scooby found work at a pharmacy on Liberty Road, one of the big streets radiating from downtown Baltimore. A gay guy named Jimmie worked there too. He was older, in his thirties, perhaps. Though Scooby wasn't bothered by a gay guy, the work was boring. Loco took a job as a cashier at a McDonald's. It wasn't exactly football and his permanent frown may have started to represent real surliness.

They all revered a slightly older guy with the street name "Murk" (Benjamin Wureh). And when they talked to him about forming a gang, he advised them, "You wanna make it real, you gotta go to Hood."

"Hood" was Timothy Rawlings Jr. He was four years older than the two Stevens. He was much smaller as well, only five-nine and 157 pounds. He looked like a kid, an extremely grave kid. His hair was cropped short, no fancy dreads or cornrows or the gumball-sized twists Loco wore. His humorless charisma was just the kind to win young men over. Small as he was, he'd been the quarterback of the Parkville High School football team. He had a still, wild form of leadership, self-conscious of his power, forever poised, permanently insecure.

Real morality was probably invisible to a guy as focused as Hood. What took its place was ritual, rules, signs, the arcana of groups and obscure subgroups like FOE: "If you rep that FOE, you about Family Over Everything."

Hood's father was a career criminal with other things than family on his mind. Hood lived just inside the Baltimore city limits with his mother, Tereia Hawkins, who'd raised him alone. She was a long-time state employee, a corrections officer, ironically. A huge, slow woman, she had an air of long-suffering endurance. Under a smattering of unprofessional tattoos, her upper arms swung like wattles when she moved.

Once the boys hooked up with Hood, things changed quickly. They would be Bloods—that is, they'd side with the American archipelago of gangs who favor red and, along with the Crips, are one half of a modern underground version of the ancient Blues and Greens, the quasipolitical hippodrome fanatics who terrorized Constantinople. (Most old pictures of Scooby show him wearing a pregang blue bandanna, not the red one that became part of his gang wear and his last outfit.)

You couldn't just be a Blood. You kouldn't just start religiously avoiding the Crips' letter *C* when you texted your boyz. History and heraldry were involved. Most gang names hark back to an address, street, or neighborhood in Los Angeles where the Crips and Bloods got their start. That's where "Swans" came from, apparently. Under Hood the Randallstown boys would become "Family Swans 92" or the "92 Family Swans." Each gang member had a swan or the name tattooed on their shoulder or arm.

When Michelle and Steven Sr. saw the tattoos Scooby had gotten on his forearms, they were furious. Scooby's father, a large man with the weary manners of millions of American husbands, grumbled with repulsion and let his wife rail at their son. She was a sharp-tongued woman. But even she ran out of words eventually, and she threw up her hands and shook her head in bitter disappointment, a pot boiling dry though still on the flame.

Scooby was a charmer and tried explaining to his parents that, yes, it was a gang, but it didn't mean he was going to have to do anything bad or illegal. It was just group friendship. Like the one between him and Loco. Nothing different. His parents challenged him: how would it look when he went for a job? He promised, he swore, it was nothing bad, not the big deal they thought it was.

Other parents had the same reaction. But how do you confront an ever-more-remote and indifferent kid? Woo's (Juan Flythe's) father didn't even know what his son was up to until he found out from a cousin. She told him Juan was hanging out with a bad crowd. So Juan's father went to his own mother, Bercille, a tough, almost mannish woman with whom Juan was living at that point. Father and grandmother discussed it. Yet they couldn't do more than discuss and worry. They certainly weren't going to talk to the police about the boy they loved, though a judge later wished aloud, idly, that parents would do just that in gang cases.

The Parrishes, at any rate, regained a little hope after the initial shock. Scooby really was an endearing kid. He was about to graduate. He went off to driving school every day around four thirty, taking that shortcut through the woods. He'd applied for a UPS job. And he was thinking about Baltimore Community College.

May 25, 2008 was Scooby's eighteenth birthday. He was a senior, school was almost over, the weather was getting warmer, he was tight with the 92 Family Swans—things must have felt good.

He had friends over to 21 Thornhurst Court for a birthday party for himself. The inner circle came: Loco, of course, and Woo and some girls—the high school crowd. Murk came, but not Hood. This party may have seemed too suburban or kidlike to him. Or maybe he thought his absence would add to the mystique of leadership. Soon enough Scooby disappeared upstairs with his girlfriend. It was his birthday after all.

Downstairs the party continued. Why someone picked up Scooby's cell phone, which he'd left downstairs, isn't clear, but the lead detective on the case wonders whether the kids weren't searching for naked pictures of the girlfriend so they could razz the pair about it later.

Anyway, they clicked their way through Scooby's cell phone, and they did find a picture. It was a shot of Scooby's penis. That might have been good—funny and embarrassing enough—but the photo was part of a text exchange between Steven Parrish and Jimmie, the older gay guy who worked at the Liberty Road pharmacy. The exchange was humorous, if anything. As recalled by the same detective, it went something along the lines of:

Jimmie, u see wat I got here? U wishin huh?

I don see nuthin much. Dat all u got me fo ur bday?

U see it good enuf.

Nobody told Scooby what they'd seen on his phone; he was still busy upstairs. Apparently the bedroom tryst didn't seem significant compared to the queer texts. Loco and Woo became confused and angry. They left soon afterward. Maybe a faint, moblike outrage filled the air, because someone also stole the girlfriend's iPod before leaving.

"Gayness" in this story is all but ungraspable. Everyone says Scooby was straight. A lot of them insist on it more than seems decent (as if his murder would make sense otherwise). He did have girlfriends. And it's not uncommon for a straight boy to get a kick out of the attentions of a gay man.

Regardless, Loco and Woo were suddenly as angry about Scooby's sexual identity as Michelle had been about his gang identity. Why they reacted this way is hard to understand. In Loco's case I imagine he felt compromised himself. Young people think their reputations echo across the world. This could have been too great a blot. The whole world knew Scooby and he were best friends. The world knew about the sleepovers, knew they'd grown up together and shared an intimate loyalty to one another.

An additional driving issue may have had to do with football and the 92 Family Swans, not so much sudden discomfort about the gray area of male bonding as the idea that any team has to have a unified purpose, and certain kinds of individuality ruin that. Destruction of a weak link isn't destruction at all. It's fortifying, honorable, sanctioned.

Loco and Woo stewed through the 26th and most of the 27th before Woo finally said, "We gotta take it to Hood."

As Hood saw it, too many people had been at the party, too many people knew. And "gay," because of its aura of submission, meant weak. Hood felt in the abstract—on behalf of the 92 Family Swans— exactly as Loco felt for himself. How would it look? Family Over Everything. The F in FOE didn't mean family, of course, except in the Mafia sense. Only brutal, gangsta irony would make a sweet-sounding slogan into an acronym like FOE.

Scholars have written about scorn in ancient times for the bow as a combat weapon. It was used, but a feeling existed from at least as far back as Homer that there was something ignoble about the arrow's power to kill at a distance compared to hand-to-hand combat, which measured man against man. ("Archery is no test of a man's bravery. A man stands fast in his rank and faces without flinch the gashing of the quick spear." Euripides, *Heracles*.) The same unease recurs throughout the developmental history of weapons. Six-shooters got the moniker "equalizers" because they made size and strength nonissues. And the problem is with us right now in its most dramatic form ever, when joysticks in Florida control drones on the Afghan-Pakistan border.

This is relevant, because Hood was about to murder at a distance. The testimony from Florida is that killing at a distance isn't like a video game at all. It feels real. So Hood, this small, serious twenty-two-year-old, was probably going to feel the reality of it too, no matter how he played it. On May 28 he called a meeting.

His gang met him at the Mondawmin Mall. The mall is a huge, cheap bilevel structure with a gleaming all-white interior. You'd never guess it was actually the oldest enclosed mall in Baltimore, dating from 1956.* It's located on the rapid transit line halfway between Randallstown and Baltimore's Inner Harbor and has the usual complement of national chains, plus a check-cashing place, a wig store. A Pakistani-run jewelry shop sells stereotypical bling while outside guys hawk African-style tribal items. But the mall has a dangerous reputation. In some quarters it's spoken of as the kind of place white people might not want to go. And despite the security guards, I saw people buying dope in the men's room.

At the center of the mall is a huge skylit atrium. A glitzy spiral staircase swoops down from a second-level balcony over a circular reflecting pool. Shops line the upper level except right at the balcony, which serves as a sort of lounge. Against a sunny wall of plate-glass windows, overstuffed neo-Deco chairs have been arranged around square fake-leather-upholstered tables or footstools. When I was there, I watched what looked like idling gang members flounce en masse onto the lounge chairs. This is likely where the meeting took place. Besides Hood, at least Loco, Woo, Scrappie, Justin Inman, and Marc Miller were present. Others may have escaped mention.

The name was borrowed from Mondamin, the Indian corn god in Longfellow's "Song of Hiawatha," whom Hiawatha wrestles to death in a strange foreshadowing of Scooby's own death: "And before him breathless, lifeless,
Lay the youth, with hair disheveled,
Plumage torn, and garments tattered,
Dead he lay there in the sunset."

At the meeting, it was made clear that Scooby, based on what was now "known" about him, was going to make the 92 Family Swans look weak or vulnerable. There had already been a few fights with Crips. Scooby himself had been involved in one or two, though they were more like schoolyard tussles than a gang war. Ultimately, the opinion of fellow Bloods may have been just as important.

Hood took all this seriously. It was his nature. Maybe he was really hoping to build a criminal enterprise someday. Maybe he was simply drinking down the experience of his own leadership in breathless gulps. Or running as fast as he could in his thoughts to remain out in front of the rest of them.

Loco was speaking about his closest friend, but he was looking at Hood, a boy quarterback wearing an expression as somber and unreadable as a lizard's. Hood was saying that they had to *do* something about this. These boys had been studying rules and rituals from the moment their gang was founded. Probably few of them dared offer more than grunts of assent when Hood gravely invoked some heartless rule. A law. He chose who would take care of it. He told them to get it done quickly.

On the 29th, the next day, a couple of people were warned to stay away from the Parrish place. Murk texted Justin Inman and told him not to go to Thornhurst Court that afternoon, even though Inman had been picked as one of the killers. "It is going to be hot over there. They are going to do that thing." Murk, who was older, may still have felt a glimmer of choice. For everyone else, choice had vanished.

It was Loco—Steven Hollis—and Woo—Juan Flythe—who went to Thornhust Court at around four thirty in the afternoon. Loco was seen approaching the Parrish place, where he'd spent so much of his childhood. He lingered by the black-painted metal door, set back like all the others in an arched recess. This was the time Scooby usually went to driving school, and he soon came out. He and Loco walked around the corner of the building toward the garbage bin and woods. Maybe Woo was in the woods already or joined them as they entered.

Woo and Loco later told a friend that they confronted Scooby about the picture and that he said he didn't want to talk about it. They dwelled on the fact that Scooby never denied the picture's implication. Loco supposedly grumbled, "We did what we had to do."

What Scooby said to them in the woods isn't known apart from the screamed half-sentence or two overheard by witnesses. The three boys got about halfway down the path, the shortcut that veers right. Whether they were arguing or sullen, whether Scooby was furious or embarrassed, he couldn't have been expecting what happened. Woo grabbed his friend and started cutting. Echoing Steve Mullins, the Alabama killer, Woo says he didn't feel quite present during the attack. Scooby was heard screaming, "Hey! Stop! Why you doing this to me . . . ? I didn't do nothing!" The pleading went on for a short while. Badly cut, Scooby broke away from Woo and hurtled toward Loco, who shoved his own knife into Scooby's chest, cutting the side of his heart.

Scooby fell. Loco and Woo now beat and kicked him. Woo says Loco was in a frenzy. He stomped on his best friend's neck, crushing the boy's windpipe. Either the cut to the heart or the crushed neck would have been fatal. But Scooby had over fifty cuts on his hands and head and body. It was about 4:50. The killers took their victim's cell phone, camera, and pocketknife. Woo says Loco also took Scooby's pants off—as if in ritual humiliation. The pants were never found, though Murk swears he later saw them and the phone at Woo's house. As a last gesture, either Loco or Woo laid a red bandanna over Scooby's face.

The killers made cell phone calls to fellow gang members at 4:55 and 4:56, probably before they left the woods. "It's done." At 5:02, Scrappie (Jasiah Carroll) texted: "So is he gone or wat?" Murk answered: "Shut da fuk up."

Fifteen or twenty minutes later, a neighborhood guy named Blaze came up the path from the opposite direction. He stopped. He ran the rest of the way to Gwynn Oaks Landing. He spotted a couple of girls he knew: "You wanna see Scooby's body? He's up in the woods!" A 911 call had been put in as soon as the screaming was heard. Not long after Blaze found the body, police arrived.

During those fifteen or twenty minutes, Loco and Woo must have walked the length of the shortcut and come out on Essex Road without running into Blaze. They later said they'd chucked their knives in one of the garbage bins. Loco and Woo kept walking to Windsor Mill Road, turned left, and strolled down the steep hill alongside busy traffic. They were probably bloodied, probably carrying a bloody pair of pants. They walked right past the police station to the parking lot of that Royal Farms store.

Meanwhile, Hood was driving around Baltimore in his gray Dodge Avenger (a sexy limited-edition model named, incredibly, "Stormtrooper"). In the bucket seat next to him sat Curtis McClean. Despite the huge wings tattooed across his back, McClean wasn't a member of the 92 Family Swans. ("That guy was so big he didn't have to bother about gangs," a detective later explained to me.) Hood got a phone call and told McClean, "I gotta pick my boys up." The agreed-upon spot was the Royal Farms store.

So there were four of them in the sporty Avenger. Presumably, team killing demands team debriefing or team congratulations. Not a happy slap on the butt so much as a grave, "You did what had to be done."

They drove downtown to the Bentalou-Smallwood neighborhood of southwest Baltimore. Christian Street is a drab-looking stretch of cheap old brick and clapboard town houses, several with fake stone siding. Dead quiet during the day, the street is home to a couple of bars. One, on the corner of Payson, has no sign except a neon *Open* in a tiny window. Across the intersection is a shabby, gray-painted place called Incognito. *Open Seven Days* and *Package Goods* are stenciled under a tar-paper overhang. The four boys went into one of these bars.

They drank. They must have reassured each other in the stiff, terse way of boys and men. You can imagine Hood drunk with fascination about what had happened but careful not to show weak-seeming curiosity.

At some point Loco and Woo left. Perhaps they went to Woo's place where the pants and phone were allegedly later seen. They were just the instruments of murder, which were now put away. For Hood the evening wasn't over.

If Hood arrived at the bar at five thirty or six, he had a long time to get grimly and pleasantly dizzy about the murder he'd ordered. Several others joined him and McClean. Michael Fitzgerald is the only one who's been identified. The next time we hear about the group it's around two thirty A.M. Hood, McClean, and Fitzgerald (plus the one or two unknowns) drove to Baltimore and South Streets. They parked two cars, Hood's and an old red Saturn of Fitzgerald's, in a parking garage on the northeast corner of the intersection.

This is the heart of downtown Baltimore. The '80s Chamber of Commerce building stands across Baltimore Street from the parking garage. City Hall is a block north and east. From here South Street runs a couple of blocks into the Inner Harbor and the berth of the museum ship sloop-of-war *USS Constellation*.

Catercorner to the parking garage is the handsome American Building, the old home of the long-defunct *Baltimore American* newspaper. The building has an ornate cast-iron façade painted dark green, which now frames the windows of a twenty-four-hour 7-Eleven. The garish red and green *7-ELEVEN* sign makes for a jarring contrast to the faded gilt of the Gothic black-letter *Baltimore American* above it.

At two thirty, the fluorescent-lit 7-Eleven must have been the brightest place around. The entrance is at the corner of the building, a vestibule with glass doors opening onto both South and Baltimore Streets. Three guys happened to be waiting near the South Street entrance: Jermaine Kelley, Brandon Sanders, and, just across the street, Christopher Webster. They were waiting on Howard and Davon Horton, who were picking up a few things in the store. The kids were dressed a little ghetto—Gucci sunglasses, diamond studs—but they weren't gang members.

From the garage across the intersection comes a group of black guys, strung out like wolves. Hood, McClean, Fitzgerald, more. One of this group, unidentified except that he was wearing a white baseball cap, walks up to Webster. He lifts the front of his shirt to show he's carrying a handgun. He takes it out.

Brandon Sanders, who was nearest the 7-Eleven entrance, ducked inside and told Howard and Davon, "Guy got a gun on your cousin, man!"

Howard looked out the window and saw Webster leaning against the granite footing of the Chamber of Commerce building across the street. Some guy in a white hat was talking to him, but it didn't look like a robbery.

So Howard steps out to find out what's going on. As he does, he sees his cousin taking off his shoes (to prove he has no money hidden), and he sees the guy in the white cap slip the gun back into his "dip area," as they call it in Baltimore.

Before he can react, Michael Fitzgerald, one of the guys who'd joined Hood and McClean, grabs Howard's arms from behind. "Empty your pockets!"

Howard figured this guy had a gun as well, so he fished four or five dollars from his front left pocket. Fitzgerald meanwhile slipped a hand into Howard's right front pocket and took Davon's car keys (Howard had been driving his brother's car), before ordering him, "Push it down the street!"

All this happened so quickly, Jermaine Kelley was still standing there at a complete loss. Fitzgerald swung toward him and grabbed the Cincinnati Reds cap from his head. Curtis McClean approached and ordered Jermaine to take out his diamond earrings. "Gimme your wallet and glasses!" Fitzgerald added. And after Jermaine gave them everything, Fitzgerald shouted, "Get the fuck out of here!"

While this was happening, Davon slipped out of the 7-Eleven and hurried down South Street. Not fast enough. One of the attackers (unknown) demanded his watch. Davon refused.

Someone yelled, "Just shoot him! Just shoot him!" This could have been Hood's second fiat for murder that day, but nobody knows who did the yelling. In any case, the attacker dutifully shot Davon three times—chest, shoulder, hip. Each bullet went clean through him. (Davon lived, barely.)

The shooter ran down South Street. The rest of them backtracked to the parking garage, where it happened a plainclothes detective was working that night. A police car was also sitting two blocks east on Baltimore Street. It made a U-turn and got to the intersection in seconds. The plainclothes detective caught Fitzgerald by his car. After more police arrived and the garage had been sealed off, officers approached a Dodge Avenger with tinted windows. Both seats were laid out flat. Two people were hiding. On the passenger's side: McClean. A hollow point bullet fell from his pants when he responded to the order to get out. Lying flat in the driver's seat: Hood. What was on that motionless, serious boy's mind as he ended his career as a leader in a shabby robbery like this?

Something rare happened in this case. Despite the baby faces involved, despite the nice Randallstown families, this was an authentic gang murder. Loco and Woo were caught easily enough, but neither they nor anyone else would name names because of the gang connection. Detectives Gary Childs and Joseph Caskey (who ran the case from the beginning) simply didn't believe Loco and Woo's gay story at first. The detectives were probably too grown-up or too sophisticated to understand or remember the bizarre, boyish ideal of impeccable manliness. Indeed, the gangs frequently mystified them. Childs shook his head when he told me about a boy who admitted shooting somebody simply because "he was mugging me," Baltimore slang for staring at him.

Woo, with his shaggy dreads, his raggedy beard coming to a point, with a heaviness around his hips that gave his thuggish appearance a trace of cowlike gentleness, eventually told his father everything—the gang, the order to kill. His father had no advice except a halting, automatic, and insufficient, "You gotta do the right thing."

If he cooperated with prosecutors, Woo would have to worry for the safety of his grandmother Bercille, his father, his entire family. He'd have to serve his time in protective custody. Out of genuine remorse, apparently, he finally did talk. He talked about the birthday party and the meeting at Mondawmin Mall and the order, mentioning a name detectives had never heard and would never have known: Hood, Timothy Rawlings Jr., a kid in jail in the city for some 7-Eleven robbery.

In an uncanny moment before Hood was sentenced to life without parole, he was permitted to review the "pre-sentencing report"—a private document full of victim impact statements and mitigating information about the defendant. Sitting at the defense table, the small, self-possessed boy bent forward studiously and turned the pages very slowly with a steady hand.

As I watched him, the question came to mind, *Is he really reading?* His lawyers whispered between themselves. The aristocratic, white-haired Judge Robert Dugan waited impassively. A court officer reminded people to keep their cell phones silent. This was mainly directed at the six gang members in the last row on Hood's side of the room. They're children, basically, slight of build and posturing in their seats with an impudence that looks as stylized as that in *West Side Story*. Yet these boys will kill.

Still, Hood turns the pages, keeping the whole courtroom waiting without any sign of self-consciousness. He hasn't been sentenced yet, but he must know what's coming. Two teachers, a ponytailed white guy and an African American woman, guide their black students—mostly girls in white sweaters—into the courtroom. The students and their teachers all wear an uplifting button that reads: *Live Your Dreams*. But as Hood continues turning the pages, reading his own life, the teachers whisper and the students are—a little disruptively—led out again. Hood keeps turning the pages.

His mother Tereia, the corrections officer, will heave herself to her feet and say her son isn't the monster he's been painted to be. "But I want to apologize for my son's alleged actions." She'll turn to address the Parrishes directly with lawyer-tutored formality.

Michelle Parrish will also go forward to speak from the prosecution table. She'll start uncertainly, then berate Hood like any mother. During her furious remarks, the gang members will suddenly be led from the room by Childs and Caskey. The detectives will explain to me later that the kids were making intimidating hand signals.

For now, Hood turns the pages, delaying his sentencing and seemingly in complete mastery of time itself.

Michelle Parrish saved her greatest venom for Loco, Steven Hollis, the best friend. His sentencing came several weeks later. The prosecutor phoned for an extra court officer in case gang members showed up again, but Loco's side of the courtroom was entirely filled by his somber relatives led by his father, a slight man in an orange shirt and a boxy pale-green suit.

The Parrishes, with one set of grandparents, sat behind a couple of reporters on the prosecution side. Though Michelle had sobbed and Steven Sr. had toyed obsessively with his BlackBerry before Woo's sentencing (Juan Flythe, who'd cooperated) and before Hood's (Timothy Rawlings Jr.), this morning the Parrishes appeared more relaxed. It was their third time, after all. Everybody was waiting for Judge Dugan and the prisoner.

A minor flutter arose among the Parrish family when Steven Sr. found he'd misplaced his free-parking ticket. As he searched his jacket pockets, laughing softly at his own forgetfulness, one of the grandparents leaned in and joked, "This happens when you get to be the over-the-hill kind." More whispered chuckles all around.

Michelle's attention crossed the aisle only once. She put her arms on the back of the bench in front of her. She leaned forward and cocked her head pointedly at the crowd of Hollises on the other side of the room. Through her stylish narrow glasses, she gave them a good long look, which none returned.

When it came her time to speak, Michelle tugged at her yellow sweater and strode forward, confident-seeming. She was wearing slacks for the first time. "I need to make sure my son . . ." And she immediately broke down. She wept. After gathering herself, she spoke faster, and her voice quickly rose almost to a shout. "I can't believe how somebody's *best friend* could kill them! To have someone you claimed to *love* as a brother, someone you *knew* was not gay . . . *You knew he was not!*" Many of the Hollises stifled sobs. "That's not love. That's hate. And no amount of sorrys can make it better." She turned to Judge Dugan: "I do not want him out!" And back to Loco: "I want every time you see me to remember that's why you're in there, because of what you did! I will never forgive you! You have *ruined* my life!"

Steven Hollis Sr. spoke on behalf of his son. He had a halting, preacherly eloquence. He clasped his hands together when he faced his old friends. "Michelle, I am so sorry. Steven was my son. Steven *is* my son. Don't let that hatred sit in your heart. If I could take it back I would. I warned him about hanging out with a gang . . ."

Mr. Hollis shifted his weight. In his effort to remain poised, he seemed to lose track of his plea for a moment. "This is his family." He gestured toward the Hollises. "And *this* is his family." Shyly, he extended his cupped hands toward the Parrishes. He recalled Thanksgivings and family gatherings they'd all shared. Soft-spoken, he wondered aloud, "If there was *any* way to . . ." Terribly diminished after his speech, holding onto a bare shred of formality, he finished, "It's all such a waste."

Loco had none of his father's gift for speaking. When he finally stood and turned, he looked more confused than ever under his frightening frown. He was no longer the 190-pound football player he used to be. In prison he'd been gradually losing weight, ten, thirty, fifty pounds. He was gaunt now. He was being eaten up. I thought of the way a wasp larva devours its host from the inside with instinctive care to keep the meal alive till the last possible moment.

Loco pressed the tips of wonderfully long, slender fingers on the defense table. They bent backward. In a voice as soft as his father's but gruffer, clumsier, he said, "I just want to make my apologies to Ms. Michelle. I hope that one day you can forgive me . . . Steven is gone, but he's still my best friend."

As if this were a Baptist church, the Parrish grandparents couldn't repress a muted response. "Hm-*mm*, hm-*mm*," they disagreed. With hushed precision they said, "No, he is not."

David McConnell is the author of the novels *The Silver Hearted* (2010) and *The Firebrat* (2003). His newest book, *American Honor Killings: Desire and Rage Among Men* (Akashic, 2013), from which this piece is excerpted, is a narrative of hate crimes in the U.S. His short fiction and journalism have appeared widely in magazines and anthologies, including *The Literary Review* (UK), *Granta*, and *Prospect Magazine* (UK). He lives in New York City.

THE ADDICT

Lacy M. Johnson

The dream goes like this: I am in a mall, or the post office, or the supermarket, or the bank, with my two children. People mill around us, each face like every other face. I am running late, or too early, to meet a friend for lunch, or I am trying to retrieve the cell phone ringing in my diaper bag. At first, I see him approaching only out of the corner of my eye—intent, purposeful, his jaw crookedly set, his upper lip snarling—and my stomach transforms from a regular stomach into a black-hole stomach and begins to swallow me and all of dream-time, which moves more slowly anyway. Sometimes I cry out in a wet, drawn-out way—a baby deer bleeding to death in my throat. In other dreams, I beg for help from the stranger nearest to me. I try to ask the bank teller to call the police, but my mouth is full of feathers. Sometimes I call the police myself. They never come in time. In one dream, I ask a kind-looking woman to pretend my children are her own. *Keep them safe*, I croak. I don't know her in real life. The kind-looking woman, my daughter, my infant son—he will kill them all and make me watch. In other dreams, terror seizes me, and even dream-time stops.

On July 5, 2000, I leave the offices of The Missouri Review, where I hold an editorial internship. I stand in the parking lot next to my car, a sandstone-colored '91 Ford Taurus, unlocking the door with an actual metal key, when I hear my name and turn around. I see him crossing the lawn, climbing the hill, walking toward me through the grass. He wears a twill bucket hat, which is strange because I have never known him to wear hats. He perspires. He looks pale, his pupils like two pinpricks. He might be high. He clears his throat before announcing he no longer wants me back. He has decided to move back to Arizona, to be close to his aging mother, to finish his master's degree at Arizona State. The implications flood me: no more looking over my shoulder to see him following me down the sidewalk as I leave the coffee shop or trailing several cars behind me on an unlit street; no more notes on my car; no more phone calls to my parents. A breath leaves my body, taking with it all reason and care. *But I still have some of your things*, he says neutrally. *Give me a ride to the moving truck—it's just up the block—and then you can follow me home*. I should know better, should ask him to mail them to me instead. But then he would make excuses. And then there would be the pleading: *Can't you just do me this one favor*? I should know better but agree.

In the parking lot where there should be a moving truck, there is only a stun gun. A struggle, a near escape and him grabbing me by the hair. There is a blindfold and a circuitous trip to a basement apartment he's rented for the sole purpose of raping and killing me. On the floor of the apartment's only bedroom are my promised "things": the down duvet he brought back from Denmark last summer for my 21st birthday in September and a chair he's constructed out of two-by-fours and four-by-fours. A hole in the seat opens to a bucket underneath. Two U-bolts are attached to the thick wooden arms with galvanized fencing staples. A choke collar hangs from the headrest. Thick blue Styrofoam covers every surface but the floor.

I'm going to rape you now, he says while I undress. *Or I'm sure that's what you'll call it anyway*. In the corner of the room, there are several sheets of paper folded into a neat square: a script he'll read to me after he's bolted me back into the chair, after he's fed me a turkey sandwich, his hands hot and sticky with his own semen. While I'm chewing, he explains that I will call my friend A. to tell her I've decided to take him back. Instead, I tell her I'll come by in a few days to pick up my clothes. She wants to know what clothes. *Sorry, I can't come by tonight. I'll come by in a few days*. Is everything ok, she wants to know: *Where are you? What is happening*? I can't speak with him sitting right beside me, demanding I hang up the phone. I want to say, *Send help*. Instead I say, *I don't know*.

Or maybe the phone call happens first.

At one point, he tells me to put his penis in my mouth—he's angry he can't get it hard—and at another, he tightens the dog collar around my neck, gesturing toward the places he's planted explosives in the walls, a camera in the corner, a detonator in the kitchen. All the while, scenes from a movie play in my head: a low-budget flick with B-list actors past their prime. I play myself. The director cues the explosion, and pieces of my body fly in every direction.

At another point, he puts his face close to mine and says, *No one can hear you. Go ahead and scream.*

It's no secret that people—some more than others—are predisposed to aggression. From an evolutionary standpoint, aggression is a necessary part of getting and keeping important resources such as mates, territory and food. Aggression is so ubiquitous in our culture that it barely merits mention: Turn on the television, make a left turn during rush hour, bump into a stranger in the grocery store, and there it is, already boiling. Conventional wisdom would lead us to believe aggression is a negative emotion, and yet, what's surprising is that the brain processes aggression in the same way it processes any reward. Aggression, rage, violence—they all activate the same set of neurotransmitters responsible for our feelings of excitement and anticipation before Thanksgiving dinner, or during intercourse, or while tapping out a couple of lines of cocaine on the marble countertop. From a chemical standpoint, there is no difference in a craving for food or for amphetamines or for violence. For some people, the craving itself becomes a reward.

I am like Superman, he tells me in an email that September. A reverse search of his IP address confirms that this email, like all the others before it, has come from Venezuela, where he fled after he discovered I'd escaped and where he holds dual citizenship with the United States. The detective stands behind me, careful not to touch, looking over my shoulder into the computer monitor. He isn't hopeful that the Venezuelan government will allow extradition but speaks encouraging words into my ear while I type: *That's it. That will really get him. That's the trick*. In my emails back to Venezuela, I play the victim, insisting the detective has bullied me into pressing charges against the man I love. *It's the detective's idea*, I write. *He thinks this could be a big case. It might mean a promotion*. In my emails, I say I wish we could still be together. I beg him to come back to rescue me. In reality, we're trying to lure him back into the country so he can be arrested and brought to trial. The police have charged him with kidnapping, felonious restraint, sodomy and rape, as well as a few lesser crimes. They have frozen his credit cards and his bank accounts. They have flagged his passport and notified the FBI and Interpol. Together, we are setting a trap; I play the bait.

Later, back in my new apartment, I hack into his email account. He's been corresponding with a South American publisher about a potential memoir deal. One chapter in the proposal is titled "Leather and Lacy"—it's the only chapter in which I appear. Other chapters cover the long circus of his life: a childhood split between the U.S. and Venezuela, an adolescence as a stuntman in a traveling motorcycle show, his early adulthood spent hitchhiking through Europe and Asia. All of the children he's fathered, all of the women he's married and divorced. In our years together, I learned the names of only a few. The first time I came to his apartment, he pulled pictures from a plain white shoebox; touching them made him sob like a child. It all started like this: with him asking me to return something I didn't know how to give.

In my new apartment, sitting at the dining table I salvaged from the curb, on a chair I pulled from the dumpster, I change the password of his email. The next day, the emails start coming in quick succession: each more frantic, more threatening, in turns more bartering, more berating, more abusive. I don't respond, and eventually, he stops sending them. I don't tell the detective what I've done. The end of our relationship was like this, too. I didn't tell anyone. I didn't fight back, or if I did, I was already lying down—bruised, bleeding, slinking out the door on my belly like a worm.

In abusive relationships, violence tends to follow the same three-phase pattern: A conflict gradually escalates, until an explosive battering incident occurs, followed by a calm, loving period of submission and reconciliation. This pattern becomes so predictable that even before the battering begins, the victim begins to dissociate emotionally and physically, muting her awareness of both fear and pain. Due to the extreme contrast between the victim's feelings of terror and helplessness during the first two phases, and the dramatic scenes of remorse, forgiveness and loving physical contact in the third phase, the victim becomes caught in two powerful cycles of reinforcement: the "arousal-jag" of escalating tension and the pleasure triggered by the extinction of violence and the onset of peace. Both reinforce the traumatic bond between victimizer and victim. They become addicted to one another and to the violence. The pattern, the interaction, the relation takes hold: The individuals become as powerless as junkies.

The story appears in the city papers a few times. It is on the local news once or twice. I never come forward to identify myself as the victim, and without a face to attach to the story, without a culprit to arrest, the public loses interest. I don't lose interest. I send a copy of a news article to his ex-wife in Denmark with only a short message attached: *This happened to me. I thought you should know.* She responds by asking for my number and wants to know if I'd be willing to talk on the phone. Her voice relates without emotion all the events of her own kidnapping, the abduction of her children, the trial and her ex-husband's deportation from Denmark. *If he comes back, he'll be arrested.* Like me, she had finally left him. *You are lucky,* she says, *that he didn't get you pregnant.*

In the weeks that follow, rumors begin to surface. An anonymous email arrives in my inbox from a woman confessing he had come to her door one night asking for sex. I hear from a friend that someone once saw him shooting up in the back room of a bar downtown. One sunny afternoon, the detective escorts me to our old apartment before its contents are emptied and either given away or destroyed. He stands outside the front door while I wander from room to room, touching only the very tops of things. I'm supposed to be looking for my belongings: a photo album, some pottery, a textbook or two. After a half-hour, he opens the door: *Everything ok?* If he comes into the bedroom, he will find me sobbing in the closet, my face buried among the hanging clothes.

Despite treatment, some victims of violence continue to re-experience trauma, finding ways to repeat it in present-day life. Nightmares are a means of doing this at a somewhat unconscious level. Individuals get to watch their traumatic events again and again—in effect, starring in their own shows night after night. *Will it end differently?* the unconscious mind of the victim wants to know. This constant and obsessive search for a different outcome, a resolution, night after night, is a normal function of the brain gone awry. Dreams always involve intensive activation of the "seeking system," an all-purpose anticipatory drive that sends all animals out into the world to satisfy their needs. The seeking system is appetite, is arousal. It's the neurobiological lovechild of Freud's libido and Lacan's lack.

The seeking system provides us with eagerness and purpose. It's what drives us out of bed in the morning in search of food, to the closet in search of a sweater when it's cold, to the fridge in search of a drink when we're thirsty. It drives us toward our mates for sex. It also generates and sustains curiosity. It's what makes us excited when we are about to get what we desire, an anticipatory state that feels so good we often seek out substances or activities that keep it engaged—cocaine and amphetamines, as well as Facebook, Google and Twitter. And in order to keep us distracted while the body repairs itself, dreaming keeps the seeking system activated even while we sleep.

According to his online resume, in the years between 2000 and 2007, he works at a variety of editing, translating and interpreting jobs, sometimes for large, international corporations. He spends time as an interpreter for the Venezuelan lower courts. He translates a Motorola cell phone product description and instruction manual from English into Spanish. He edits several titles on conflict management for The University for Peace. Meanwhile, I marry. I divorce. I marry again. I change addresses at least once every year. I give birth to a child. Less and less frequently, I email the detective to ask about the case. On Oct. 31, 2007, an email appears in my inbox. It's him. He has just been released from jail in Venezuela after a failed extradition attempt and wants me finally and officially to drop the charges in the U.S. *I hope you'll consider my plea*, he writes. *And I would like to hear back from you even if it's just to say that you're sorry. Even if you decide not to respond to this message, I wish you all the best.*

I close my laptop screen and draw the blinds. I lock all the doors and turn off the television. I pull my daughter out of bed and call my husband in a cold sweat. We're hiding on the floor in the kitchen when he finally bursts through the front door, dressed as Clark Kent for Halloween, his tie loosened and pulled to the side, his shirt half-buttoned, the blue fabric of his Superman T-shirt visible underneath. I call the detective, who now works as a lead investigator for the county's prosecuting attorney. He wants me to respond to the email, to try one last time to lure him back to the U.S., but I can't bring myself to do it. I have too much to lose.

Now, I've lost track of him. He has disappeared or changed his name. I know that two of his sons still live in Denmark. One has a pretty girlfriend the whole family seems to like. I imagine that everyone hopes they will get married. His ex-wife and half-brothers are "friends" on Facebook, a fact that gives me inexplicable hope. Maybe one of them knows where he is, whether he is still living, but I can't bring myself to write to them and risk exposure. Instead, I look in the back seat of the car before I pull out of my driveway each morning. I search the rearview mirror while driving my children to school. I scan the parking lot before unbuckling them from their seats. Back home, I sit at my desk, and instead of writing, I watch for him out my window. When I pick up my children, we do not go to the park but instead go back to our house and close the blinds. I do not leave the house after dark. I turn off the lights at bedtime and lay awake in fear that he will come into my house and kill me while I am sleeping. If I sleep, it's the same dream every time.

I tried to quit smoking about a dozen times before I actually quit smoking. Every time, I'd tell myself the same bullshit stories: *I'll just wean myself off. I'll only smoke when I'm out drinking. I'll only smoke X cigarettes a day. I'll only smoke on Tuesdays and Fridays.* The problem with this approach was that the enormous anticipation of each next cigarette made the smoking of it that much more addictive. When I finally did quit, I told myself that I would never smoke, ever again. Not one cigarette. Not one butt. Not one drag.

For two whole years, I was addicted to diet pills. It was partly the manifestation of an eating disorder and partly my love of the constant and perpetual neural and metabolic hum. Like time travel: The world slowed; I sped.

And then there's coffee. And alcohol. And pot. I'm also addicted to sex, though not as much as I would like. I'm addicted to picking the fleas off my dog and dandruff off the base of my scalp. It's disgusting. I lie about things that don't matter. I can't help myself.

At some point, I also have to admit I'm addicted to the dream. I'm addicted to the memory. I'm still addicted to him.

It's in the process of working on this essay, when I read about the seeking system, that I have a revelation: *All this time spent seeking him has only sustained my addiction*. The implication is not lost on me: *I can quit*.

What if, for example, instead of thinking of taking my children to the park, I actually take them to the park? They will play and laugh, and because their happiness is infectious, I will also laugh. If, instead of sitting at my desk, waiting for someone to arrive at my doorstep, I draw the blinds wide open and begin typing, stopping only to enjoy the taste of my morning coffee (I'm not quitting that), I will delight in watching the words accumulate.

If I quit the bimonthly internet searches, the annual emails to the detective; if I quit cyber-spying on his half-brothers and looking in my rearview mirror; if I quit lying awake in fear— maybe I can also quit the dream. Which means I have to quit seeking resolution and, instead, let the present be the outcome I've been looking for. Which means I have to quit letting that past experience define me. Which means, at some point, I must decide never to write about this ever again. Not one paragraph. Not one sentence. Not one word.

I quit. A solution so beautiful in its simplicity. The simplicity rippling outward toward something akin to euphoria.

Tonight, for the first time in a long time, I will go to sleep thinking only of the present. And tomorrow night. And the next night. And the next. Until that becomes a craving. Until that craving itself becomes a reward.

Lacy M. Johnson is the author of *Trespasses: A Memoir* (University of Iowa Press, 2012). She worked as a cashier at WalMart, sold steaks door-to-door, and puppeteered with a traveling children's museum before earning a PhD from University of Houston's Creative Writing Program. She has been awarded fellowships from the Kansas Arts Commission, the Mitchell Center for the Arts, and Millay Colony for the Arts. Her work has appeared in *Creative Nonfiction*, *Sentence*, *TriQuarterly Online*, *Memoir Journal*, *Gulf Coast*, *Irish Studies Review*, and elsewhere. She is currently at work on her second book, a memoir about violence, memory, and recovery.

GIRL, FIGHTING

Laurie Lynn Drummond

The first time I got punched in the face—punched, not slapped or shoved or struck or thumped by a flying elbow gone astray, but punched as in fist landing squarely on the lower quadrant of my right cheek—it was delivered just after midnight in an apartment parking lot off Airline Highway in southeast Baton Rouge by a man at least five inches taller and a good seventy pounds heavier than me.

I was not his intended target. He intended to hit his wife. She ducked. I didn't.

A heavy throbbing spread quickly from the point of contact midway between cheekbone and jawbone; my jaw buzzed with bees, all armed with tiny hammers. My ear whooshed like a huge underground river.

For several seconds the three of us shared a common emotion: shock—shock that he'd gone and hit a cop. We all froze. His wife, a tired-looking girl with a mass of dark curls, crouched at my feet. His face went slack: mouth dropping open to reveal crooked lower teeth, eyes expanding and softening above drooping pockets of flesh. I have no idea what I looked like; I was still processing the fact that she'd ducked and he'd hit me. My face felt like an overripe watermelon on fire. For a second I was tempted to giggle: it was so ludicrous, him standing there appalled, knowing what was to come, unable to turn back time. *What a friggin idiot*, I thought with a glee that quickly turned to righteous anger.

He back-pedaled, hands crossed in front of his face, saying, "I'm sorry, I'm sorry, I'm sorry," as I cleared the huddle that was his wife. He provided little resistance when I body-butted him up against the hood of my police unit, turned him around, cuffed him, frisked him, placed him in the back seat, then spoke my first words since his fist had landed: "You're under arrest, mister." It hurt to talk.

My backup, Carolyn, had been talking to neighbors, her back turned to the scene. "Damn, you got popped," she said. "What happened?"

I waved her off, my right hand gently probing my jaw for altered topography, and turned to the wife. "Are you okay?"

Fine, fine, fine, his wife said, he hadn't laid a hand on her. Her face was swollen and bruised, and she worked her wedding ring round and round below an enlarged knuckle, begging me not to arrest him, said he hadn't intended to hit me.

"Oh, I know that," I said. "He was aiming for you."

"But he didn't hit me," she said. "We was just arguing. The neighbors shouldn't of called, it was just an argument."

"Well, he hit *me*, lady. You can't hit a cop and not take the fall for it."

"But YOU got in the way," she said.

No arguing that one; it was my job to get in the way.

After I'd processed him at downtown booking—fingerprints, mug shot, inventory of his belongings—and endured some ribbing from the guys doing jailer duty, I headed over to Lady of the Lake Hospital to get my face checked. It throbbed like a hip-hop band had taken up permanent residence in my bone marrow.

"Yowzer, girl," said Miceli, the wiry Italian doctor I knew from working extra duty at the Lake emergency room every Friday night. "What's the other guy look like?"

"Wearing orange," I replied, referring to the parish prison garb. "Not a scratch on him."

"Really?"

"Miceli, I don't hit people unless I have to."

He nodded slowly, as though carefully processing the concept of a cop not hitting people unless she had to, and after X-rays determined I had no broken bones, he sent me home with an ice pack and pain killers.

• • •

I'd been a cop since 1979, almost three years by that time: two years as a plainclothes officer at Louisiana State University and nearly a year in uniform as an officer with the Baton Rouge Police Department working out of Broadmoor Precinct, which was then a mostly white, middle- to upper-class area.

In all that time, I'd never had a reason to hit anyone. Get physical, yes—it's nearly impossible to arrest someone without shoving, pulling, turning, or frisking. I'd had to tackle some men, but there was never any need to hit—with my fist or nightstick or PR-24.

Certainly I'd worried about getting hurt, but hurt in the sense of shot or stabbed. I'd worried about my gun being taken from me: I was barely 5'6" and fluctuated between 122 and 128 pounds. I was twenty-four years old. And I was female.

I had no illusions about my physical abilities up against the average male, so I'd pushed myself hard in the City Police Training Academy during the two hours of PT in a gym without air-conditioning every afternoon for twenty weeks in the dead of a muggy Louisiana summer. I lifted weights. I practiced takedown holds. I was triumphant when I performed twenty push-ups properly (not the girly knees-on-floor version). I could handle Lt. Martello's full weight on my stomach for five seconds during leg lifts. I even conquered the damn rope climb.

Out of a class of forty-seven, I graduated second in academics and second on the firing range, which earned me an expert marksman badge. I ranked in the bottom half physically—I'd failed to make the six-minute mile by forty-eight seconds, and I completed only fourteen chin-ups of the required twenty. But I passed all the other physical agility tests and graduated in my best physical shape ever.

Three months out of the academy, I took up White Crane Kung Fu. My younger brothers, both over six feet tall, had been training for several years, and I was impressed with what they were learning despite the cultist feel I'd picked up from their conversations: they practiced the forms obsessively and seemed to view their Sifu, or master, as some minor deity. I wasn't looking to become anyone's Little Grasshopper. But I couldn't deny they were good at sparring. I couldn't deny that either of them could whip my butt if so inclined.

So one day I drove over to Sifu Illar's studio. Illar was a short, slender man with dark hair and a wisp of a mustache who nodded constantly and barely let me finish sentences. He let me know, several times, that he had a deal in the works with Chuck Norris to write a movie script.

Illar assured me that the practice was primarily defensive, but he'd work with me on take-down holds, reading body language, taking weapons away, and more effective ways to use my nightstick. The practice would improve my physical agility and strength, he told me, and eventually I could move into sparring and tournament fighting.

"No tournaments, no fighting," I said. "If you can help me improve my street skills, fine, but that's—"

"No pressure," Illar said. "Work at your own pace. Come try out a class."

I walked into that first class fairly confident. We started with floor stretches. Everyone but the newcomers wore baggy black trousers with white strips up the side, black or white t-shirts, and black slippers or tennis shoes. Many wore white sashes, some green, a few black. We ranged in age from ten to sixty. Two students with spina bifida were in wheelchairs. Sifu Illar roamed the room, grinning a lot despite his intensity, correcting posture and occasionally telling someone to try harder.

My partner for the wall stretches was a green belt, a tall woman about my age who'd been doing this for three years. It took all my strength to get her leg up over her head. "More," she kept saying in between deep breaths, and I'd brace my hands further down her thigh, move my feet back some, and push harder.

My foot never passed my shoulder. "That's enough," I'd squeak, and she'd say, "Breathe," and then push some more until I thought my groin muscles would ignite.

Next up were the stationary forms. Five minutes into the standing seated position, The Horse, fire ants took residence in my thighs and every muscle below my waist trembled. But when we started defensive maneuvers, I quickly picked up the response to both a left and right jab: stepping into the oncoming punch and twisting the wrist back and down as I applied pressure between the thumb and forefinger. I was thrilled to bring a green sash to his knees.

I went home that night, took a hot bath and applied ice to both wrists. The next morning, I could barely walk, and lifting my arms induced agony.

By the time I got punched in the face on Airline Highway, I'd been taking classes for seven months, had become adept at holding The Horse for the full ten minutes, my foot touched the wall in stretches, I'd mastered the finer points of kicks and achieved fluency in the basic forms, and I was ready to take the test for my white belt.

But obviously this wasn't enough. I'd been lucky that the angry husband had frozen, that he hadn't followed with several more punches. The problem, as I saw it that morning after as I stared at my swollen cheek turning more eggplant-colored by the hour, was I didn't know diddly about being hit in the face. And I needed to learn before the next time came around.

I'd fought physically only twice before I became a cop, both times with girls. I don't count tussling with my younger brothers, which mostly involved holding each other down and tickling until the victim peed, or the afternoon I punched my fist through my bedroom window when I was sixteen.

The first time I took a swing at someone I was nine. Eve Trow was the yin to my yang: she was shy, agreeable, studious, smart, an only child raised by sheltering older parents who thought I was a bad influence on Eve. I was talkative, rebellious, bossy, an often-perplexing child to my conservative parents who thought Eve was a good influence on me. But Eve and I shared a love of books, words, learning, and imaginary games, and so from third grade on, we were close friends, despite the occasional disagreement and one full-blown fight.

I have no recollection what or who started it. First we were yelling and then screaming and then one of us hit the other and the other hit back and next we were rolling around on the recess blacktop, scratching and smacking, with Miss Thorburn, our 4th grade teacher who wasn't much taller than us, stamping her foot and ordering us to stop in her thick Scottish burr. That earned us both five demerits, lots of Mercurochrome, and in my case, my mother's accusing silence for several days.

Five years later Allison Mitchell and I faced off. Allison and her sister, Sallie, lived across the cul-de-sac where I grew up in Northern Virginia. Their younger brother, Tad, was the same age as my brother Finlay. We all played together regularly, along with three to eight other kids, depending on who was around. Within twelve years, Allison and Tad would be dead—Allison from an overdose, Tad from suicide—Sallie would be divorced with two children, Finlay would be clean from the drugs that briefly wrecked his life, and I would be working Plank Road Precinct on the dog shift.

But on that day, our only concern was some petty, perceived injustice. Sallie, Allison, and Tad had ganged up on Finlay. So I stepped in, something I didn't normally do.

A shoving match between Allison and me ensued, and soon we were slapping each other and pulling hair, pulling hard. When our scuffle turned into body slams against the walls and over furniture, Finlay yelled, "I don't need you to protect me."

I burst into tears and ran home.

My mother found me huddled on my bed and stroked my head. Gobs of blond hair came out in her hands. I don't know which was more unsettling: seeing the physical damage from my fight or the glorious adrenaline kick I'd gotten from whaling away at Allison, just letting go.

• • •

I discovered early on in my career that I excelled at talking, specifically negotiation. The myriad calls—family fights, bar fights, disturbances, man with a gun calls, heated confrontations between drunken motorists, barking dogs, suspicious persons, attempted suicides, kids who played their drums too loudly for the neighbors' tastes—required a level of finesse with words, especially if I wanted to avoid raising the threat level or getting hurt.

By nature, I was a pacifier, not an agitator. Although I went through a brief John Wayne phase like most rookie cops, I preferred to find a solution that didn't involve jail or a misdemeanor summons. I dumped small amounts of marijuana out on the ground, drove the juvenile home, negotiated between angry neighbors, made referrals to counseling centers and psychiatric institutions, sent the upset husband to a friend's—if that was a viable alternative to jail. I prided myself on my restraint, compassion, professionalism.

One of my partners, Marian McLin, who I teamed up with for nearly two years near the end of my career, used to tell me I talked too much on calls, did too much counseling.

"Sometimes," she'd say, "you just gotta arrest their ass, Laurie."

I decided David Wallace could teach me how to get punched in the face and not freeze. Wallace was a motorman out of the Traffic Division who taught self-defense and takedown holds at the Training Academy, a black belt in karate who'd won some boxing tournaments when he was younger. A good-looking man with a wide-open face, strawberry blonde hair, sharp blue eyes, he was confident in his abilities, looks, and maleness. I'd first met him while I was still a cadet in the training academy.

An urgent whisper next to my ear during a lecture on what constituted reasonable suspicion and probable cause startled and alarmed me. "You're Drummond?"

I nodded to the perspiring officer crouched by my side.

"Step out to the hallway," he said, and I did.

He stuck out his hand and introduced himself. "I'm Wallace. You're the one writing that proposal for mounted patrols?"

I nodded and shook his hand.

His face went momentarily slack then he grinned. "Give me your hand again."

I obliged and shook his hand once more.

"Amazing. You shake like a man. Great grip. I want a copy of your proposal when it's done. I'll be back in touch."

When David came to the Academy several weeks later to work with us on basic self-defense maneuvers, he had several officers shake my hand. "Can you believe the muscles in her hand?" he'd ask. Then he'd put me on the mat—hard—with a quick flip of his wrist. "Anchor your body weight in your gut and go with the motion," he'd say.

I figured any man who appreciated my grip might be willing to give me a few pointers about boxing, and I was right. David quickly agreed, both amused and, he admitted later, impressed. This was years before kick-boxing became the yuppie-rage and Muhammad Ali's daughter slipped on gloves; women boxing in 1983, even female cops, were not the norm.

I cajoled another female officer, Pat, into joining me for a boxing lesson, using my now nearly healed face as evidence as to why we needed tips on taking and giving punches. Our first lesson took place on a wet winter morning. What struck me first was how big those gloves were, how intricate they were to strap on—first the wrappings, then the tugging for a snug fit, then tying them off— and how powerful and bizarre it felt to see my hands quadruple in size. The mouthpiece reminded me of years with a torturous orthodontist.

David started us out on the bag. He explained the rhythm of working the bag, how to hold our hands and arms—wrists straight, fists clenched, elbows slightly flexed—the bent knees, what part of the glove we should be striking with: thumb down and square on the bag.

"Turn with your shoulders," he'd say. "Push with your hips and toes."

The next several lessons focused on technique: how to stand, body position, the jab, straight right, hook, and uppercut. Foot placement felt awkward and unnatural, like I was a prehistoric bird learning to walk. Pat and I danced around each other, throwing jabs, working on combinations, looking serious, and trying to remember the multitude of instructions. Too focused on technique, our punches lacked much power.

"Move your left foot towards your right foot so that your left toes meet your right toes at an angle," David told us. "Keep your hips forward."

I tended to let my shoulders lead, and my feet continually fumbled for the correct stance as I tried to sort out left foot from right foot and keep my weight anchored.

One day, Pat didn't show up for our lesson. David shrugged and said, "I'll put on gloves."

David's jabs came much quicker than Pat's and with more force. Pat was several inches shorter than me while David was nearly six feet tall, so I had to adjust my punches upward and keep my left hand higher to protect my face.

"Step into me, don't look at your feet, don't bounce around so much," he said, commands similar to those I'd heard over the years on the tennis court: step into the swing, watch the ball, don't bounce around so much.

I landed a few blows, mostly ineffectual; David had an uncanny ability to bend out of the way. I swung my arms too wide, easy for David to read and counter with a straight punch. And I kept stepping off the mat, partly from trying to avoid David's nonstop punches, partly as a result of the weight of his blows. I felt like one enormous bulls-eye, which was exactly what I'd asked for: teach me how to be hit and not freeze.

He grinned. "A little different than boxing with a woman, huh?" he said as he deflected one of my punches and landed a solid thunk on my left collarbone. "Keep your shoulders back."

I nodded, and resolve tightened in my gut.

"Watch my hands and eyes," he said. "Come at me with all you've got."

Whap. My left hand dropped and David's punch caught me on the chin. My eyes watered, my chin stung, but I didn't freeze and I didn't back down. I got pissed. And in that moment, I realized that I could combine what I knew about Kung Fu with what I was learning about boxing. Who said fighting had to be by the rules?

I moved back into stance, bent my right knee, dropped my right shoulder, and kept my arms tight to my face and body. I let David move, shifting my feet only slightly to keep my right foot back and anchored on the ball of the foot. When I saw an opening, I rotated my hips forward with the motion of my right hand and landed a solid uppercut on David's chest; his upper body fell forward slightly, and I followed with a quick uppercut to his chin: an exquisite, whammy of a punch that sent him backwards several steps. Without even thinking, I followed him, kicking out straight into his stomach, dropped down to my right foot, spun around backwards and brought my left foot up in a sweeping side kick that landed—beautifully, powerfully—on the left side of his face.

He went down. On his ass. Mouth open, legs splayed, hand to jaw.

"Jesus." He rose carefully to his feet. "Where'd you learn those moves?"

I smiled widely, my gloves resting on my hips. "Good teacher."

"Uh-uh."

I gave a small shrug. "I've been doing some Kung Fu."

"Kung Fu." The words came out of his mouth slowly. He settled back into a stance. "Alright. Again."

I don't remember seeing David's punch, or feeling it land on the right side of my head just beside my eye, or crumpling to the mat. I was conscious only of my brain, the eerie, indescribable sensation of my brain bumping against the inside of my skull, first the right side—tap—then the left side—tap—a slow gentle wave of fluid carrying it like a swing suddenly abandoned on the playground, traveling from one side to the other, with me acutely along for the ride, every thought and sensation centered in that small, moving space, totally disengaged from every other part of my body. For several seconds, I was my brain and nothing more.

Then I passed out.

• • •

Over the next few days, I felt woozy, wobbly, had the sense that I wasn't quite in control over my body. Stupidly, I never went to the hospital. I was exceedingly fortunate, something I didn't truly appreciate until Dr. Terry Smith with the Head Protection Research Laboratory in Los Angeles spelled out all the possibilities for me many years later.

Put an ice cube in a glass of water. Put the glass on a table and slide it away from you very quickly, then stop it abruptly. The ice cube will bang off of the near side; immediately after you stop the glass, it will hit the far side—a simple illustration of what I came to call my brain bump. The clinical term is *contre-coup* injury, French for "opposite side."

The brain is surrounded by cerebrospinal fluid, or CSF, which protects the brain by keeping it suspended and preventing direct contact between brain and bone. The only problem with this ingenious physiological engineering is that brain motion tends to lag behind skull motion. When David's fist landed, my skull suddenly accelerated, moving quickly away from his fist. The skull motion rapidly reduced the distance between my skull and brain; consequently my skull banged into my brain, causing a contusion at the impact site. This same phenomenon happened when my skull stopped at the end of its motion; my brain, still moving in the CSF, bumped my skull opposite the point of initial impact.

If the forces are high enough, or hard enough, one of the parasaggital bridging veins or the middle meningeal artery that passes between the skull, through the CSF, and into the brain can rupture, and an acute subdural hematoma may occur—in which case, death arrives within thirty minutes.

The brain can also sustain injury if it is rotated. Nod your head vigorously up and down, and you are, in fact, also rotating your brain. Get in a high-speed, head on collision in a car without airbags while wearing your seat belt and your head will rotate forward at a rapid rate while the seat belt assembly stops your chest.

Most likely, my brain did rotate some when David's punch landed. This type of head motion is the most deadly in terms of brain injury because the axons, nerve cells responsible for transmitting information around the brain and up and down the spinal cord and then into the muscles and other systems, are stretched. When they stretch too far, the body of the axon snaps like a fishing line and there is cessation of nerve transmission.

Stretch or damage several axons and the brain has enough collateral ability that you won't detect the difference. Damage a few more, and you might notice a change in mood or memory, perhaps some vestibular or balance problems. Damage several more and the system starts to break down dramatically: you have problems remembering and walking, problems with stimuli like loud noises or bright lights; you may have significant motor problems.

Damage a number of axons, and you experience what is known as DAI or Diffuse Axonal Injury. The clinical symptoms are usually long-term coma or death.

David's punch ended my enthusiasm for boxing. I'd learned how to take a punch and not freeze. I'd also learned that with some punches, you just don't get back up.

But the most valuable lesson was more subtle, a coming to consciousness of something I'd already known instinctively: mental conditioning is paramount. Officer performance theory holds that strong mental conditioning accounts for 75% of an officer's survival, whereas physical conditioning accounts for only 5% (technical skill is 15% and sweet lady luck is 5%). Mental conditioning isn't simply courage—courage can get you killed just as quickly as stupidity if you aren't using good judgment. And it isn't simply confidence. A relaxed, unaware officer confident in his or her capabilities breaks down a bit differently on the survival scale: luck is 75%, mental 5%, technical skill 15%, and physical 5%.

Mental conditioning comes from being alert and ready for danger; not making assumptions; not becoming lax; not letting anger win out over calm, solid judgment; and continual, repetitive survival skills in a variety of situations. Research has shown that in a crisis, officers resort to the shooting stance they practice most often—so if you practice only at the range, standing up, out in the open, in daylight, one hundred yards from a target that does not return fire, when you encounter a night-time shooting situation that calls for running, rolling, using available cover, and you're only fourteen yards from the person who's shooting back, your chances of survival diminish significantly.

I refocused my efforts on the mental and technical aspects of police work. I started attending Street Survival Training seminars and Combat Shooting sessions, and I assisted with monthly Shoot Don't Shoot training sessions. I wore my bulletproof vest every shift, no matter how hot or humid the weather. And I wore my St. Michael's medallion, the patron saint of police officers, 24-7. I figured I had most of the bases covered, *most* being the operative word.

Seven months after my brain bump, I was dispatched to a family fight in the projects behind Memorial Stadium and the State Capitol.

I'd been transferred to Plank Road Precinct several months earlier, a high-crime, poverty-stricken area, where my exposure to the underbelly of the city tripled overnight. Officers rarely went out on a call without back up, even during daylight. But on this late spring morning, no other units were available.

I pulled up to a rickety, brown, shotgun house squashed up against other rickety, shotgun houses. I grabbed my five-cell flashlight and slid the portable radio into its holder.

A heavy-set woman the color of nutmeg met me halfway up the sidewalk. "She be beatin my head in," the woman screamed, every fat cell in her body jiggling in her agitation. I saw no immediate signs of injury.

"Who is?" I said.

"Sharleen. She used dat phone beatin me. I want her ass in jail."

"And you are?"

"Jasmine."

"Anyone else in the house, Jasmine? Any children?"

"Nah."

A woman, slender as a rifle and almost the same color with a tight cap of curls, stepped onto the porch, yelled several epithets, then disappeared inside.

"You better run, girl," Jasmine screamed.

"Any guns in the house?" I asked.

"There ain't no guns up in there, jist Sharleen. Git her ass outta my house."

"You own this house?"

"Yeah. She moving out. But then she start beatin on me, thumped me upside my head." The woman leaned down and revealed a large lump on her skull.

I learned that they were breaking up, that Sharleen was in the process of moving out, that the fight had started over who owned what property.

Before I set foot on the porch, I heard Sharleen in the back bedroom throwing things, muttering in a high, screechy voice. I did a visual of the living room, kitchen, bathroom, carefully working my way toward her, making sure there were no weapons, no other humans.

Sharleen stood in a room filled with half-packed boxes, clothes slung on the unmade bed, an overturned lamp, glass shards on the floor, phone ripped out of the wall by her feet. Her hands were empty. She was tall and skinny—long arms, legs, and face interrupted only by the bumps of elbows and knees and one sharp chin that preceded every move she made. She couldn't have weighed more than 100 pounds.

I attempted to negotiate. They screamed at each other over every sentence I spoke. No, Sharleen couldn't just get her things and leave with me watching; Jasmine wanted her thrown in jail. Sharleen was a bitch; Jasmine was a crack head. No, Sharleen couldn't return tomorrow to collect her belongings with an officer present. Jasmine wanted her arrested now. Sharleen wasn't leaving without her stuff.

Sometimes, you do just have to arrest their ass.

I said, "Okay, that's it. You're going downtown for battery."

I reached for Sharleen's shoulder and turned her suddenly complacent body against the wall as I Mirandized her and patted her down, keeping half an eye on Jasmine. Sharleen started crying, her body seemly devoid of all bone now, as I reached back with my left hand to unsnap the keeper holding my handcuffs, my right hand firm against the small of her back.

"Baby, don't do this to me," Sharleen sobbed over and over.

Just as I slipped the first cuff on Sharleen's wrist, a huge weight hit my back. My hat flew off and my knees hit the hardwood floor with a painful crack.

Jasmine had jumped me.

"Noooooo!" Jasmine wailed in my ear. We rolled end over end, me trying to shake Jasmine loose—one hand protecting my gun, still snapped in its holster—Jasmine holding on like a koala bear as we wedged up against the bed.

Sharleen smiled. I remember that clearly. She smiled as she picked up the phone receiver and walked over to me. I struggled to sit up, Jasmine heavy on my shoulders, came to my knees, braced hard against the floor with my left hand. Sharleen raised her arm and swung.

Tap.

Just one gentle bump of skull kissing brain this time, although a second one might have occurred as my skull stopped and my brain kept moving, but I didn't feel it. For even as I was registering, "I'll be damned, brain bump again," my body took over and triggered massive amounts of adrenaline.

I staggered to my feet, Jasmine still clinging to one of my legs. I kicked out with the other leg, catching the back of her locked elbow, heard it snap and her yelp as I shifted my hand to the portable radio, yelled "1D-79, Signal 65" before Sharleen came at me again, a snarl replacing her smile. I managed one finely placed punch on her jaw—it hurt much more without gloves—which drove her back, and then she came at me again. A pressure point takedown hold flipped her on her back, but she slithered between my legs and bit down hard on my calf.

In the midst of this, I heard an "en route" to my Signal 65. I'd chosen this carefully even in the panic of the moment: not Signal 63 which meant, "drop everything, officer's life in danger," or a simple "Headquarters I need back-up" but the in between call for help, Signal 65, which roughly translated meant "come as quickly as you can, things are really fucked up."

I don't remember much of the next five minutes or so that Sharleen and I grappled—no punching, no perfectly executed kicks, just simple grappling—except that Jasmine stayed huddled on the floor crying and Sharleen was hard to get a good grip on. She bit, she slapped, she scratched, she pulled hair, and she screeched the whole damn time. Every takedown hold I used on her, she slipped out of, wiggled free or bounced back up from. I figured she had to be on some powerful drugs, but blood tests later revealed no traces in her system.

By the time Andy Crause ran through the front door, we'd careened into the living room and knocked over two tables; I had somewhat trapped Sharleen on the floor against a wall, my knees on her back, trying to get one of her sweaty, undulating arms back so I could cuff it.

Andy is a big man, six foot and over two hundred pounds, and we'd worked many calls together, but it took us several minutes to get the cuffs on Sharleen. We bounced and rolled over half the room. Finally, he sat on her, dug his boot into the flesh of her upper arm, while I clamped my knees around her head and reached over to put one cuff on; Andy shifted and we brought her right hand down and secured it with the other cuff.

I put out a Code 4—everything under control, no further assistance needed—then we sat there on Sharleen, now suddenly quiet and sobbing again, and looked at each other, breathing hard, half smiling. Both of us bled in various places—from Sharleen's teeth and nails, from the struggle with the cuffs. My face hurt. I was tempted to tell Andy about not freezing after getting walloped with the phone, but some things are better left unsaid; start bragging to fellow officers that you held your own and they'll start worrying that there's some question as to whether you *can* hold your own. Cop machismo is a fine art.

"Damn," Andy said.

"Glad to see you," I said.

"You look like you got slugged."

I nodded gingerly, wondering if the side of my head looked as bad as it felt, wondering if Miceli at the Lake would once again ask me what the other guy looked like. Sharleen didn't appear to have a scratch on her.

"What happened?"

I laughed. "Just girls fighting."

By the time I placed Sharleen in my unit, she'd regained her spunk. She hissed, she cursed, she screamed and screeched. She repeatedly kicked the back of my seat and the wire screen behind my head as I drove down North Boulevard to Central Booking.

I ached, I hurt, the adrenaline wore off, and I made a rookie mistake: I let anger win. I returned her taunts with taunts of my own. I escalated the situation, and I knew better.

When she spit, a huge wad of phlegm landed in my hair. Then she kicked hard, jolting me forward; my chest hit the steering wheel. I don't remember making the decision to do what I did next. I simply checked my rear view mirror—no traffic behind me—and pulled what I'd seen other officers do, but until this moment had never done myself, what cops called the dog swerve. Oops, there's a dog in the road: swerve and hit the brakes, hard. Someone in the back seat of a unit with her hands cuffed behind her has no way to brace herself.

Sharleen's face hit the wire screen with a loud thud. Blood gushed from her nose. She gasped and choked. White foam oozed over her lips and down her chin.

My first reaction was to get her out of my unit to minimize the blood and vomit I'd have to clean up later. I grabbed paper towels and jammed them under her nose, tilted her head back.

My second reaction was pure horror—a horror that I can still tap into today—at what I was capable of. I hadn't wanted to *hurt* her, I told myself; I only wanted her to shut the fuck up.

I held her forehead as she spit and cleared her mouth, then I helped her back into the unit, wiped her mouth and nose, leaned her head against the back seat. The bleeding stopped.

"I'm pregnant," Sharleen sobbed.

"Pregnant?" I said, thinking of her and Jasmine, a pregnancy not computing.

She nodded. "That's what me and her were fighting about."

"I see."

"My nose hurts."

I probed it with my fingers. "It doesn't feel broken. We'll get it checked out at the jail."

"You shouldn't have done that," she said.

My gaze shifted away briefly before I gave her a look that brooked no disagreement. "Will you be quiet? No more of this nonsense?"

She nodded.

And she was quiet, docile really, all the way to Central Booking. Inside while I fingerprinted her, took her mug shots, listed her charges as Simple Battery, Resisting Arrest, and Battery on an Officer. While I explained to the guys on duty that she'd put up a fight and needed her nose checked, that she might be pregnant. She just looked at me, eyes big and expressionless.

She looked at me the same way all through the trial, as I testified to Jasmine's injuries, Sharleen hitting me with the phone, how long it took Andy and me to get the cuffs on her, my brain bump. Her lawyer mostly tried to trip me up on procedure: whether I'd Mirandized her, whether I'd given her a chance to leave the house, whether I'd instigated a fight before she swung the phone. I answered all his questions honestly.

Sharleen was not pregnant; her nose was not broken. She spent six months in jail. I never saw her again. As far as I know, she never told anyone what happened on our ride to Central Booking. Until this moment, I have never spoken of it either.

Miceli was not working the ER when I went to get my head checked. No one asked me what the other guy looked like. The attending doctor's gentle fingers smelled of vanilla lotion and antiseptic. He signed a slip of paper that excused me from work for several days. I suffered only a mild concussion, a three-day headache, and eighteen years of fierce deep shame.

Laurie Lynn Drummond is a former uniformed officer in Baton Rouge, Louisiana, and the author of the linked-story collection *Anything You Say Can And Will Be Used Against You*, a finalist for the PEN/Hemingway Award. Her essays have appeared in *Creative Nonfiction*, *River Teeth*, *Fourth Genre*, and *Brevity*. This essay is an excerpt from her memoir-in-progress, *Losing My Gun*.

THE DEATH OF A FAMILY

David Updike

In June of 1973, when I was sixteen, something terrible happened in my hometown. It was my mother who first gave us the news, with that look of suppressed anguish that came over her at such moments: there had been a murder in town, it seemed. A mother and her two children.

"Where?" we asked.

"Out off Topsfield Road, somewhere, in one of those new developments." She couldn't picture exactly where.

"Who?"

"Well, they don't know, exactly. But they're talking to the husband—they took him into the station for questioning."

Later, more details emerged: they had all been suffocated in their beds, with plastic bags and tape. And another peculiar thing: the husband was White, the wife Black.

"In Ipswich, this happened?"

"I'm afraid so," she said. "It's just awful—tragic."

"Why do they think it was him?"

"I really don't know the details. I just hope it wasn't one of those racist groups, the KKK or something. Who knows?"

As far as I knew, nothing like this had ever happened in town—a murder. Odder still was the strange specter of race. The only African Americans I knew in town were a couple of teenaged boys who had lived, for a time, with the family of my best friend, whose father was then minister at the Ascension Memorial Church.

The following morning, Wednesday, June 27th, Mr. Gordon Haas of Ipswich shared the front page of the *Boston Globe* with a photograph of John Dean testifying before the Senate Watergate Committee. In the photograph, Haas appeared to be a young and handsome man with sideburns, horn-rimmed glasses, a jacket, and a wide-collared seventies shirt, and he was being escorted from police headquarters with his hands shackled behind his back. After coming home from work and being questioned by the police, Haas had been charged with murdering his thirty-two-year-old wife and their two young children, Gordon Jr., 4, and Melissa, 2.

The next day, the two local papers came out—the *Ipswich Chronicle* and the *Ipswich Today*. In the *Chronicle* was a photograph of Mr. Haas arriving back at the house, walking toward it while being restrained by Eddie Rauscher, a longtime local cop, and wearing Bermuda shorts and no shoes. The articles described the shocked neighbors milling around in the rain; the family dog still tied to its tether in the backyard; the tearful babysitter of the night before—a classmate of mine—who had learned that the children she had put to bed the night before had never woken up. In a neighbor's house, "The women sat stunned, weeping quietly among themselves, while their children played in the recreation room down in the basement."

Shirley, the papers reported, had been a popular woman in town: a member of the League of Women Voters and the Cable Memorial Hospital's auxiliary board, as well as a secretary for the Sunday school at Ascension Memorial Church, of which her husband was president and their children pupils. She had spent the evening of the 26th with friends at a book club in neighboring Essex, and was dropped off at her house at eleven o'clock. That evening, a friend said, "She was happy, joking and laughing as always."

In the *Ipswich Today* of June 29th, there is a soft-focus and three-quarter-view picture of Shirley, a young woman gazing off into the middle distance with a dreamy, questing expression on her face. She is classically beautiful, her hair done up in the swooping style of the fifties. There is, too, a heartbreaking photograph of the two children, Melissa and Gordon Jr., smiling outwards at someone— the mother or father who is urging them into shy, tentative smiles. The Haases had been the perfect "inter-racial couple," and an entire article is dedicated to the normalcy of their life together. Shirley was the more gregarious of the two and, one article states, herself the product of a mixed-race marriage, a claim for which I would find no further corroboration. The articles describe the case as I vaguely remembered it, with one additional detail I had been unaware of: at the time of her death, Shirley was seven months pregnant with what would have been her third child.

Of her husband Gordon, a few years younger than she, the collective response to the tragedy was sympathy, not suspicion: "Disbelief that Mr. Haas would kill his attractive dark-skinned wife and two children spread throughout the town." After the arraignment, the Reverend Edward French of the Ascension Memorial Church said that Mr. Haas could not possibly be guilty. "They were good people; they were beautiful people. He was a good man."

And Ipswich was a good town, full of good and well-meaning people, leftward-leaning Democrats, mostly, open to all. Gordon and Shirley Haas had moved to town two years earlier, and Gordon worked in the personnel department of Lechmere Sales in Cambridge, thirty-five miles away. He had grown up in Barrington, Rhode Island, and attended Williams College on a football scholarship, and it was there in the registrar's office that he met Shirley Grant, a pretty, light-skinned African American woman from neighboring North Adams. It was there, in St. John's Episcopal Church, that they were married in 1965.

The couple then moved to Marion, Massachusetts, and worked as teachers and counselors in the Youth Corps program in New Bedford. Two years later, Gordon got a job at John Hancock Life Insurance Company in Boston. They moved to Watertown for a couple of years before buying a house in a new development in Ipswich. On a quiet residential loop off Kennedy Drive, 13 Hodgkin's Drive is a split-level ranch house typical of the era, similar to the prototypical home we saw each night on reruns of *Leave It to Beaver*.

In town, the murders had been met with incredulity, at first, but they soon began to cast a pall of doubt over the town's image of itself. Reverend French continued to defend Haas despite what many found to be compelling evidence against him. For my parents and their friends—many of whom had been active in the civil rights movement and had been members of the Ipswich Fair Housing Committee—the case presented a local contradiction to all they stood for and believed. For even if Haas had killed his wife and children, what had driven him to it? Could it have been that the town itself had made him—them—feel unwelcome? When I began to look back into the case thirty years later, friends of my parents and even my own stepfather asked "Why are you so interested?" or stated, more to the point, "It seems like you want to blame the town." When a remembrance of the case and the family was proposed at the Ascension Memorial Church, some members reacted with angry and adamant opposition and wanted no part of "digging up the past." Three decades later, many wanted to continue forgetting that anything like this had ever happened here.

The morning of June 26th, 1973, had been a rainy one, and Gordon Haas drove into work, leaving his house at about six thirty, as usual. At about ten A.M., he called the Ipswich police to say that he had received a call at work: someone had advised him to "check on your family" and made the unsettling comment that "Blacks and Whites don't mix." The police drove to the house, found the back door ajar with a key still in it. The family dog, Samantha, was tied to a tree in the backyard. Upstairs in their bedrooms were found the bodies of Shirley, Gordon Jr., and Melissa, plastic bags taped onto their heads. (I was later told by an Ipswich policeman that the bodies of the children were held entirely *within* the plastic bags.) One of Shirley's fingernails was broken.

The police then called Mr. Haas and, without telling him precisely what was wrong, told him that he needed to come home. A colleague, Robert Christensen, drove him Ipswich. Haas arrived to find a throng of policemen, neighbors, and news people at the house. He was told that his wife and children were dead, but he was not allowed upstairs. Scratch marks were observed on the side of his neck. He was asked to come down to the police station to answer a few questions. On his way to the station he reportedly said, "I want to be helpful," but he did not ask—it would be noted later—what exactly had happened to his wife and children. Later that day, based partly on his responses to their questions, partly on notes found in his pockets and at the scene, he was arrested.

At first, people were skeptical; Haas was a friendly, well-liked man in town. But when they heard the details of the case, most began to gradually accept the validity of the arrest. One of the notes found in his pocket was a shopping list that included some of the items used in the murder—"ether, mask, tape, bags, gloves"— and another, more mysterious, was a quotation of William Lloyd Garrison that had been taken from the abolitionist's anti-slavery newspaper, *The Liberator*: "I am in earnest. I will not equivocate. I will not excuse. I will not retreat a single inch. I will be heard." Despite the notes, the police were eager to dispel any notion that there were any racial "overtones" to the case. And the neighbors, too, assured reporters that there was "no obvious bias in the family or neighborhood." Nonetheless, the police had been concerned enough to alert several Black families in town, urging them to stay inside in the event that there was a "maniac on the loose." The arrest of Mr. Haas alleviated such fears, but not the smoldering sensation that the town had been somehow tainted by the crimes. As Haas himself would tell me later, "things like this just didn't happen in a place like Ipswich."

In the months and years to follow, the case would drift in and out of the news. Haas was tried and convicted of the murders in 1975; two years later, the verdict was overturned by the State Supreme Court on the grounds that some of the evidence used to convict him had been obtained illegally. The second trial ended in a hung jury, but he was convicted again in the third and sentenced to three consecutive life sentences in Walpole State for the "plastic bag killings of his wife Shirley, 33, and the children, Gordon Jr., 4, and Melissa, 2 1/2."

I had been in prison before—Walpole, in fact—as a college student volunteering to teach English to inmates. But in 2002, Gordon Haas was in neither Walpole nor another prison where he spent time (in a town named Shirley), having been transferred to the Massachusetts Correctional Institution at Norfolk, where Malcolm X had lived when he began his self-education and conversion to Islam. I had forgotten the great heaviness that comes over you as you approach a prison. As you work your way through the mechanisms of entry, through the steel doors and past the surly guards, the feeling is distilled into a kind of dread.

But then I was walking across an airy courtyard, a kind of moat, alone, and into a well-lit, relatively pleasant room where visitors, children among them, were waiting for their loved ones. Although we had never met, I immediately recognized the casually dressed, medium-sized man striding purposefully towards me with a pleasant, open face. I stood up and we shook hands. He was wearing thick glasses, the kind that magnify the eyes unnaturally large, like fish in a bowl. I was surprised, for some reason, by his strong New England accent, presumably that of his native Rhode Island. He looked younger than I'd expected—he had been twenty-nine at the time of the deaths, so he was close to sixty.

The red plastic chairs were bolted down in diagonal rows, so we had to turn awkwardly in our seats as we talked. He never seemed angry—about his life in prison, about life in Ipswich when he had lived there, about the prison itself. Norfolk was designed to be like a college, he told me, and indeed it looks a bit like one: three- and four-story red brick buildings, for the most part, and laid out like a campus, albeit one with walls, guards, barbed wire, and watch towers. Indeed, he earned a master's degree here in an educational program once run by Boston University but no longer available. Everything's been cut back or cut out, he explained, despite the fact that the recidivism rate for inmates who earn college degrees in prison is close to zero. At one time, he made model ships that were sold, along with other things that inmates made, at a prison gift shop. He now worked in the library and was very active in a Catholic Church group—the "Lifer's Group"—and a program called Project Youth, which brought high school students into the prison for a tour and a cautionary talk with some of the inmates. Sometimes, he helped fellow inmates who were doing legal research on their cases.

Before long, the discussion drifted in the direction of his case, his reason for being there. He had no difficulty listing the mistakes that had been made: it had been raining since the night before the murders, yet the police never closed the yard to pedestrian traffic—"people were walking all over it"; the spare house key had been found in the door, yet fingerprints were never taken from it; the funeral director, Dave Carlton, had embalmed the bodies before a full autopsy could be conducted, which is illegal.

But the greatest problem, as he described it, and one that had been a major issue in court, involved body temperatures: taken that morning, the readings determined the estimated times of death. The first examiner had encountered a problem with the thermometers, and when the temperatures were finally taken, Shirley's temperature, along with one of the children's, was 78°F; the other child's was 84°F. The human body, he told me, cools at the rate of one and a half degrees per hour, and a smaller person, with less mass, would cool faster than an adult. Assuming that they had died at approximately the same time, the two children should have had the same temperature, and his wife another. The medical examiner, a Mr. Katz, had not written down the temperatures at the time but an hour and a half after the examination, in his car as he drove home. This fact brought the whole validity of the evidence, and hence the time of deaths, into question.

The family, Gordon maintained, was still alive when he had left for work at six thirty in the morning, waving to some of his neighbors in parting. Here he paused and added, "I don't know how someone could do such a thing and then act normal afterwards. No one who saw me at work that morning said there was anything different or abnormal about me, the way I was acting." They had, however, noticed the scratches on his neck, and had asked how he'd gotten them. He told me the same thing he had told them: his wife had been startled when he'd bent over to kiss her goodbye, and she had reached up and scratched the right side of his face. Had they taken any evidence from beneath her fingernails? "They didn't do any of that. This was before the days of DNA testing."

If critical of the police, he also seemed sympathetic, and he repeated what he had told me in his letter: the police were not really prepared for this kind of case, and they shouldn't have been expected to be. For "things like this just didn't happen in a place like Ipswich." The chief, he felt, had wanted to prove something, to advance his career, when he should have handed the case over to the state police, who were better prepared to handle a murder. One of the first officers on the scene, he said, "was practically crying on the stand, walking in on such a horrific scene." (According to Officer Rauscher, the photographer who took the pictures of Shirley and the children wept.)

As the clock on the wall inched its way toward four o'clock, the inmates and their guests began their protracted goodbyes. Privately relieved that our time was up, I stood and thanked him for his time. He couldn't walk me to the gate, he explained, so he said goodbye and thanked me for coming. He seemed genuine in his appreciation. He had told me that he had no other regular visitors aside from his sister, who only made the trip from Las Vegas every couple of years. "Keep in touch," he said. I told him I'd visit again, and we headed off in our respective directions. Once outside in the parking lot, I was surprised by the lifting weight of my own relief and by the sight of two deer grazing in a nearby field.

• • •

North Adams, Massachusetts, lies at the foot of the Berkshires in the western part of the state. From the top of the mountain, along the "Mohawk Trail," a road descends sharply through a series of switchbacks and hairpin turns before sloping dramatically into a once-working-class mill town of brick and stone, former factories turned into apartments and businesses, and, more famously, MASS MoCA, a museum of modern art. A block from Drury High School's former location is the public library, a handsome nineteenth-century brick building.

It was beautiful late-summer weather when I arrived. In the public library, a friendly woman told me that she vaguely remembered the story of a local woman murdered along with her two children in the eastern part of the state. The articles in the *North Adams Transcript* carried the same sad news as the Ipswich papers, the same photograph of Shirley Haas, formerly Shirley Grant of 23 South Street, North Adams—a soft, formal portrait of a young woman wearing a dark dress and an expression of mild, unassuming confidence.

The facts of her life were essentially the same as well: she was "a light skinned black," the paper said, and after her graduation from Drury High School in 1958, she had won a one-hundred-dollar scholarship to attend the Chandler School for Women, in Boston, from the local branch of the NAACP. Afterwards, she had returned to town and worked at the Cascade Paper Company, then at Williams College. Only a few weeks before her death, she had been in town with her two children, visiting her mother and attending the fifteenth reunion of her graduating class. She was survived by a brother, two sisters, and her mother, who worked at the Sprague Electrical Company. She had been married in town at St. John's Episcopal Church on August 28th. I checked the date: I had arrived on the thirty-sixth anniversary of their marriage.

I asked the librarian if they carried copies of the high school yearbook from 1958, and she directed me toward the school department offices a few blocks away where, in a busy superintendent's office full of pre-school bustle, I met a woman named Barbara Dowling. They didn't have the 1958 yearbook, she said, but she had one at home because that was her husband's class. She paused for a moment, looking startled. "Yes, I knew Shirley—not very well. She was in my husband's class. We were all horrified. He learned of it while he was coaching a little league baseball game." If I came back after lunch, she would Xerox some pages for me.

When I came back in the afternoon, she already had them; her husband had helped her find the pictures that included Shirley. She was on the student council, and she appears in a montage of photographs of the cafeteria, leaning forward on a crowded table of students who are listening as she talks. In each of the photographs, she appears as the only Black student, a light-skinned woman with a round, pleasant face. The yearbook picture itself appears on a page typical of an American high school yearbook circa 1958, a page she shares with some other students whose last names also begin with "G," other smiling teenagers with quaint nicknames: Alfie George, Sandy Giardi, Betty Giusti, Gret Cousins. Of Thomas "Gibby" Gibson, not much could be said: "Has no cares or worries . . . drives father's Plymouth . . . works at Jack and Harry's . . . likes to hunt."

But Shirley Ethel Grant, with her bright eyes and broad smile, was a busy student: "Thumbs Up Club; Banner; Chorus; Sophomore Talent Show; Sophomore Frolic; Freshman Reception; Football Dance 3; Volleyball 3; Tennis 1, 2; Soccer 2; Ski Club; Miss Personality . . . Our little hot rod from South Street. Shirley Ethel Grant. Shirl"

Shirl. I thanked Mrs. Dowling and walked back into town, where I asked a passerby for South Street. Not far away, as it turned out: down the hill, past the church, and then another couple of blocks to South Street—the well-trod path between the house and school that Shirley and her siblings must have walked countless times. Only a block or two long, it is a typical-looking street of a typical

New England town and could have passed for any number of the streets in Ipswich. Number 23 was halfway down on the right, a large, off-white house with a front hedge, two front porches, an American flag, and a dog lounging in the driveway. Roused from its torpor by my knocks, it would not stop barking until a young woman came out, looking at me suspiciously. I introduced myself and asked if this was the house where the Grant family had once lived. It was.

She had bought it a couple of years ago from one of the sisters; the mother had lived there until she died, and then the daughter had held on to it for a couple of years before selling it. Yes, she did remember the sister's name—Miriam Royston. She still lived in Williamstown, she thought. A very nice woman. The family had lived there for years, but she didn't know them, only the sister. She had never heard of the case, the story about Shirley. She wasn't from there, originally. The dog resumed its barking, and the woman seemed eager to get back inside. I thanked her and left.

I spent the night in town and, in the morning and with some misgivings, called the phone number I had found in the Williamstown phone book the night before. A woman answered and listened to my halting self-introduction. I was a teacher living in Boston, I explained, but I was from Ipswich, originally, and I had become interested in the story of Shirley Haas and her family; I'd been given her name by a woman who lived at the house on South Street where she had grown up. I mentioned that I was in an interracial marriage, as if to justify my interest.

She paused before answering, surprised, no doubt, by this call from the past. "Yes, I'm her sister," she said, and politely continued, "I'm sorry. I'd like to help you, but even after all this time it's still too painful to talk about."

I asked if there was anyone else I might speak with, anyone who had known Shirley.

"No, there are only two of us left, and I'm sure my sister would feel the same way I do."

Her tone was pleasant but resolute. I thanked her, and before she hung up, she added, oddly but not unpleasantly, "I wish you good luck in your marriage."

Accompanied by his four-year-old son on a bicycle, Gordon liked to walk downtown on Saturday mornings and have breakfast at the Williams Bakery on Main Street. "We loved Ipswich," he told me more than once. And Gordon loved his children: some of his neighbors had once suggested to him that he was too affectionate with Gordon Jr., nicknamed "G-II," and that this was not how a father should act. "They told me I shouldn't kiss my son, and I just said, 'go away.'"

"He spoiled—they spoiled—the kids to an extreme," remembered Reverend French. "All suggestion is [that] he really cared for them and spent a lot of time with them. Shirley's family, as far as I could see, accepted him as loving husband and father before and after— an easy group to have felt deep suspicion. They helped him even financially, in the early days, and they stayed with him more than once."

When they first started dating, Gordon wrote to me, "Shirley's family was very loving, and welcomed me as one of the family. There were some who had reservations but Shirley's immediate family—her mother, brother, and sisters—were very supportive. My family was not, and did not attend our wedding. My father was a vocal racist, although I could never fathom why, save that he was not the success he thought he should have been and was very bitter. He could and did make life miserable for many. He and I had not gotten along well when I was growing up and the divide just widened after Shirley and I were married."

When his father had found out that they planned to marry, in fact, he went "ballistic." He forbade Gordon from attending graduate school at the University of Rochester on the theory that the presence of Gordon and his Black wife would be too disruptive to Gordon's brother, an undergraduate at the school, who he feared would be persecuted by association. Gordon obliged and did not attend. Instead, both found jobs in a Youth Corps jobs program in New Bedford. After the marriage, Gordon's father had virtually no relationship with either him or the children.

While growing up, things at home were "very tense": his mother was afraid of her husband, who was very mean and hard on his sons, particularly Gordon. He was so unpleasant to be around, in fact, that Gordon stopped inviting his friends to the house for fear that his father would "cause a scene," embarrass him and them, and send them away.

The family lived outside of town, isolated, and Gordon ended up spending much of his time alone. Although he was a good student and a football star, his father taunted him, telling him, "You're not good enough. You're never going to make it." In spite of this bullying, Gordon helped lead Barrington High School to the Class C state championship in his senior year, even as his father continued to predict he would not make "all-state." When the newspaper announcement came, Gordon walked into his father's bedroom and—in a scene that could have been taken from a father/son melodrama, the embittered son finally proving his father wrong—threw the paper on the bed, said, "There's your paper!" and stalked out.

"People told me he was proud of me, but I never saw it. . . He told me he didn't want me to get a swell head," he chuckled ruefully. "Well, it worked."

Education—or lack thereof—was not the issue. His father had gone to Brown, graduated Phi Theta Kappa and, after various jobs, taught math at Moses Brown School. Gordon's happiest times growing up were spent with his grandfather, who had once been the vice commodore of the Newport Harbor Club. Unlike his son, Gordon's father, he was a kind and loving man who would come to their house on Sundays to spend time with his grandsons.

Even after the children were born, Gordon's father would not come to see the family. Gordon's mother didn't drive, so she had to secretively ask her other son to drive her to town if she wanted to see Gordon Jr. and Melissa. Nevertheless, Gordon went to Rhode Island several times to see his parents. Once, while he and Shirley were visiting in the early spring of 1973, his father used a "racial epithet." They left immediately and drove back to Ipswich; more than thirty years later, the hurt of this moment is visible on Gordon's face as he tells the story. He does not repeat what this exact racial epithet was, but we may safely imagine.

And then, in mid-June of the same year, on Father's Day, Gordon drove with Shirley and the children to visit his parents in Rhode Island. His parents were about to move to Georgia and had invited them to see if there were any books they might want. His mother was also eager to see her grandchildren before the move. "It was the only time my father saw his grandchildren," Gordon said. "We went not for my father, but for my mother who so wanted to see my children before she and my father went to Georgia to live. I was not expecting any reconciliation or changes in my father's attitude, and there were none." But there was one moment that Gordon found amusing: Hearing himself addressed by his grandfather with "Hey, kid," G-II had turned around and said, "'My name is not Kid; it's G-II.' It was a precious moment."

It was the last time his father would see his son or grandchildren alive: a couple weeks later, a strange sort of reality intervened. One can only imagine the emotions that must have flowed through the old man's heart when he heard the news that his daughter-in-law and his two grandchildren had been murdered, suffocated with plastic bags, and that his own son had been arrested and charged with the crimes. He might have found it odd, too, that a note found at the scene, written with a red crayon, said "Black and White don't mix"—if not his own words, exactly, then his own sentiment, his strongly held belief that he had been trying to impress upon his oldest son for years.

Among the odd details of the case is the fact that Shirley's mother apparently believed in Gordon's innocence for the remaining years of her life. She posted bail for him the first time he was let out of jail, and when the second trial ended in mistrial and a new trial was ordered, Gordon moved to North Adams to live with her, in the house where Shirley had grown up, for almost two years. He worked in town at a factory, and also as a taxi driver.

There was initially "some negativity" shown toward his presence in the town, but he "never had a problem." He kept a low profile, and in his spare time he drove to Albany and spent a lot of time in the medical library of the state university, studying the grim science of the recently dead; "lividity": what happens to a human body after it dies. At the time of the deaths, he told me, "I couldn't bring myself to read the pathology report. I'm very squeamish— still, I couldn't stand things like that. But I should have."

It is hard to envision, living with the mother of one's murdered wife, the grandmother of one's late children, while waiting to be tried for their murders. And yet, when I first met him thirty years afterward, he was still in touch with one of Shirley's sisters, Marion, with whom he exchanged cards on the holidays.

Whatever preparations he made at the medical library were of no avail. In the third trial, a new witness was called, a woman I will call Mary Frances. She had been a secretary for Gordon Haas at Lechmere Sales, and in the weeks preceding the murders, they'd had a "whirlwind relationship" involving "luncheons, dinners, and nighttime walks along the Charles River . . . during which they professed their love for each other." At the time of the murders, she was no longer working for Mr. Haas, but they had continued to see each other and had been together in her apartment on the evening before the murders. Among the things they had previously discussed was the inconvenient fact of Gordon's marriage. In the trial, she testified that Gordon had asked her, two weeks before the murders, what effect a "catastrophe" would have on their future relationship. Members of the jury were said to have "gasp[ed]."

In such a scenario, love and the desire to be with Ms. Frances, to start a new life together, could have combined with other sources of stress and confusion—money, the labor relations at work, a lifetime of racial venom absorbed from his father, and perhaps Ms. Frances' threat to end the relationship—to cause a major break with reality, a psychological environment ripe for cracking up, and a delusion that he could continue on love's course with Ms. Brown if only his wife and children were out of the picture. And if Ms. Frances had tried to put a stop to their relationship because he was married, this could have caused him to panic, to respond with a sudden but deluded attempt to make himself available and ensure their future together.

"But why the children?" I asked a friend, Steve Bergman, a psychiatrist with a side interest in the psychology of murderers.

"Because how could he live with them after he had killed their mother?" Bergman said. "There was too much guilt." And of Ms. Frances, he asked me, "Was she White?"

"Yes—why?"

"Because on some level that's what he believed—Black and White don't mix." On some level, that is, he was still trying to please his father.

In the evenings, Shirley used to walk through the neighborhood with her children and talk to the neighbors, among them Sharon Scobert, with whom she had planned to go clothes shopping for their children on the day of her death. When Sharon had called in the morning, the phone appeared to be out of order, and she called to report it to the telephone company. Shirley was a lovely, gregarious woman who had "every friend in the world," Sharon said, and she described the kids as "adorable." With a slight hint of embarrassment, she added that Ipswich was a town with a lot of Greeks and Italians, who could get very dark in the summer; Shirley was light skinned, like someone with a "good tan." It was not until Sharon visited the house one day, saw a photograph of some of Shirley's uncles, and asked who they were that she realized Shirley was "Black." Miryam Williamson, who had been in the League of Women Voters with Shirley, told me the same thing—for some time after meeting her, she had been unaware that Shirley was African American.

Shirley's mother was African American with some Native American blood, Gordon thought; her father, also African American, died in his sleep on Christmas Eve in 1945, when Shirley was five. Her mother never remarried, raising her three daughters and a son alone in North Adams while working at Sprague Electrical Company. Shirley's childhood was spent in this loving family on South Street and ended in my hometown of Ipswich while I slept, at age sixteen, a couple miles away. I am moved by the few photographs I have seen of her: as a happy teenager in 1958, an ebullient high school girl, "our little hot rod from South Street"; as a glamorous young woman in her early twenties, soft featured and beautiful, gazing off into the middle distance; and then later, in Ipswich, working for the "Sweetheart Fair," raising money for the Cable Memorial Hospital, a mature, handsome woman of the seventies, wearing beads and a wide-collared shirt.

She married in 1965, a time when interracial marriage was still illegal in eighteen American states and frowned upon, to be sure, in all of the others—Massachusetts included. Her relationship with Gordon Haas, I feel sure, was born of love and respect, and together, with *her* family's blessing but not his, they married and moved across the state to its southeast corner, New Bedford, and then to Ipswich with their two young children. Two years later, an incomprehensible murder took her back to North Adams for her own funeral, then to Williamstown—only a few hundred yards from the campus where she and Gordon had met—the final line of a triangle drawn, the strange geometry of her life complete.

"Race" had not been the reason for Shirley's death, but a weakly offered explanation for some greater human failing, and a jury of fellow citizens decided that this murder had been committed by her own husband. It was a story, Miryam Williamson wrote, "of nearly overwhelming human tragedy." Of his guilt, said Williamson, who had also known Gordon and had covered his second trial for the *Salem Evening News*, "My heart tells me he didn't do it, but my head tells me he did." The sentiment also expresses my own. Yet, even thirty-five years later, Reverend French was still not fully convinced of Gordon's guilt. French died in 2008.

For the town, he wrote to me, "Tragedy surely concluded what might have been a gentle beginning, an exploration of a new kind of joining, new then if less unusual now, in our country. Those words left by someone opened the door we would not like to go through . . . Were there time, I'm not sure how I would address the explaining of such events. I thought then that I believed in [Gordon and Shirley], believed in Gordon, that they enriched the community, and that tragedy we could not make sense of had somehow concluded a chapter full of promise."

I returned to North Adams a few years later, not on a beautiful summer's day but a cold November one. I drove past the old high school, past the house at 23 South Street—still there—through the semi-bustling Main Street of North Adams, and then headed back toward Williamstown. But my memory failed me, and although I had found the graves with ease on my first visit, they eluded me now. I took several misguided trips around the cemetery and even wondered if I was in the right one before I came upon the family again. But something had changed: once well-tended and honored with fresh flowers, the graves were now neglected. Melissa's headstone was tilted, akimbo, as if being pressed upwards from below. The engraved letters of their names were filled with pine needles and decaying bits of seed and leaves and the castings-off of trees. Lichens had formed in greenish patches on the stone. I scraped some off with the flat side of a key and cleaned some of the letterings with my fingers and a twig. Shirley's sister, it seemed, no longer came to visit—perhaps she had become too infirm, or had lost the heart to do so, or maybe she, too, had passed away.

As sad as the deaths themselves, almost, are the deaths of those who had known and loved Shirley and her children, so that with time even their memory fades away, and with it the ineffable bonds of love that once held them all together, as family.

David Updike teaches English at Roxbury Community College in Boston and lives in Cambridge with his wife, Wambui, and son, Wesley. A collection of his short stories, *Old Girlfriends*, was published in 2009 by St. Martin's Press.

SPEAKING OF EARS AND
SAVAGERY

Steven Church

Round 1

> "Like Dempsey, he has the power to galvanize crowds as if awakening in them the instinct not merely for raw aggression and the mysterious will to do hurt that resides, for better or worse, in the human soul, but for suggesting the incontestable justice of such an instinct . . ."
>
> —Joyce Carol Oates, "On Mike Tyson"

On June 28, 1997, in Las Vegas, during the rematch fight between Evander Holyfield and Mike Tyson—a fight billed as "The Sound and The Fury"—things weren't going well for The Fury.

Tyson had already been beaten badly by Holyfield in the previous fight, suffering a TKO, or "technical knockout," in the 11th round after a sustained pummeling. That match had shown Tyson to be vulnerable, and he looked every part of the sports cliché "a shadow of his former self." He made excuses afterward, claiming Holyfield had used intentional head-butts to cut and daze him when the two fighters entered into a clinch. Most people believed Tyson had lost his edge, had grown fat on the largess of his life or been corrupted by the influence of Don King—all of which was true.

Tyson's complaints, however, were not totally without merit. Holyfield had long been known as a master of the subtle head-butt, a tactic that, while common, is hard to spot and is potentially devastating. A head-butt in boxing is not the exaggerated forward strike you see in professional wrestling or movies, but a more subtle tactic of close-in, hand-to-hand combat, a swift strike with the crown of the head to the thin-skinned brow, cheek, chin or forehead of an opponent. Done correctly, discretely, it can quickly disable an opponent by knocking him stupid or by causing swelling to the eye or excessive bleeding, which blinds the fighter.

Intentional head-butting is against the rules of boxing, a violation similar to a punch below the belt. The head-butt is considered a "dirty" tactic—just the sort of trick you'd think a man like Mike Tyson, not a man like Evander Holyfield, would use to gain an advantage over his opponent. Perhaps because of this, all of Holyfield's head-butts were judged to be "accidental."

As the rematch fight entered the second round and Tyson's furious efforts to slow the fundamentally sound and patient Holyfield seemed fruitless—several clean punches failed to deter Holyfield's steady advance—the two men entered into a clinch, and another head-butt from Holyfield opened a sizable gash above Tyson's right eye. With blood streaming down his face, Tyson complained bitterly to the referee and admitted later that he was dazed and scared, feeling vulnerable, but the referee, Mills Lane, ruled the head-butt was unintentional.

Angered by the head-butt and Lane's refusal to intervene, Tyson came out for the third round and unleashed a barrage of punches at Holyfield, but his rally barely fazed the champ. The two men clinched up, and again Holyfield head-butted Tyson, who, at this point, became convinced Lane wouldn't protect him. He was desperate, angry and determined to defend himself.

Tyson, despite all his fury and bluster, always spoke with a lisp, and his characteristic high-pitched, nasally voice made him sound like a man-child, a curious mix of innocence and aggression. Tyson always, always fought as if he'd been beaten back into a corner and told to stay there. Like everyone else in the world, I'd come to love Tyson for his naive ferocity, for the brutality with which he dispensed opponents, often exploding as if he'd been unchained and turned loose from his corner. He didn't just beat his opponents; he went out there in his black trunks, black shoes and short socks, and he humiliated his opponents. We loved every terrifying second of the carnage, especially when he threw his uppercut, a punch that seemed capable of knocking a man's head clean off. Most of us wanted him to destroy Holyfield, to show the world that Iron Mike was still a force to be feared. But something was wrong from the beginning. Tyson wasn't himself, wasn't the Fury we expected. Instead, he became something else entirely, something much worse—a mirror, a reflection of our own bloodlust, a vessel for our collective savagery. Tyson lost the artistry that made his brutality beautiful. It disappeared into the fog of fear.

Lane separated the two men, and the fighters exchanged a few punches before locking up again. As they did, Tyson spit out his mouthpiece. When Holyfield's head came up, Tyson twisted his neck, tucking into the side of his opponent's face almost as if to kiss him on the cheek or nuzzle his neck.

Tyson opened his mouth wide. He bit down hard on Holyfield's upper right ear, severing the helix, the outer section of cartilage. Holyfield jumped back, shoving Tyson, who spit out the chunk of ear onto the canvas. As Lane tried to figure out what had happened, Holyfield hopped around the ring, gesturing at his head with his glove as blood poured from the wound.

The boxers were sent to their corners. Everyone watched. Then, perhaps caught up in the moment and not fully aware of the extent of the damage to Holyfield's ear, or perhaps so sucked into the adrenaline of blood-sport that he was blinded to the reality of what was happening, Mills Lane allowed the fight to continue. He wanted it to continue.

After exchanging a few punches, the two fighters locked up again. This time, Tyson bit down on Holyfield's left ear—not as hard as the first bite but still hard enough to cut and leave a mark and send Holyfield jumping back, flailing his arms hysterically and pointing first at Tyson and then at his own head with his cartoonish red gloves.

Lane again sent the fighters to their corners and finally ended the fight, waving his arms in the air and disqualifying Tyson, who exploded in rage and rushed at the Holyfield corner, throwing punches at anyone who got in his way. Soon, the ring was flooded with thick-necked sheriff's deputies in beige uniforms.

As Tyson exited the ring, boos erupted from the crowd. The whole place seemed to surge and pulse with adrenaline. Tyson bulled his way toward the exit, and a fan threw a water bottle at him. He jumped over the barrier, charging into the crowd, screaming profanities and pointing at people, raging at anyone near him. Members of his entourage and security personnel dragged Tyson out of the stands and pushed him toward the exit.

Unable to look away from the television screen, I watched the spectacle unfold from a safe distance. Red gloves. Black men. The bloodied helix. The noisy physics of Tyson's fury. And part of me wanted to be waiting in the locker room as Tyson came back. Part of me wished I could get close enough to touch his unchained violence, but most of all, I wanted to see the severed ear, the bloodied helix, lying on the canvas or cupped in a white towel, nested in a bucket of ice.

Round 2

"I just want to conquer people and their souls."

—Mike Tyson

David Lynch, the mind behind such cinematic creations as "Twin Peaks," "Eraserhead," "The Elephant Man," "Dune" and "Lost Highway," also wrote and directed 1986's "Blue Velvet," a movie that changed forever the way I thought about ears.

In particular, it changed the way I thought about ear-related savagery, about the meaning of severed ears. Such thoughts aren't something you always want. Perhaps you unwittingly stumble into Lynch's vision. You're simply watching a young man walk through a field of overgrown grass in the opening scene of "Blue Velvet," and you have no idea what to expect. Perhaps you watch him closely, this tall, pasty-faced man in Lumberton. Everytown, America.

Innocent but curious. A man, but just barely. Jeffrey Beaumont. He's cutting through this overgrown lot after visiting his dying father in the hospital. He's not expecting any complication to his life. He has no idea how quickly things can change, how one small discovery in a field of secrets can crack open his world.

Jeffrey finds an ear in the grass. A human ear. Severed from the skull, it becomes like a window, or a rabbit's hole. Lynch said of this scene, "I don't know why it had to be an ear. Except it needed to be an opening of a part of the body, a hole into something else . . . The ear sits on the head and goes right into the mind, so it felt perfect."

The brilliance of the scene is captured in the dilemma it hands off to the audience: The question put before them is "What would you do?" It implicates us in everything that follows—the twisted search for answers that leads to Isabella Rossellini and the infamous scissors, Frank and the mask, hiding in the closet, the car ride, the dancing, the drinking, the kidnapped boy, Dean Stockwell, nitrous oxide and Roy Orbison—all of it spinning madly out of control. And it all begins with curiosity, attention to an ear and a lingering question: What would you do? Could you stop yourself from falling, too? It's strange how a subject overtakes you. This thing that Jeffrey cannot leave alone, this thread he cannot stop tugging, makes everything come undone. Lynch's camera takes you down into the ear, and you fall into the darkness. Your life is never the same.

Again and again, I fall into the severed ear in this scene, disappearing into its rabbit's hole. This ear replaced Van Gogh for me—the easy, comforting allusion of aberrant emotion Lynched forever after, corrupted and complicated in ways that are so much more unsettling than the anecdotal violence of Van Gogh's severed ear. Now, when I hear "severed ear," it's not golden sunflowers and unrequited love I think of, or even a drunken quarrel between rival artists, but, instead, the mess of Mike Tyson or David Lynch's particular brand of savagery.

• • •

Round 3

"Everyone has a plan until they get punched in the face."
—Mike Tyson

The word "earmark" appears to have originated in the 15th century, referring to a notch cut into the ear of cattle or sheep to indicate ownership. When I was 18, done with team sports, I pierced my left ear to declare some small measure of independence from my parents' shepherding influence. I marked the other a year later because I appreciated symmetry. I kept my ears adorned for over a decade and only took the jewelry out when I had my first job interview for a teaching position. I don't wear jewelry in them any longer, but I don't need the decoration for them to get noticed. I have large ears with prodigious lobes, which dangle down like tiny saddlebags.

Next time you're in a classroom or a restaurant or some public place, look around and see how many ears you can spot. Pay attention to how people wear them, cover them and show them off, however subtly or unintentionally. Pay attention to size and angle of articulation. Pay attention to gender. Ask yourself—if you can stand the self-consciousness—how much effort you put into your own ear display.

Aside from some new mysterious hair sprouting from them (and inside them!), I don't have to worry much about my ears. I live in a climate where frostbite is a concern only for fruit. I might suffer the occasional sunburn if I'm not careful. Most of the time, though, I take my ears for granted. If they weren't attached to my head, I'd probably leave them in coffee shops and bars, drop them on morning walks, lose them in the cushions of the couch. I'd probably find the dog in the backyard, chewing on one of my ears, or have to scold my toddler daughter for depositing my ear in the fish tank. I'd buy extra pairs of ears—the cheap kind you get at convenience stores—just to have some backup pairs.

I have large saucer-like auricles, maybe a little too big for my head, a little like costume ears. Some people in my family—but not me—have ears that stick straight out from their heads; my dad jokes that they "look like they're driving down the street with their back doors open."

Some people crack their knuckles or chew their fingernails (which I also do when I'm forced to sit still for more than a few minutes). My whole life, I've played with my ears. I can't help it. I like the stiff leathery feel of them; the soft, squishy, peach-fuzzed lobes; even the cheesy stink you get sometimes behind the ear. They feel cool and stiff sometimes, like plastic props or like, I imagine, a dead body; other times, they're warm and pliable as bat wings. If I'm having a really hard time—say I'm at a particularly odious meeting or poetry reading—I'll tug hard on my ears, yanking them down and twisting them, sometimes rocking back and forth in my seat. I'm sure I look like some kind of mental case, but it's the only way I've learned to stay in my seat.

Most of all, though, I like to fold one of my auricles (usually the right one) down and stuff it into the ear canal. If it's cold, the ear will stay folded and stuffed for a few seconds or until I flex a muscle in my face and the ear pops out. I do this sometimes absentmindedly or, if I'm in a class, when trying to sit still and pay attention.

I can also wiggle my ears, causing them to wave back and forth subtly—a trick that unnerves some people and makes others say, "Oh, that's easy," as they begin the pained effort of attempting to do the same, which usually just results in them raising their eyebrows up and down in an exaggerated motion, looking even sillier than I do.

It's not easy. I trained myself to wiggle my ears, practicing in front of the bathroom mirror, staring at myself, pinching and flexing face muscles until I got it right, until I could move them on command. My father can do it, too. As a boy, I stood awestruck before him, demanding he repeat it over and over again, just as my daughter does to me now about my ear-stuffing trick, saying, "Daddy, I want an ear trick," and giggling hysterically when my ear pops out.

The truth is all human ears are somewhat interchangeable. They share physical characteristics, the same language of structure—the "helix" and "antihelix" ridges, the subtle "antihelical" fold between them, a small canyon of flesh; the shadowy "scapha," "fossa," "concha" and the somewhat superfluous "lobule"; and before you reach the "external auditory meatus," you have to negotiate the "tragus" and "antitragus." The differences between one person's outer ears and another's are subtle, slight and usually a matter of inheritance, aesthetics and centimeters.

We may take it for granted, but the human ear—the first sensory organ to develop in the womb—is responsible for a surprisingly complex mission of protection and service. On one level, the outer ear, also known as the "pinna" or "auricle" (yes, sounds like "oracle"), is basically just a large sound-wave deflector, which keeps noise from zipping past our listening holes, but the ear's shape and design is far from arbitrary.

The curves and folds in your pinna are designed to funnel sound waves down into the inner ear's more subtle and delicate machinery, which lies just beyond the "tympanic membrane." It's here that the more complicated work of hearing is done, where the waves are translated into electronic impulses, which fire neurons and other brain receptors, generating what our brains recognize as sound.

While the inner ear is responsible for our sense of balance and equilibrium (something else we often take for granted until we lose it), the outer ear also works to help regulate body temperature, with our auricles serving as thermometers and heat transference devices. Perhaps most striking, the outer ear is surprisingly, often embarrassingly, responsive to emotion.

If I get embarrassed or nervous or scared, my auricles flush red and feel hot to the touch, erupting from the side of my head like flares or flags signaling emotions I want to keep bottled up. I've often been told I have a terrible poker face. This is true. My ears are part of the problem.

Still, I appreciate their personality. I need my ears, and for more than just their necessary physical functions, more than hearing. I need them for the physical act of thinking, for listening to myself and essaying one tangent or another. Just as my kids did when they rode on my shoulders, I often use my ears as handles, places to put my nervous fingers. I tug and twist them. They are touchstones for me. Talismans. Tangible things I can use to keep my hands and brain busy, to help me find thoughts lurking at the edge of clarity, to keep me grounded and listening for more.

Round 4

"To come to a scene and you see a fellow human being ripped apart, I feel for that."

—Officer Frank Chiafari, Stamford Police Department

Travis, a 200-pound, 15-year-old chimpanzee, lived in a private home in Connecticut for most of his life. His owners, the Herolds, operated a tow truck business, and Travis used to ride along in the truck to help stranded drivers. He was something of a local celebrity, an animal that acted the role of family member and friend. He drank wine, ate steak and enjoyed many of the finer things of human life, but it seems Travis was also a sad chimp— perhaps even a depressed, anxious and fed-up chimp, frustrated with his own brand of captivity, tired of the expectations that he be so tame, so unnatural.

On the last day of his life, Travis was particularly agitated and was given Xanax for his rage. It didn't help. He'd gotten outside the house, out of control, and he was angry. His owner, Sandra Herold, called her friend Charla Nash as a last resort. Travis knew Charla and seemed to trust her. She had a calming way. Charla pulled up to the house and stepped out of her car. All she wanted was to get Travis back into the house, to get him to calm down and feel safe again.

But Travis had crossed over. He'd escaped the role assigned to him.

Charla barely made it a few steps before Travis viciously attacked her in the driveway. By the time he'd finished, he'd bitten or ripped off Charla's nose and lips, her eyelids, part of her scalp and most of her fingers. One of the first responders on the scene said he couldn't believe an animal had done that and said it looked as if her hands "went through a meat grinder." For his part, Travis had suffered a stab wound to his back when Sandra Herold plunged a steak knife into him in a futile attempt to stop the attack.

Officer Frank Chiafari was among the first responders. He'd known Travis and liked him. But as Chiafari pulled into the driveway, Travis was no longer endearing, no longer an innocent pet; he'd become something else entirely, a manifestation of savagery unchained, the worst side of nature.

Charla lay semi-conscious and horrifically maimed on the ground. Before Chiafari could react to her condition, Travis approached his car, knocked off the side mirror as if "it was butter," grabbed the handle and yanked open the door. In some awful approximation of a horror-movie scene, Travis stood there covered in Charla's blood, opened his mouth to shriek and bared his teeth.

Chiafari, cowering in his car, shot Travis four times with his service revolver. Travis stumbled away from the car, back into the house, crawled into his bed and died where he slept most nights.

Afterward, the officer was haunted by what he'd seen and by what he'd done. He couldn't visit a mall or an amusement park without being haunted by images of faceless women. He avoided zoos or the circus or any place where he might see a chimpanzee, an animal that Chiafari knew was capable of perhaps the most human and natural instinct of them all, extreme violence and savagery.

For some reason, Travis didn't touch Charla's ears.

During her appearance on "The Oprah Winfrey Show" in 2009, Charla's ears were, in fact, the only feature that allowed you to recognize the thing on top of Charla's shoulders as human, the only recognizable facial feature on a head that looked more like an abstract sculpture of a head. Charla's eyes had been removed, and she drank through a hole in her face. She had only one thumb remaining.

Charla Nash could still hear just fine. And this, it would seem, was both a blessing and a curse. She still felt like the same person inside, and because she couldn't see or touch her face with anything besides her one remaining thumb, her main understanding of how she looked was gained by listening to other people's reactions. She could only hear what others saw—or didn't see—in her face, and she wore a veil to protect us. She said she still felt like the same person—still felt like a person.

"I just look different," Charla said.

Round 5

"My style is impetuous. My defense is impregnable, and I'm just ferocious. I want your heart. I want to eat his children. Praise be to Allah!"

—Mike Tyson

Fifteen years later, Mike Tyson is only mildly repentant for biting off Evander Holyfield's ear. Basically, he's sorry he was forced to do what he did. A recent documentary on Tyson's life seems to support his claims that Holyfield used head-butts for a tactical advantage in each of their fights and that, for whatever reason, the referee in each fight mostly ignored the tactic.

Is it possible that Tyson became a victim of his own image— the mad dog fighter, the Fury? If everyone else believed it, why wouldn't the referees also buy into the hype, the belief that Tyson represented something animal and primal while Holyfield symbolized the Sound, the humble, soft-spoken gentleman boxer who would never intentionally head-butt an opponent?

You can watch videos of the incident online. As bizarre and grotesque as it is to see the ragged tear on Holyfield's ear and the blood pouring down his head, to watch Tyson spit out the chunk of helix, and to think about what it would take to bite through flesh and cartilage, to sink your teeth into someone's ear, it is also strangely unsurprising. Normal. Even predictable and, in some ways, entirely justified if you think about it. You might have done the same if you were in Tyson's shoes. Really, what would you do? How would you defend yourself from head-butts?

Aside from the impulse to self-defense, the instinct to bite is ugly, but it makes sense. It's natural. As someone who obsessively chews his fingernails and his pens, who has watched his babies' faces contort with teeth-pain relieved only by chewing or biting down into something, who has seen a frustrated toddler bite because she can't do anything else, I can recognize that the urge to bite is not always an urge to hurt but sometimes an effort to find comfort and security, intimacy and escape from pain. It's a desperate effort at self-soothing. My daughter has bitten me when we are playing happily, rolling around on the floor. She's not trying to hurt me. She just gets overly excited. She's trying to hold me, to be close to me. She wants a connection closer than touch, wants to feel safe and secure.

Tyson's no child, and I don't mean to infantilize him, but I believe his actions were not so much those of a violent man but instead the existential jaw-clenching of a lonely, frightened human being— desperate, tragic for sure, but not necessarily chaotic or aberrant, certainly not inhuman. To me, watching the videos of the incident now, Tyson looks like a man who wanted to be held. I hope that if I had been there in the locker room, if I'd been a different person, someone in Tyson's inner circle, I would've recognized that need in him and pulled him close, wrapped my arms around his broad, sweaty back, pressed my cheek against the rough nap of his hair and whispered in his ear, "It's all right, Champ. It's all over now." Sometimes, we all need such touch.

Perhaps you think I'm an apologist for brutality. And perhaps I am. Perhaps I simply want to accept the possibility in each of us. Was the blood or gore or pain of what Tyson did any worse than a head-butt? Tyson, too, was bloodied. Tyson, too, had cut flesh, bruising and swelling. But I understand the difference. There was, in fact, something about putting his mouth to another man's ear, his teeth into another's flesh, something so intimate, the severing so desperate and personal, that it made us recoil and call Tyson an "animal," "psychotic," "savage," or, worse, "inhuman. " I believe what burned us most was the naked humanity, the unfettered vulnerability of what he did. What frightened us was his fear. What disappointed us was his weakness. We are so awful in our love for fighters.

Several years later, in an interview after a warm-up victory against Lou Savarese before a 2001 bout with Lennox Lewis, Tyson seemed juiced with rage, charged full of adrenaline as he barked at reporter Jim Grey a series of mumbled prayers to Muhammad. Grey, already looking ahead to Tyson's bout with Lewis, asked if the fight, which ended in a TKO after only 38 seconds, had been Tyson's shortest fight ever.

Tyson then launched into a monologue wherein he talked at least twice about having to bury his best friend, about how this fight was for the dead friend. He was grieving publicly, painfully, and you could see him focus his grief and his rage on Grey's question and on his role as Tyson the Fighter. You could see the switch flip, a manufactured persona rising to the surface, and Tyson seemed to rev up even more, comparing himself to Alexander the Great, Sonny Liston and Jack Dempsey, calling his style "impetuous," before eventually threatening to eat Lennox Lewis' children.

Lennox Lewis did not have any children when Tyson said this, but the line, delivered at the end of an outpouring of grief over the loss of his friend, has become, in popular memory, another tag, another mark—further evidence that there is something wrong, something dangerous about Mike Tyson.

It makes me love him even more.

You see, I liked to nibble on my children's ears. Sometimes, I even did it in public. I did it with my lips curled over my teeth so it wouldn't hurt. I nibbled gently like a dog biting a puppy's ears or a monkey grooming his baby. When I carried my daughter on my hip, her round, soft face and ears sat right at mouth-level, and it was all I could do most times not to nuzzle her cheek, kiss her face and nibble on her ear, rolling the flesh and cartilage between my incisors, the helix of the outer ear between my lips, never my uncovered teeth, never that sharp. It was a way to hold her and keep her close. It was like a kiss, a cuff and a tug to tell her I love her.

Round 6

"Tyson suggests a savagery only symbolically contained within the brightly illuminated elevated ring."

—Joyce Carol Oates, "On Mike Tyson"

Sadly, the ear is an often forgotten, underestimated or disregarded appendage. You're not likely to respond to "I love your ears" as a pickup line. Nonetheless, we depend on the symmetry and subtlety of our ears, their unobtrusive presence as counterweights to each other and aesthetic accessories to our skulls. We notice only when something is wrong. Some of us need them as talismans and triggers for tangential thinking; and nearly all of us know of Van Gogh, the tortured artist and lover who cut off his own ear. We keep this story close as a kind of parable, a lesson or warning, perhaps a story of mythic love—at least, until it begins to mingle with other stories, other parables of severed ears, savagery, mystery and madness; until it is replaced by Lynch and Tyson, and Travis. For me, there is as much gravity in the story of Van Gogh's desperate act as there is in that image of Holyfield's bloody helix, that small curve of cartilage severed from the rest, and as there is in Lynch's ear cradled in a bed of grass, or Travis' choice to leave Charla's ears alone, a kind of aesthetic and ethical weight that shakes up our measure of the balance between human and inhuman.

We'd like to be able to dismiss Tyson as "animal," a mentally deranged savage who is nothing like you and me. We don't want to admit it, but perhaps it's not that easy to separate us from him. Tyson is no animal, no inhuman fighting machine, no simple boxer; instead, he is perhaps more honestly and innocently human, more vulnerable and real and dangerous than most of us can ever hope to be. To me, Tyson always seemed to be fighting himself with as much savagery as he fought his opponents, and he always seemed sublimely, purely alive in the ring in a way I could never dream to achieve in any context. We want to believe that we're not like this Mike and that we're far from Travis and his brand of savagery, too, but try as we might, we cannot always remove ourselves completely from the urge to bite, to sink our teeth into something substantial, something firm but forgiving, tangible or terrifying or terrestrial—especially when we are at our weakest and most vulnerable, or when our plans collapse and we just want to be close enough to hold someone closer than seems physically possible, to consume that person and keep him inside us forever.

Steven Church is the author of *The Day After The Day After: My Atomic Angst*, *Theoretical Killings: Essays and Accidents*, and *The Guinness Book of Me: A Memoir of Record*. His essays have been widely published, and anthologized in *The Fourth Genre: Contemporary Writers of/on Creative Nonfiction* and the 2011 *Best American Essays*. He's a founding editor of the literary magazine *The Normal School* and teaches in the MFA Program at Fresno State.

ORIGINS OF A
MURDER

Alexandria Marzano-Lesnevich

1.

The boy wears sweatpants the color of a Louisiana lake; later, the police report will note them as blue, though in every description his mother gives thereafter she will always insist on describing them as teal.* On his feet are the muddy hiking boots every boy wears in this part of the state, perfect for playing in the woods. With one small fist, he grips a BB gun half as tall as he is. The BB gun is of the Daisy brand, with a long brown plastic barrel the boy keeps as shiny as if it were real wood. The only child of a single mother, he is used to moving often, sleeping in bedrooms that aren't his. His mother's friends rent houses along the same tucked-away string of half-filled lots that the landlord calls Watson Road whenever he wants to charge higher rent, though it doesn't really have a name and even the town police department will need directions to find it. The boy and his mother stay with whoever can pay the electricity bill one month, whoever can keep the gas on the next. Wherever the boy lands, he takes his BB gun with him. It is his most prized possession.

·This month, they are staying with a woman who has a child of her own. The baby is two years old, which is old enough that he wants to play with the boy and screams when he doesn't get his way. Today the baby is wailing. Six years old, just off the yellow school bus home from kindergarten, the boy eats his after-school snack in a hurry, dreaming of getting away from the noise, dreaming of the fun to be found out in the woods. Behind the weathered white

---

This work is not authorized or approved by those persons criminally charged or their attorneys, and the views expressed by the author do not reflect the views of anyone other than the author.

house at the end of the road lies a thatch of woods of the dense, deciduous, swampy kind, the kind in which rotting leaves mingle with the earth and the land gives soft way beneath the boy's feet. Though the thatch is very small, with only a single long ravine like a scar in the earth, a single place in which to prop up the BB gun and play war or dream of hiding away forever, these woods are the boy's favorite place to play. He asks his mother for his BB gun. She takes it down from the shelf that keeps it safe from the baby and she hands it to him. The boy runs out the door. Two children near his own age, another boy and a girl, live in the white house, and while the boy likes exploring on his own, he has more fun when the other boy can join him. He goes to their door and he knocks.

A man answers. The man wears thick glasses. He has sparse brown hair and big ears. At twenty-six, he is small for a grown-up, but he is still much taller than the boy. The man rents a room from the family of the boy's friend. He babysat the boy and his friend a few days prior. He helped them take a bath. Now the boy asks the man if his friend is at home. No, the man says, but the boy can come inside and wait, if he likes.

Now, they've met before. The boy knows the man. And yet the boy pauses. Something in the man's face just then makes him unsure. The man asks again: Why don't you come in, he presses the boy. He opens the door wider. The boy walks into the house, props his BB gun up against a wall near the entryway, and climbs the stairs to his friend's bedroom. He sits down cross-legged on the floor and begins to play.

The man climbs the stairs after the boy. He wants only to watch the boy play; he will say this later, later he will swear to it. But the watching does something to him, changes something in the man, and from then on it is like he is in a dream. He walks up behind the boy and he hooks his forearm around the boy's throat. He squeezes. He lifts the boy into the air. The boy goes limp. Maybe now the man touches the boy, maybe he can finally admit to himself what he's wanted since seeing the boy in the bath. Maybe he doesn't. In all that will come from this moment, the three different trials and the four different confessions and the DNA testing and the serology reports and the bodily fluid reports and the psychiatric testimony and all the sworn sworn sworn truths, no one but the man will ever know for certain.

Now the man picks up the boy, cradling the child as though he were simply asleep, and carries him into the man's own bedroom. He lays him out on the bed. He covers the boy—no, it is a body now, he covers the body—in a blue blanket printed with the cartoon face of Dick Tracy, detective. Then he sits on the edge of the bed and pets the blond hair.

A knock comes on the door downstairs and the man goes to answer it. In the entryway stands a young woman. Her hair is the shade of light brown that is often a childhood blond. Has he seen her son, she asks. (When she asks this, another son rests inside her, just three months along, too early for the pregnancy to show. Inside her, another story has begun.) Who's your son, the man asks. Jeremy, the woman answers, and the man realizes that he already knew. No, he says. I haven't seen him. Oh, says the woman. Well, maybe the boy is at her brother's. Maybe, the man agrees. Would she like to come in and use the phone? She could call her brother, he suggests. He opens the door wide for her.

Thank you, she says, and steps inside. To her left, propped up against the wall, is a Daisy-brand BB gun, its long brown barrel shiny and smooth. The woman steps to the right. She does not see the gun. The man offers her the phone and she dials, looking for her son.

The year is 1992.

2.

The year is 1984 and the Louisiana mental health clinic caseworker's notes (notes that will later be entered into the court record) describe the nineteen-year-old, brown-haired man before him as depressed, submissive, "overly compliant." The man is eager to please, the caseworker writes, but seems to sense he may not know how.

Behind the thick glasses he wears, his brown eyes stay too steady, constant in a way that suggests a fundamental disconnect with life, a fundamental hopelessness. He doesn't get excited and he doesn't get mad, he just is. The caseworker gives him a mimeographed sheet listing problems the man could be experiencing and asks him to circle which ones he is, right now, experiencing. The man circles: NERVOUSNESS, DEPRESSION, GUILT, UNHAPPINESS, WORTHLESSNESS, RESTLESSNESS, MY THOUGHTS. He does not circle: EDUCATION, ANGER, FRIENDS, SELF-CONTROL, FEARS, CHILDREN. He begins to circle STRESS but stops. The pen leaves an arc on the page. He begins to circle SEXUAL PROBLEMS, then stops and crosses that arc out—but then he is rebuked by his mind, by the better part of his knowing, and makes the acknowledging circle. The page becomes evidence of the struggle: What he has, what in his better moments he can admit to himself he has—does he consider it a sexual problem? The circle around WANT TO HURT SOMEONE he draws so tightly it nearly touches all the letters, so tightly it strangles the idea even as it admits it, so tightly it wants to be its own undoing.

Between two clinic appointments the man runs away. He hitchhikes his way across the Louisiana swamplands, through the piney woods of Texas and into the dry Arizona desert where vistas of red rock burn more like the sun than any rock the man has ever seen. The man burns red himself but he does not care. The desert is beautiful. Here, the air fills his lungs with lightness, nothing like the choke of the Louisiana heat. Still, it's funny that he should come here, that he should be drawn back to the place where history would tell him never to go. It is like he needs to find the beginning. He keeps going. When he reaches California, he will stop. California, where his parents lived before he was born. California is where the happy photographs come from, the photographs his mother kept hidden in a heavy trunk when he was a boy. The photographs of the son, long dead, who came before him. Will this trip be a homecoming, a homecoming to a righter life? He means to live with his uncle. He'll find himself a job out there. He will make for himself a life.

But his uncle refuses him. He cannot stay in California. Instead the uncle buys him a bus ticket undoing the whole journey he's just made, and when the man gets back to Louisiana, he suffers the indignity of having to call his parole officer. The officer says, next time you're going to leave, tell me first.

The thoughts start again. When he sleeps he sees a child. The child is naked and he touches the young, unmarked skin and not until afterward, after the touching, does he wake, the sheets twisted, his panting guilty. Which means he's done it again, if only in the dream. When he tells the caseworker about the thoughts, he describes them as nightmares—not wishes, not fantasies. But once a week he masturbates. He can only masturbate by thinking about young children, he says. The man has never been on a date. He is a virgin. His only friend is a sixteen-year-old girl and he says the friendship is platonic. Sometimes he's made young children, boys and girls both, take off their clothing and perform fellatio on him, he says. Then he removes his own clothing. He performs it on them. Last time the boy refused and he told the boy he'd shoot him. "I don't know what I wanted to do that for." The boy was seven years old. His father reported the man to the police. That's why he's at the clinic now.

But all of that is in the past, the man says, all of that is over. He is done with that life. (He must be. He is only nineteen. If he is not done, what will his life hold?) He would have a job now if he'd stayed in California, he tells the caseworker, he tells his mother, he tells anyone who will listen. "Long as I got something to do, I'm all right." But for all the times he says this, and for all the times the caseworker records it, the man never does say what that job would have been. He begins a correspondence course in small engine repair. He wants to "acquire a trade," he says. He wants to move out of his parents' trailer and live alone. It's not right that a grown man should live with his parents and baby brother, not right that a grown man can't stand on his own feet. His brother is sixteen years old and his brother is normal. The man knows this the way he knows that he himself is not. Years from now, after the trials, when the state penitentiary prints a list of the nine names the man has requested be allowed to visit him, the man's parents and sisters and even his sisters' husbands will be on the list, but the brother's name won't. An odd number, nine, short of the round numbers the prison system tends to prefer. Likely the man could have asked for more. But his brother's name won't be on the list.

A month passes before the man's next appointment at the clinic. He's just turned twenty. He reports that he took a job at an auto dealership but then quit it two weeks later. He tells the caseworker he doesn't know why he quit, he just felt like quitting. The caseworker asks again, why. This time he tells her: Each day he walked to the job, he passed schoolchildren playing, then passed them again on his way home. He'd see the children and he'd want. He'd want. The man wants to stop wanting. He quit the job just to never walk by those children. Long as he's got something to do, he's all right—but now the man does not have something to do. He is not all right. He's been thinking about "dying or getting someone else to kill me," he says. He's drinking whole bottles of peppermint schnapps at a time. Last week he drank fifty dollars' worth. "I warned him that drinking might impair his judgment," the caseworker notes.

Of everything I must read to write about the man named Ricky Langley—the murderer, the pedophile, beloved son of Bessie Langley, killer of a six-year-old boy named Jeremy Guillory, and lifer, now, in the Louisiana prison system—of every way in which I must get to know the man, these notes are the most difficult for me. The notes are in the 8,000-page court record, a record I initially obtained thinking that the murder, so plainly committed, was simple.

But at 8,000 pages, the record is not simple. The notes were handwritten by different caseworkers in 1984 and then 1985, one year before Jeremy Guillory was born. A caseworker writes that when Ricky says he's taking a correspondence class, the caseworker tells Ricky that he should check the program out with the Better Business Bureau. BBB, the caseworker writes. And here is where my mind goes: to Jeremy Guillory's Daisy-brand BB gun. Here is what the caseworker does not do: He does not say, *Ricky, do you think a correspondence course is enough of a plan to keep you from molesting a child? Or, Ricky, BBB, it is only one letter off from BB, the child you kill, he will have a BB gun.* The caseworker writes that he "decided to review with the patient" the effects of sexual molestation on children. Patient seemed, he writes, "genuinely concerned" to be told that molestation harms children. "He may now have greater motivation to eradicate this behavior," the caseworker writes—and I read those words in the record of a murder.

What do we do with Ricky at this point in the story, while Jeremy, one year away from being born, seven years away from being killed, can still be saved? Now, as I write, Ricky sits in a cell in St. Gabriel, Louisiana, sixty-eight miles from the hospital where he was born and 138 miles from the house where Jeremy Guillory died. Writ "denied," wrote the Louisiana Supreme Court this past January, when after three trials over twenty years, a death sentence pronounced and then overturned, the court declined his lawyers' efforts to ask again what should be done with him. But in 1985, none of this has happened yet. In 1985, twenty-year-old Ricky, five-foot-three, virginal, strange and he knows it, off and he knows it, bad or sick and he knows it, weighing just 120 pounds, is sitting on a chair in the Lake Charles Mental Health Center, explaining to a caseworker that ever since he was twelve or thirteen, he would just "go with" young children. He sounds tired, the caseworker writes. "He seems to be looking for help. . . He seems to exaggerate his problems," but "he seems to be looking for help."

Scrawled in the corner of a completed form is a note: "Ricky had another close call."

What do we do with him? Now, at this point? Between the margins of this written page, he is the story, the story's center. In the Lake Charles Mental Health Center in 1985, he is simply a folder, likely manila, and his is the folder amongst many identical manila folders that holds the name of a man who will soon be a killer. But not now, not yet. Now at twenty he seems to be confused and sad and he claims to want to kill himself, says last year he tried but he couldn't pull the trigger. Twenty years ago, the doctors wanted to abort him. In 1985 he says he'd like to do the job himself. In seven years he will kill a boy and when they arrest him he will write a letter to his jailer and ask that he himself be killed. Ten years after that he will claim to a doctor that the jailer agreed to help him. Help him die. Help him. That is why he is here in this clinic office, talking to a caseworker who holds a pen and diligently scribbles notes: because he is asking for help. He wants to be helped.

And thirty years into the future, with Ricky still alive having taken a life, alive and serving a sentence of life, I keep reading these notes as though in them I will find the answer to whether we could have helped him. When did this story begin? When could it still have been rewritten?

3.

Outside the town of Red Rock, Arizona, a man steers a station wagon under the high midday sun. In the distance rises the eponymous rock, red and orange and closer to fire than any horizon the man, born a child of the wet swamp, has seen. Before him stretches the desert, and to the man it must seem not vibrant, like the hopeful greens and blues he left behind in California, but desolate. He is twenty-four years old, he is the sole support for his wife and their five children, and one month ago he lost his job at an auto plant outside of Los Angeles. He cannot find another job. The year is 1964 and this morning his wife, once his high school sweetheart and now a woman of twenty-three, rose early and packed the children and everything the family owns into the station wagon. Now he is driving them back to southwestern Louisiana, to the small cluster of rural towns their families are from. He is driving her away from the new life he promised her and into a life that the man knows contains as little hope for surprises as the unrelenting desert. For seven hours he has driven toward this leaden future;

for twenty hours still, he will. Beside him, his wife rests, and if she has a lap belt in her seat (for the year is 1964, and seat belts have only begun to come standard in the front, and are rarely in the back) she has left it undone. In the rear-view mirror he can see his eldest, a boy, five years old and dark-haired like both the man and his wife. The boy is his parents' darling, nameless his whole first month of life because only the perfect name would do. Then the three middle girls, close in age and just plain close. And the baby girl, only a few months old, smushed in with the others, the girls helping to give their mama a break. The baby has only a few more minutes left to live, but the year is still 1964, and the man cannot know that yet.

It is winter, but this part of the desert is hot at midday and the man sweats in the sun. There is no air conditioning, not in the car in 1964, and the air outside the rolled-down windows blows as hot as a heater. The windshield and the press of the man's worry intensify the heat. The children need food, the children need clothing, the children need. He cannot give the children what they need. Maybe now the sweat stings his eyes and he reaches one hand up to wipe the sweat away, and this—just this instant, when his hand cups his eyes, when his eyes are not on the road and his hand is not on the wheel—maybe this is how it happens. Almost thirty years from now, when the lawyers talk about this moment at the murder trial of his unborn son, they will question whether the father was drunk. Does he now have a flask hidden under his seat, a flask that holds liquor he must balance the wheel to gulp down, but that makes all the long hours of giving up—of steering his family right toward giving up—possible? For some acts the heart must be steeled. But the year is still 1964, and as the man is about to lose so much, I must find a kinder way to tell this story: The man sweats in the heat.

He does not see the bridge. What happens next a lawyer will move to the pitch-black middle of the night when she tells the story, as though it is unthinkable by daylight. But in 1964 the two-o'clock sun beats brightly down on this last moment.

The station wagon hits the bridge, throwing the family from the car. The boy, the only boy—beloved boy, named for his father's dead brother, lost in a car crash years ago—his head is severed clear off. The baby girl dies. The middle sisters live. And the man lives; the sisters will have a father. And his wife, who now lies unconscious in the concrete ditch at the bottom of the bridge embankment, right now she is sliding into a coma that will keep her in dark sleep for days to come—she, too, will live. They will have a mother.

The woman's hip is smashed. Her pelvis, smashed. She will require thirty operations on her right leg before the doctors give up and amputate it—but that does not happen yet, not for a long time. When she wakes from the coma the man takes her the rest of the way back to Louisiana and it is there, in the place she tried to leave, that the doctors construct a cast to hold her body. They lay thick white strips of plaster in rows from her ankles to the top of her chest, until all of her is imprisoned in stiff white. A hole over her genitals allows waste to exit. Her legs they fix splayed open, with a metal bar running between her ankles that the hospital orderlies will yank on to move her. Only her arms are free, and when her daughter comes to see her in the hospital (this daughter is three years old in 1964, but someday she will be the one who rises and walks to the front of the courtroom to tell the story of her family) the woman lifts her arms and pulls the daughter's warm, alive body to her. The daughter will remember that hug forever: the familiar pull of the familiar arms, the familiar mother's familiar love, and instead of the soft familiar lap, the cast.

Inside the hospital, months pass. One month, then two months, then three. The woman lies in the cast and waits. The hospital is overcrowded; wards meant for twenty hold forty. At most a thin curtain separates the cots, but it cannot hold back infection. Writing in a book decades from now, a doctor will remember back across the years to the night eight women died on just one ward, and give thanks that those times are over. But now in 1964 they are not over, and the woman lies on her back in her ward and listens to the moans from other cots. What she cannot see, she can hear.

Sometimes orderlies come and wheel her to be X-rayed. Sometimes the orderlies bring her new drugs, which she swallows still lying on her back on the cot. Drugs for the pain, drugs for the infections, drugs to help her sleep. Mostly, drugs for the pain. The drugs do not take away the pain. Her husband brings her liquor. That helps.

When Christmas comes, the doctors let her leave the hospital for a few days. Her husband is back on the road, having found work as a truck driver, and while he is away her brother and his wife have taken in the children. Now the couple moves out of their bed for her and sleeps on the sofa in the living room. The woman's husband comes home. She is still in the cast, but for the first time since before, husband and wife can share a bed. She can see her children. For the first time since before, they are all together again—all of them, that is, who will always now be all who were left. When the year turns 1965, they celebrate, then the woman goes back into the hospital.

Five more months she spends on her back encased in plaster, five more months of the X-rays and the drugs for the infections and the drugs for the pain that do not work and five more months of the drinking. For five more months the woman's body withers inside the cast, until she is less than seventy pounds. She is the size of a child.

But while the woman gets smaller, the cast gets tighter. Not everywhere. Only around her midsection.

The woman is pregnant.

How happy the woman is when the doctors tell her! Her baby is dead and her boy is dead and the year has brought grief and pain unimaginable and somehow out of all this pain, on one Christmas bed, new life has begun. This is a miracle.

But no, the doctors correct the woman, no it is not a miracle. Somberly they stand by the bed and explain to her and her husband what the woman already knows: the drugs, the hard plaster of the cast, the X-rays. This baby, they say, cannot be born. Perhaps the woman and her husband hold hands as they listen, and perhaps between their pressed, complicit palms passes the knowledge of what the doctors may not know: the drinking. The year is 1965, eight years must pass before *Roe v. Wade*, and still the doctors insist: This baby cannot be born.

(Inside the woman, the fetus's heart beats. It has legs now, it has ears, ears that will always look large against its too-small head. Its fingerprints have refined themselves so that someday they will leave marks behind that can belong to no one else. And the fetus has arms now, arms that will strangle a boy named Jeremy—but the year, remember, is still 1965.)

This mother is not going to let her child go.

And so the doctors do what they must, and take a saw to the cast, cutting a wide moon into it to halo the mother's stomach. The mother does what the mother must: inside her cast, she waits. And the baby does what babies do: he grows.

He is born on September 11, 1965, weighing seven pounds, two ounces. Ricky Joseph Langley, his mother names him, the boy who will live in place of the boy dead. The father comes to the hospital to bring him home where his sisters wait, giddy.

I will keep reading, I will keep searching for the beginning of this story, but in 1965 a proud older sister lifts the corner of a blanket and peeks at the brother who is now hers. "Two arms, two legs, five fingers, five toes," she will say years later, remembering this moment. That baby was perfect. She checked.

Alexandria Marzano-Lesnevich is working on a book of combined family memoir and literary journalism about a Louisiana murder and death penalty case, from which "Origins of a Murder" was adapted. The essay originally appeared in *Oxford American*. She has received awards and fellowships in support of the book from the MacDowell Colony, Yaddo, the Rona Jaffe Foundation, and other organizations, and published work in the *New York Times*, *TriQuarterly Online*, *Fourth Genre*, and elsewhere.

SPECTACLE:
THE LYNCHING OF CLAUDE NEAL

Ben Montgomery

Allie Mae Neal pushed through the screen door and found a shady spot on her porch where the summer sun didn't bite. Kittens purred at her feet and wasps flitted in and out of holes in the roof. The few neighbors who passed by saw an old woman in a wheelchair, blue eyes lazy and unfocused behind thick glasses. She'd wave and they'd wave back. Black or white. She has never held a grudge.

"I never blamed nobody," she said. "I never knew who to blame."

She never knew because nobody was ever charged with a crime, and because no man spent a single second in a cell for the things they did to her father, with knives and rope and hate.

Seventy-seven years have passed. She can't remember his face. If she ever wanted to look, she could study the single photograph of him that exists. But in it, he is hanging from a tree.

The story of her father's death ran in newspapers from New York to Los Angeles, detailing how a small band of men killed him, and how a mob mutilated his corpse. They called it a spectacle lynching, and historians say it was perhaps the worst act of torture and execution in 20th century America. The killing became Florida's shame. President Franklin D. Roosevelt knew her father's name.

Claude Neal.

But America moved on, all except for Allie Mae, who is still jolted awake by nightmares, and the other descendants of Claude Neal, who are still scattered and broken, and a few historians, who have never told the story whole. In the Panhandle town of Greenwood, the lynching of Claude Neal remains in some families a dark legend. Those who could remember it outright are mostly dead. The ones who inherited the stories have kept them secret, safe.

A car pulled up outside Allie Mae's little house. Out stepped her cousin, Orlando Williams. He is 64, too young to remember his uncle. But he has seen the way the violence ripped through generations of his family.

He's young enough to keep hoping, if not for justice, then at least for answers.

He climbed the steps and kissed Allie Mae on the cheek.

"I promise," he whispered.

"I know," she said.

For 25 years he has vowed to bring amends. He has fired off letters to lawyers, congressmen, governors, presidents. After decades of rejection, there came, this summer, a knock at his door. The Justice Department had opened an investigation into the 1934 lynching of Claude Neal.

Whether because of Williams' efforts, or simply because the world has kept turning, one of the most atrocious chapters of Florida history is getting another look. The six men who tortured Claude Neal in the woods have never been publicly named. Those who kept his severed fingers in jars as souvenirs have not had to explain. Greenwood, a place where the names on the church rolls haven't changed, has not had to face its history. Its people—the shrinking number who know—are still protecting the reputations of killers.

Jackson County, Florida, 1934: Drip coffee, Purity Ice Cream, turnips, chuck roast, mustard for 15 cents a quart, 26 cents for a dozen eggs. Sun-bleached overalls, Baptists, Methodists, kerosene lamps, screen doors, mosquitoes, pine trees, knee stains, brick chimneys, K & K Grocery, and cotton, 12 cents a pound. Cotton on the roadside and cotton in the ditch and cotton in forever rows stretched across fields flat as tabletops.

Greenwood, 9 miles north of the county seat, was a one-telephone town of 1,300 farmers and sharecroppers staked to the Florida dirt against the tide of the Great Depression.

On the afternoon of Oct. 18, 1934, a white girl went out to water the hogs and did not come home.

Lola Cannady was 20 years old, 5 feet tall and 90 pounds. She had brown hair and thin lips, and she was pretty for a farm girl raised in a clapboard shack. She was engaged to a boy who lived not far away. Their wedding was close.

She was last seen heading to a pen across the dirt road from the only house she had ever known. When she didn't return, her family began to search. Neighbors joined, and the hunt stretched through the night, with guns and dogs and lanterns. They scoured the woods and set bonfires in the fields. The next morning, the sun rose on a commotion.

At 6:45 A.M., Sheriff Flake Chambliss, a big and burly man who was well-regarded, inspected the scene. Lola's body had been covered by pine boughs and logs. When he pulled away the brush he could see that Lola, fully dressed, had been beaten over the head. Chambliss found a piece of torn cloth nearby. He kept it as evidence.

He called upon two doctors to examine the body. Both agreed she had been murdered and that she'd had sexual intercourse. One called it rape.

Talk among the Cannady family and their neighbors turned to Claude Neal.

Neal, a 23-year-old farmhand, had grown up with Lola. He was short and scrawny. He couldn't read or write. He scraped by, picking peas and cotton, mending fences and tending to hogs. He had a wife and a young daughter named Allie Mae. He lived with his aunt, who had inherited 40 acres near the Cannady place.

A sheriff's deputy found him in the corn crib of an employer, where he had spent the night. The local newspaper reported that the sheriff found Neal's bloody clothes in his aunt's wash, and the swatch of cloth found in the woods was fitted to his shirt.

The sheriff hauled Neal to the jail in Marianna, the county seat, but he sensed something stirring. This was a place where church pews filled on Sundays, but Jackson County wasn't past dark days. It was still scarred by a bloody Civil War battle and a Reconstruction-era race war. Six blacks had been lynched here since 1900. The headline in the local paper after Lola Cannady's death read: *Ku Klux Klan May Ride Again, Jackson County Citizens May Rally to Fiery Cross to Protect Womanhood.*

Sheriff Chambliss had just two deputies, so his tactic was to hide Neal the best he could. The next 24 hours were a game of cat and mouse. Chambliss moved Neal to the jail in Chipley, then Panama City, then Camp Walton. The gun-hung whites of Jackson County split up to search a 75-mile radius. By 9:30 that night, 100 farmers, unmasked and drinking, swarmed the Bay County jail, moments too late. The next morning, 50 men surrounded the sheriff's house, demanding to know Neal's whereabouts. The sheriff wouldn't tell. The authorities smuggled Neal across the state line to Brewton, Ala., more than 150 miles from Greenwood. They booked him in as John Smith from Montgomery, charged with vagrancy, and placed him in the best-protected cell.

By then, another crowd had gathered at George Cannady's house. The old man talked to a reporter from the local newspaper. He said his daughter had been choked so hard her eyes were coming out of their sockets.

"Lord, but you can't know how it hurts," he said. "The bunch have promised me that they will give me the first chance at him when they bring him back and I'll be ready. We'll put those two logs on him and ease him off by degrees.

"When I get my hands on that nigger, there isn't any telling what I'll do."

Inside the jail in Brewton, in the double-locked cell in the back, Claude Neal was alone. The sheriff from Escambia County had questioned him twice and produced a confession signed with an X.

It said Neal had gone into the field behind his mother's house with a relative, Herbert Smith, to catch a sow. He had noticed Lola Cannady cleaning out a hog trough. She asked for help and Neal washed out the trough and pumped it full of water. When Lola turned to go, Smith caught her arm. "How about me being with you?" he asked.

"You must be a fool," she said.

Smith grabbed her, dragged her to the edge of the woods and told Neal to hold her arms. He raped her, then said, "Come on, Claude, and get yours."

When they were finished, the confession said, Smith broke a small, dead oak tree and hit her on the head. They covered her with pine boughs, still alive.

The confession didn't jibe with the way Chambliss laid out the story in the local newspaper. And when Smith was brought to face Neal, police said, Neal recanted and said he had acted alone. The Escambia County sheriff, who took Neal's statement, told the press he had never wanted to kill a Negro so bad in his life.

Herbert Smith was never arrested. And even with a new confession, the case against Neal had holes.

Whether he was guilty would be lost to history, for he would never face trial. Men were already rushing toward the jail at Brewton. They arrived after midnight on Oct. 26 and held a shotgun on the jailer. They found Claude Neal, tied his hands with a plow rope, stuffed him in the backseat and slipped out of town into the darkness.

In New York, Walter White was incredulous. The secretary of the fledgling National Association for the Advancement of Colored People watched from a distance. By his tally, Claude Neal was about to become the 5,068th person lynched in the United States since 1882, and the 45th since Franklin D. Roosevelt entered the White House. He was about to become the 16th lynching victim that year, and there was little White, or anybody, could do.

A story about Neal's abduction ran on the front page of the *New York Times* that Friday, Oct. 26, seven days after Lola's body was found, four days after the confession signed with an X was produced. Papers across the country focused the nation's attention on Greenwood.

Mob Holds Negro; Invitations Issued For Lynch Party
'All White Folks' Invited To Party
Thousands In Throng To See Florida Mob Murder Negro

White, 41, sent a telegram to Florida Gov. David Sholtz at 5:22 P.M.

EVERY DECENT PERSON NORTH AND SOUTH LOOKS TO YOU TO TAKE EVERY POSSIBLE STEP TO AVOID THIS DISGRACE UPON THE STATE OF FLORIDA (STOP) DOTHAN ALABAMA EAGLE ALSO ANNOUNCES THAT NEGRO IS BEING HELD BY MOB FOUR MILES FROM SCENE WHERE HE IS TO BE BURNED AT STAKE (STOP) WE URGE UPON YOU TO TAKE IMMEDIATE STEPS TO RESCUE NEGRO FROM MOB AND PLACE HIM IN SAFE CUSTODY

Gov. Sholtz said he couldn't send troops to Greenwood without a request from Sheriff Chambliss. Chambliss had not asked for help. He would say later that he couldn't even find the mob.

White didn't trust the local press, so he called upon a friend, a liberal Southern preacher named Howard "Buck" Kester, to investigate.

He wanted to know who was responsible for taking Neal, and he wanted them brought to justice. In a place so small, with so many watching the events unfold, maybe an enterprising white man could sort through the chaos and come up with some names.

Cars lined the dirt road in front of the Cannady home for a mile in both directions, splitting cotton patches and hog pens and woods of black jacks, water oaks, dog fennels and persimmon bushes. By 7:30 P.M. more than 2,000 people from 11 states had gathered, according to a *Dothan Eagle* reporter there. They passed jugs of moonshine and stood around bonfires.

George Cannady, 70, paced his property, patting a revolver stuck in his belt. The Cannady clan stepped forward, 14 of them, some carrying knives.

"The womenfolk will do what they want to the nigger," one man said, according to the *Eagle* reporter. "Then the men will get him."

"Alright!" the crowd shouted. "We want the Negro!"

Neal was being held several miles away, in the woods, on the banks of the Chattahoochee River. The six men who had abducted him—who referred to themselves as the Committee of Six—sent word that the mob should disperse. They feared someone would be injured if they introduced Neal into the drunken, chaotic crowd.

About 1 A.M., headlamps danced through the woods as a line of cars rolled into the yard. Behind one, a rope jerked as the car hit bumps. The body on the end of the rope was covered with dust and blood. A man standing on the back sliced the rope, and the body slid limp.

Lola Cannady's mother and sister were first to the corpse. They slashed it with their knives. Her brother cut off a finger. George Cannady, crying, pumped bullets into Neal's body. Men, women and children, some just toddlers, walked past the corpse and stabbed it with sticks. They kicked the dead man's body, spit on it and drove their cars over it.

When they had finished, the men threw the corpse onto the running board of a car and left for Marianna. At the courthouse square, they hung Claude Neal's body from a strong oak. A newspaper reporter counted 50 gunshot wounds. Souvenir seekers cut off his fingers and toes and skinned his body with knives.

At 6:32 that Saturday morning, Sheriff Chambliss cut down the work of the Jackson County mob.

The governor's phone wouldn't stop ringing. One man in Marianna called it a "day of terror and madness." The messages piled up.

Mayor of Marianna called and advises that help is needed at once.

Doc Baltzell—Bad situation, worse than can be imagined—need 2 companies. Threatening to burn out all Negro quarters tonight.

Clake Hotel Calling. Fist fights going on spasmodically. Crowd peeved at Sheriff. Surely need help—running all negroes out of sight.

The whites had burned the homes belonging to Neal's kin. They chased blacks through the streets. Two hundred stormed the jail to get a man accused of throwing a bottle at a white man. They didn't relent until an officer produced a machine gun. Some white employers held the mob at bay with rifles, protecting their workers.

The black people hid. They hid under houses. They hid in their employers' closets. They fled in droves, some driving, some running.

Those cursed with the last name of Neal abandoned the lives they had known and ran. A Neal relative brought his wagon down from Donalsonville, Ga., and told the children to hide under corn and hay until they'd made it safely away.

In a thicket outside town, a pregnant woman laid low. She was scared and in pain. The baby inside her would not survive. It is impossible to know whether she knew this. What she did know, what she must have known, is that her life would never be the same. Hunkered beside her was her 3-year-old daughter, Allie Mae.

C'mon now, she whispered to the girl. *Go with me.*

Allie Mae Neal is 80 now, and she has no memory of those thick woods save for the stories her mother told. She remembers that the doctors had to cut the fetus from her mother when she couldn't deliver.

She doesn't remember how it happened, but as they ran, Allie Mae was hurt.

"The doctors said they couldn't tell what was wrong," she recalled. "They said, 'When they was dragging you around, something must have happened to you.'" Still, if she tweaks her neck or back, she can't move for several days. She remembers missing school because of it. She remembers her mother having to cut clothes off her back.

Her childhood was filled with worry. She walked 3 miles to school, and each passing car was a threat, so she'd hide in the woods. Each white neighbor was a possible predator, so she rarely got close. She hardly left her mother's side.

"She was all I had," she said, "and I was all she had."

Her teachers favored her. They'd catch her quietly sobbing when the fathers would show up to escort her playmates home, and they'd give her Tim Tam cookies and sing to her, *Sally Go Round the Moon*. They never talked about it, but it seemed like they understood.

When she was older, she cleaned homes in Marianna. Some made the connection. They'd tell her it was a damn shame those men killed her daddy.

She can't remember her father at all. Her mother would tell stories about how, after baths, he'd dress her up and tie bows in her hair.

She sees him now in the empty spaces. He looks like her Uncle Grady, handsome and smiling. At night, she lies in bed, staring at the ceiling and thinking about him. She has lived 77 years with a tangible void. Nightmares still interrupt her sleep, but she keeps all the bad inside.

"I never have been full of hatred," she said. "Just every little thing that go on I'd say, I wish I had a daddy. If my daddy was living, so and so. If I had a daddy, I could go such and such a place. I kept that up all the time. My daddy wouldn't let this happen. My daddy wouldn't let that happen.

"I never had a father to take me to a school party or nothing. I never had the joy of a daddy. Never did."

She has never seen the photograph. It steals your breath.

It was snapped before sunup, on Oct. 27, 1934. It shows a thin, short man hanging by his neck from an oak tree in front of the Jackson County courthouse. The man is naked and mutilated. Blood streaks his skin.

A rope is tied crudely around his neck. It is not a noose, not meant for killing, for he was dead when he arrived. This hanging

229

was for display. His missing fingers and toes were community keepsakes. At the edge of the frame stands a white man wearing a jacket and hat and a blank stare.

The photograph sold for 50 cents on the street that day.

That photograph stoked public outrage the way that images of police dogs and fire hoses would 30 years later. The NAACP mailed the photograph and Buck Kester's investigative report to 15,000 politicians, editors, academics and preachers. Claude Neal's naked body appeared in newspapers across the country. Men and women put stamps on their anger.

"I realize that to you a nigger is probably less deserving of pity than a dog," a Michigan man wrote to the Florida governor, "but could any decent man stand by and see a dog mutilated, burned, shot, kicked and hanged without making any attempt to save its life?"

"Things like this make me almost ashamed of being white," wrote a woman from Massachusetts. "How long are these mobs of Southern white trash going to get away with their cowardly, inhuman persecution of colored people?"

Writers, teachers and clergymen prodded the government to investigate. Newspaper editorials urged the governor to arrest the lynchers, and when it was clear he wouldn't, they turned to the Department of Justice and the president. But they deferred to the people of Jackson County, saying no federal law had been broken. This stirred progressive politicians, and the next year was the closest Congress ever came to passing antilynching legislation.

The need soon faded. Lynchings, already on the decline nationwide, dropped from about 15 a year to fewer than five. There would never again be a lynching in America as large or grotesque.

As for the people of Jackson County? A grand jury met three times. It concluded that Claude Neal undoubtedly raped and killed Lola Cannady, and that he was killed "by persons unknown to us."

So civilization marched forward, but it left behind a secret. The killers remained nameless as their crime faded from collective memory.

"Most all of the old people who might remember are gone," said Lizzie Long, 81, who still lives in Greenwood and remembers seeing people running through the woods.

"I just can't go back that far," said Laura World, 96. "I remember enough to know we were all scared."

"All I know is the stories I've been told," said Doyle Green, 83. "I just know why they killed him was to send a message. If you cross the line, you're going to die . . . And they ain't many people who wants to die."

A few people have tried to break the silence. But each backed off in fear for his safety.

When Buck Kester, the NAACP investigator, showed up at a church to meet a black minister, he found the house of God swarmed by white men with flashlights. Cover blown, he left town as quickly as he could, but not before getting a few names "rumored in Marianna to have had a good deal to do with the affair": Bowen Griffin, Bruce Carter and "Peg-leg" Brown.

In the late 1970s and early '80s, a professor tried again. He was threatened. Some talked on the condition of anonymity. His sources became "psychotically paranoid and frantic."

Later, a sheriff who wanted to take another look was warned: "You just leave that alone."

George W. Cannady's grandson lives in an old mobile home less than half a mile from where his Aunt Lola was killed. The folks at the courthouse had suggested visitors approach with caution. The Cannadys are "peculiar," they said.

The property is littered with junk cars and rusty farm implements. A young woman came out of the house. "Y'all should just let sleeping dogs lie," she said. Then she disappeared inside.

A few minutes passed before a man emerged, shirt unbuttoned, Velcro shoes, and introduced himself as George Cannady. He stood in the dirt and swatted gnats. His family has its own version of events: The whole thing started over an unpaid debt and a family feud about a milk cow.

His grandfather went mad because he had wanted to kill Neal himself.

Cannady, 62, said he has always been interested in the lynching, and even did some of his own research in the state archives. He said he knew the Committee of Six, but he wouldn't identify them.

"I ain't going to go there," he said. "I even had conversations with some of 'em, years later. They was decent people. I think they felt so bad about her. It is a little 5-foot girl weighs 90 pounds being brutalated and raped by such a monster, you know?

"I think the people just said, 'Well, if we let this go on, then somebody else, it'll happen to them.' They just didn't want it to go on, you know?"

Cannady said the primary lynchers are all dead. He mentioned one of their names, and when pressed for more information, he retracted, said the man has descendants and he wouldn't want them angry.

"If I find out you put that name in that damn paper," he said, "I'm going to look for you, boy."

John P. McDaniel is 70, retired now, a proud Democrat still living in Jackson County, where he served as sheriff for nearly three decades.

In the early 1980s he began quietly studying the Neal lynching. He had grown up hearing the rumors and always wondered. He asked the county historian for help.

The two returned to the crime scene. They found a pad of ash, all that remained of the Neal family home that was burned to the ground five decades before. They photographed the dilapidated Cannady house nearby. They scoured handwritten notes and evidence logs. Sheriff McDaniel, known to locals as Johnny Mac, talked to an old man who claimed to have been present when Neal was killed—not involved, but there. He named names. One of the names belonged to a man who was still alive.

The man was old, ill and senile.

And then, nothing. McDaniel dropped it.

"His memory had gone," McDaniel said. "It was just of no value to talk to him. He wasn't going to tell me nothing."

The sheriff felt conflicted.

"If I could have solved the case and brought the men to trial, I would have, but it would have taken a lot of evidence," he said, "and it just wasn't there."

Plenty of people claimed to know who was involved, but their stories fell apart under scrutiny. He talked to a woman who remembered seeing the silhouettes of chickens flying through the air as the Neal family's house burned. But when it came to what happened on the Chattahoochee, most of what he heard was hearsay.

"If you can't prove it, you just have speculation," he said. "And if you speculate, you might harm an innocent person."

Locals are still sensitive about the lynching. Jackson County has been painted as a racist backwater before, and McDaniel said it's not like that.

"I love this county very much. I gave this county 34 years of my life. I love every person in it, black, white, green," he said. "I'm not going to do anything that will hurt this county. It's been too good to me."

There is one other person he can think of who knows more than he does.

On a blistering August afternoon, Dale Cox bounced in his pickup down a dirt road, outside a fall-down hamlet called Two Egg, east of Greenwood. Tall pines rose on the roadsides. Cox grew up here. A reporter turned historian, he has spent much of his life digging into the past of Jackson County—Civil War battles, ghost towns, racial violence.

He has been collecting information about the Claude Neal lynching since he helped Sheriff McDaniel investigate in the early 1980s. He has unearthed new material, unseen photographs, evidence reports.

He finally arrived at a boat launch on an inlet near the Chattahoochee River, a stone's throw from the Georgia border. He parked and found a small opening to a thickly wooded area north of the launch.

"Through here," he said.

He walked a crooked path through the thick forest, glancing up occasionally at the canopy. He came upon an overgrown road that once led to a steamboat port called Peri Landing. Not far away, he spotted a tall post oak rising above the pines.

"This is it," he said, touching its bark. Only five or six people alive know where this tree is, he said.

"People who came out here after the fact told me that it looked like a deer had been slaughtered," he said. At the base of the tree, the vegetation is sparse. "The folklore is that nothing will grow where his blood was spilled."

While the crowd of thousands waited at the Cannady farm, the Committee of Six brought Neal here, Cox said. They bound him to this tree with trace chains and held him for eight hours. Cox thinks there should be a historical marker here, but he doesn't think the community is ready to open up about what happened, to be linked publicly and forever to such an act.

"In a way, 1934 was a long time ago," Cox said, taking a seat at the base of the tree. "In a way it isn't, because people still remember it. Locally, there's still a lot of sensitivity."

He has looked at enough evidence to draw some conclusions.

"The physical evidence tells me Neal likely committed murder." He pointed to Neal's confessions, the sheriff's report that says Neal's mother admitted washing his bloody clothes, the footprints at the crime scene leading to Neal's house, the piece of cloth that the sheriff said fit Neal's shirt.

It's easy to question the integrity of the investigation. But Neal's guilt or innocence isn't really the point. A group of men usurped the legal system and butchered him in a way that was unusually depraved, even for the time.

Cox interviewed two of the Committee of Six. They were his neighbors, men who knew his father and grandfather. He said he knows the names of the men responsible, and this has put him in an uncomfortable position. The last of the men died a few years ago, but their descendants are still around. If he makes their names public, he said, it could harm people connected by blood to a crime they had nothing to do with and may know nothing about. Not just the lynchers' children, but grandchildren, nephews, nieces.

"I'm conflicted about it, almost from an ethical standpoint," Cox said. "These guys never had their day in court, they're not around to defend themselves, and now, if we name them, their reputations—their families' reputations—are tarnished forever, nationwide."

He has also wrestled with the question of proof. He wasn't there.

"They were never indicted," he said, "and to my knowledge they were never named in any of the reports back then." The men named in Kester's report for the NAACP—Griffin, Carter and Brown—were not directly involved, he said.

Cox, 48, has spent much of his life trying to uncover truth, recording the past in all its nobility and wretchedness, so we can better understand who we are and who we aspire to be. It's ironic, he knows, that now he can't tell his hometown's biggest secret.

He has been diagnosed with ALS, a terminal illness known as Lou Gehrig's disease. His body is shutting down. Already, he grows dizzy and has to rest. He'll lose the ability to move his arms and legs, the ability to speak and, eventually, to breathe. He knows this, and it's why he has been working hard to finish a book he started long ago: *The Claude Neal Lynching*. He will tell everything he knows, except for the names of the men responsible.

He is willing to name names only if the FBI asks, so someone else can responsibly vet the information. But he has shared the transcript of one of his interviews. This is the first time it has been published.

He was scared to begin with, telling us he didn't do it but that he would point out the man that did. Stuff like that. But then after he got relaxed he started to get mad and uppity. He said he had done it and if she weren't dead he would do it again. We was supposed to take him to old man Cannady's house and let him do the killing, but we heard from our man there that there was so many people that showing up with him would just get people hurt. So instead we took him down to Peri Landing and chained him to a tree on that little rise there where the road cuts down through the hill back from the river. Know where I mean?

Cox: Yes, sir.

Well, we kept asking him weren't he sorry for what he had done, but he kept saying no sir, he wasn't. We beat on him some, I reckon, and started cutting him and letting the blood run then burned the blood with a torch. We did a lot to him, I reckon.

Cox: Like what?

Well, I guess we was pretty liquored up and I ain't like that no more, but we cut off his balls and made him eat them and say they was good. Then we cut off his pecker and made him eat it and say it was good. Burned him up some. Whipped him some. I know everybody says we cut off his fingers and toes and all that but we didn't really do that. Other people did that later. After he was killed.

Cox: How was he killed?

Oh, well, we decided we couldn't risk carrying him alive up to Cannady's place, so somebody shot him.

Cox: Who did the shooting?

I don't rightly recollect for sure but I think it was (name withheld). He had his pistol with him and I recollect he or (name withheld) shot him in the head.

Cox: What happened then?

Well, we put him up on the back of the car and carried him in slow procession I guess you could say up to Parramore and then on up the Bascom road. We stopped there at your granddaddy's and showed him what we had done. You ever hear of that?

Cox: Yes, sir, my dad and uncles have talked about it.

From there we went on up the old road near abouts to Bascom then on over to the Cannady place. When we got there we kicked him off the bumper and drug him on up there. The old man and old woman came out and was pretty mad with us. He kept saying that we had promised him he could do it, but we hadn't promised nobody nothing. (Name withheld) came out and shot a round of bullets into him but he was already dead. (Name withheld) cut off the little finger on his left hand too. Everybody that wanted to took a look and some of the kids poked him with sticks or kicked at him. Somebody then said that if old Flake wanted him so bad, we should take him on up there and give him to him. So we took him up to the courthouse and hung him in a tree right outside Flake's office. That's pretty much what we did.

Cox: How do you feel about it now?

Well, I don't think much on it. It just seems like it were something that happened but it don't seem so real nowadays. I mean I don't feel bad about it because he raped and killed that girl. There weren't no doubt about that. He were a bad man. A bad man.

Late summer 2010, Jackson County. A light rain was falling. The sign outside the Greenwood Chapel A.M.E. Church said WELCOME SMITH AND NEAL FAMILY. Up the road, under low-hanging clouds, inside a little club called Paradise, a family gathered. It was a strange reunion. Most of them had never met. They came from places like Caryville and Madison and Donalsonville, towns that adopted them after their parents and grandparents were chased away.

Claude Neal's nephew Orlando Williams had brought them together. He hoped a reunion, with barbecue ribs and a chance to talk about the story they've whispered about for generations, might bring some kind of closure. The Electric Slide and family secrets.

Neal's niece, Ruth McNair, 80, rode the Greyhound up from Tampa, the first time she had been on a bus since the 1950s. She sat in the front seat because now she could.

"I'm just so happy I don't know what to do," she said. "Somehow God took care of us. Who would have thought I'd ever be able to meet my family?"

Seeing each other made them realize what had been lost. It didn't take long for them to understand they had all been changed by the crime that had driven them apart.

"It don't ever get erased," McNair said.

When Claude Neal's brother Joseph was on his deathbed in 2001, he had a talk with his son-in-law. It was a quiet moment, and the old man began to cry. Long ago, he said, some white men were harassing him. They thought he looked familiar. Thought he looked like a Neal.

He told them he wasn't. To save his own life, he denied his name.

"He had carried that with him," said Jerrund Sheffield of Caryville, "for a long time."

Orlando Williams stood behind the turntables, headphones over his ears. The family he had never known danced and hugged into the night.

He wants to shake skeletons from closets. He has dedicated an hour a day for 25 years to getting answers. Who killed his uncle? Why was nothing done to stop it?

He was encouraged when President George W. Bush signed the Emmett Till Unsolved Civil Rights Crime Act of 2007, which authorized up to $13.5 million a year to investigate old racially motivated killings. But prosecutions are difficult. Witnesses die and memories fade and many of those crimes, no matter how awful, are never solved.

Even if the Department of Justice can't prosecute, agents deliver a report of their findings to the victims' families in an attempt to bring closure.

Williams is obsessed with exposing the truth. There were dozens of victims of the Committee of Six. Their crime chased entire bloodlines from Jackson County, tormented his elders and robbed him of his childhood.

The lynching broke his own mother.

"She was traumatized when her brother was killed," he said. "She went through total hell, and she put us through total hell."

She would leave her five children with relatives and disappear for months, sometimes years. She'd return out of guilt and whisk them off to some tiny house to try to make a home. When she was sober, she was okay. But she always slipped back into dark places.

She'd start talking about what the men did to her brother. She'd smoke Camels and drink moonshine. She'd hit and kick her daughters. She'd make the kids read the 23rd Psalm out loud while she drank and cried. "She just couldn't take what happened," Williams said.

They found her dead, face down on her bed, on Valentine's Day 1961. She had suffocated.

Orlando Williams was 14. After they took her away, he stood in the room where she died. He saw a calendar on the wall above her bed and an indentation on the mattress, the empty place where his mother had been.

The knock sounded official.

One afternoon in early August, Orlando Williams' wife peeked through the window of their house in Virginia and saw a man in a suit and tie standing at their door. The man flashed a badge and introduced himself as an agent with the FBI. Williams thought he was in trouble.

What did I do? he asked.

The agent said he was there to talk about the murder of Claude Neal.

The two men sat at Williams' kitchen table. The agent said a case had been opened and that the Justice Department intended to learn all it could. The agent took notes as Williams told him about his mother and his grandmother, shreds of stories of how a family was torn apart, and how it had come back together in search of justice.

The agent said the results of the investigation would be sent to a cold-case prosecutor, and that if the evidence showed that there was a prosecutable violation of any federal statutes, appropriate action would be taken. Names would be named.

When the agent left, Williams called Allie Mae to share the news that someone had finally listened, and that the rest was only a matter of time.

Ben Montgomery is an enterprise reporter for the Tampa Bay Times and founder of the narrative journalism site <u>Gangrey.com</u>. In 2010, he was a finalist for the Pulitzer Prize in local reporting for a series called "For Their Own Good," about abuse at Florida's oldest reform school. He lives in Tampa with his wife and children.

I DIDN'T WANT TO WRITE
CRIME PORN

an interview with Erik Larson
conducted by Donna Seaman

Hailed by the *New York Times* as "a master of the telling detail" who can take "an unlikely historical subject and [spin] it into gold," journalist turned narrative historian Erik Larson's dynamic books often capture an individual caught up in a pivotal historical moment. His first commercial success, *Isaac's Storm*, chronicled the massive Galveston hurricane of 1900—responsible for the deaths of as many as ten thousand people—as well as the story of the Texas weatherman, Isaac Cline, who utterly failed to predict the storm's potential strength, and the murder of businessman William Marsh Rice, the founder of Rice University in Houston, Texas.

Larson turned to the more sinister details of history in his subsequent book, *The Devil in the White City*. On one level an exploration of Chicago's 1893 World's Columbian Exposition, the book also tells the story of hotel-owner and serial killer H.H. Holmes, who lured unsuspecting attendees of the fair to his custom-built hotel equipped with acid vat, dissection table, and crematorium. An Edgar Award winner for best "fact crime" writing and a National Book Award finalist, *The Devil in the White City* stayed on the *New York Times* bestseller list for over three years. In his next book, *Thunderstruck*, Larson shadowed another notorious murderer, Hawley Harvey Crippen, whose ultimately futile attempts to evade Scotland Yard became an international source of fascination via Guglielmo Marconi's newly-invented wireless telegraph.

Larson's most recent book, *In the Garden of Beasts*, delves into the darkest period of the twentieth century: the rise of Adolf Hitler's

Third Reich as it was witnessed by the United States' unlikely ambassador, William E. Dodd, and his romantically intrepid daughter, Martha. An instant bestseller, the book's paperback release in May 2012 brought Larson back to Chicago, where senior editor for *Booklist* Donna Seaman caught up with him at a quiet, not-yet-open hotel restaurant to discuss topics ranging from the ethics of nonfiction to Larson's unusual coat of arms. The interview originally appeared in the Summer 2012 "True Crime" issue of *Creative Nonfiction* magazine.

SEAMAN: What did you love to read as a boy?

LARSON: It depends on the phase. I loved the Tom Swift series, and I actually loved Nancy Drew books. I think I read them all. And then I graduated pretty quickly to the Dumas books. I loved "The Three Musketeers." I loved "The Count of Monte Cristo." And when I was quite young, I got into reading Dickens. I'm not sure I really understood "Bleak House," but I thought it was great. I was not a voracious reader, though. I was more interested in drawing.

SEAMAN: Do you think your passion for drawing helped you develop your observational skills?

LARSON: You know, my glib answer is "no." But possibly. I mean, I've sworn to get back into drawing and painting. If you think about it, once you've spent a lot of time drawing, if you look at a building or a house, for example—and this is going to sound stupid—but you look closely at the interior framing of a window, and you see that window very differently than somebody else sees it. I'm looking at that window—I often find myself doing this—and I see the many lines that comprise the window frame. I actually count them sometimes. It's amazing how complex windows are. So that's a tiny example of how it could be the case. It can't hurt. It's got to go in the mix.

But in terms of detail, the thing that helped me more was that I got really lucky with my newspaper jobs, ending up pretty quickly at The Wall Street Journal in the days when you could spend a lot of time writing short pieces. I always tried to do the funny pieces. You can't be funny; you have to let the details be funny for you. So you have to collect the details. That gave me a really good eye for what details worked and what details didn't work. Because what it comes down to with the sort of historical writing I do is finding those little details that make a scene come to life, that make a scene tighter. It doesn't take a lot. I think sometimes just one sentence can really do it.

SEAMAN: It seems you lost patience with newspaper journalism.

LARSON: Yeah, well, first of all, I got into it totally by accident and for the worst motives. I studied history at the University of Pennsylvania, but that's because the history professors were some of the best. I got lured into Russian history, in particular, by a fantastic professor. I got so drawn into Russian history by this guy that it changed my whole college plan. Suddenly I was Russian history, Russian language, Russian literature. I had intended to go to law school; then I took a business law course, just to see what it was like, and I realized: no way. I couldn't get through the reading. I hated it. I hated it with every ounce of my body. So I worked in publishing for a while, like a year. I was an editorial assistant, which meant on my lunch hour I would clean my boss's office and desk. I had to make her telephone calls because she did not know how to operate a punch phone; she couldn't deal with long-distance calls.

Then I saw the movie "All the President's Men," and I just loved it. I thought to myself, that's what I've got to do. So I went to journalism school at Columbia University, and I got my first newspaper job as a reporter at the Bucks County Courier Times in Levittown, Pa. It was a good first job. I covered the cops on Saturday nights, and then I wrote features the rest of the time— long features, Sunday specials. So that was good for getting me started in long-form journalistic writing. And I got really lucky there because I was passed over for a promotion. I got so pissed off that I sent my resume to all my friends in the business. One was at The Wall Street Journal, and I was hired.

I loved The Wall Street Journal for the time I was there. I loved the writing, and I enjoyed the community of writers. Writing was "it." Anybody could do business, but if you could write, they wanted you. Then the emphasis began to change markedly to hard-news coverage of business. You could still do features, but it was no longer the case that you could make a career doing the kind of stories I did. I was never in it for the business writing. I never liked writing about corporate assholes. That's what it came down to, and I was having to do too much of that. So I was ready to give journalism up. But I suppose if, you know, The New Yorker had stepped up and said, "We want you as a staff writer," I would have stayed in it.

SEAMAN: So you gave up a secure gig. Then what?

LARSON: Then I got married. After a blind date and three broken engagements. So dumb luck became a factor. Then we made a huge mistake. I don't know if you've ever seen those stress scores—you know, for what causes over-the-top stress. We did precisely what's on that list. After we got married, I left my job. I had been working, at that point, at the San Francisco bureau. We left San Francisco to go to Baltimore. So everything was in upheaval. I was so adrift. I totally lost what I refer to as my cocktail identity. Do you know what I mean? People ask, "What do you do?" I could say, "I write for The Wall Street Journal." I lost that. So I had nothing. I had no friends in Baltimore; I had no identity. It was actually very hard.

So to keep my name out there, I started doing freelance pieces for whatever magazines would take my stuff because I discovered, early on, that magazines had a prejudice against news reporters. I wrote some stuff for Harper's and for The Atlantic, and that was very satisfying. But at one point, I also realized that given the amount of work I was putting into each stupid little story, I could probably write a book. Didn't it make more sense to write something that would stay on the shelf for longer than 24 hours or a week? This was a gradual realization, and I vividly remember the day it came to a head. I had a contract with a magazine (that you would recognize, but I'm not going to tell you what it is), and the editor was a very good editor. And this contract paid the bills with an annual fee; plus, they paid a certain amount on top for each piece. But one day, I'm on the phone with my editor, talking about ideas. We talked a lot. I was sinking to my desk as I was talking to him, and I fell asleep. But here's the thing: I woke up a few seconds later, and he was still talking. He had no clue. So after that conversation, I thought, "This has to stop." That's when I wrote my first book proposal, which became my first book, "The Naked Consumer," which nobody read. And nobody bought. If that had been my first book today, my career would have been over. Because nobody gives you a second chance now with new books.

SEAMAN: The full title is "The Naked Consumer: How Our Private Lives Become Public Commodities," and you were prompted to write it by the avalanche of targeted junk mail you and your wife began receiving as new parents even before your first child was born. It came out in 1992, making you a pioneering observer of how companies invade our privacy to advertise their products.

LARSON: Yes, I was very early on the subject of how companies spy on consumers, writing about it at a time when people were not paying much attention. I thought that book was going to be the next "The Hidden Persuaders," which came out in the 1950s, before my generation, and was hugely successful. "The Naked Consumer" sure was not. It received zero support from the publisher, zero publicity. It was a nightmare experience. But I did love doing the book. It satisfied a lot of things that hard-core journalism did not.

SEAMAN: If you revisited that subject now, you would have to tackle an enormous amount of high-tech and corporate information about online surveillance and data-mining and advertising strategies.

LARSON: I would not even be tempted to revisit it now. I really liked that first book, but there was no story. That's where I went wrong. I started evolving toward story in my second book, "Lethal Passage: The Story of a Gun." Funny enough, given the subject, my youngest daughter told her friends I wrote "Lethal Weapon," and they were like, "Wow!"

SEAMAN: "Lethal Passage" is another remarkably prescient work. You were the first to trace the journey of a certain handgun model as a way to illuminate the sources of gun violence in our society. The criminal use of handguns remains a complex and tragic problem.

LARSON: The sheer number of illegal guns used in crimes is not getting worse, but I don't think the numbers tell the story. What happened with that book was that I was living in Baltimore, where there was a lot of crime. The show "The Wire," unfortunately, gets it right. It was in the mid-1980s, and there was a real surge in drive-by shootings. I was always struck by the fact that 13- and 14-year-old kids had these sophisticated handguns. At the time, nobody ever wrote about where the guns came from, how the kids got the guns. It was completely absent from the story. I just wanted to find out how these things get into these kids' hands.

So, I started looking for a case and pitched it to The Atlantic Monthly. I wrote about the model that had become the most popular crime gun. I traced its history, and the history of a boy and a school, and how he and the gun came together. I thought it was a very good piece, and The Atlantic did, too. I was so worried about that piece. It must have been about 30,000 words, and I remember telling my wife, "I'm so depressed. They're not going to buy it. It's too long, but I can't cut anything. It's all important to me." So I sent it in, and 48 hours later, I get a call from the editor-in-chief of The Atlantic, and he says, "We really like this piece. We're going to run the whole thing, but if you can find any places to cut, we would love it." So they ran it as a cover story, this gigantic piece; it was great.

I thought, I have all this stuff; I'm going to turn it into a book. It wasn't successful financially; it didn't become a bestseller, but it was successful critically. And more importantly, it really helped change, for a time, the gun landscape. It really did. Police departments kept calling me to say thank you for giving them a way to look at this, to deal with it. In the Justice Department, somebody I can't name would bounce ideas off me for what needed to be done. All this was reversed in a heartbeat by John Ashcroft. Everything. If there's a gun problem today, it's on John Ashcroft's shoulders. Nothing has been done to counteract the trend. But it will happen. Something will, at last, get people's attention, and things will change for the better.

SEAMAN: You wrote two very topical books about current trends and issues, with a growing interest in telling a story. What inspired you to return to your love of history and start writing narrative nonfiction about the past?

LARSON: On some level, I knew that what I wanted to do was to write narrative nonfiction in order to tell true stories from the past. The way it came about: I had read a novel, in 1994, "The Alienist" by Caleb Carr. It's about a serial killer in old New York in the 1890s. What I loved about it was the way he evoked that era in New York. I came away feeling like I'd lived there. So I started thinking: Wouldn't it be interesting to write a nonfiction book about a historical murder? So I very deliberately started looking into historical murders. I actually came across Holmes, the serial killer in "The Devil in the White City," fairly early on, but I didn't want to write about him at the time because I didn't want to write crime porn. I was looking for something along the lines of the film "Gosford Park." I came across a murder that involved William Marsh Rice, who founded Rice University. He was murdered in New York in 1900 by his valet and an unscrupulous attorney. And there was a hurricane connection to this story. I got enthralled with this hurricane because I've been a hurricane junky from way back, growing up on Long Island.

At this point, I had a new agent, David Black, who was crucial to steering me onto the right path. He really was. He has a tremendous, instinctive sense of narrative. You know how it works with nonfiction: You do a proposal, and then they say yea or nay, and then you get an advance and go off to do the research. So I submitted a proposal for a book about the hurricane. My agent liked the idea broadly, but he said, "You need to do something more." He wanted a stronger story. I went back and did some more research and gave him another proposal, a little closer, but not quite there for him. He's renowned as a proposal Nazi. So I kept going and going and going. I must have gone through eight drafts of this damn proposal. I was so ready to dump him, and he knew it. He wasn't going to push me too far. Finally, we got down to the last, essentially typographical, nuanced edit, and he said, "We're ready." So we sent it out. People did love it. We sold it to Crown. A very nice offer. It was great. That was my first step into narrative history.

SEAMAN: The writing in "Isaac's Storm" is so rich.

LARSON: It's my wife's favorite of my books.

With "The Devil in the White City," we went through the whole process again. David was instrumental in getting me to concentrate on what makes a powerful story: Where is the conflict? Where is the suspense? We're not talking about making things up; we're talking about where the story is in real life. Who are your characters? Find the right characters, and you'll have your story.

SEAMAN: The stories you've chosen involve the worst of crimes. What draws you to tales of murder?

LARSON: I don't necessarily hunt for dark subjects. It just happens that the darker events of history are often the most compelling.

SEAMAN: Are social and moral concerns important to you when you're selecting subjects to write about?

LARSON: Not really. I simply look for whatever historical event or situation offers the best opportunity for nonfiction storytelling.

SEAMAN: Is grappling with evil a great challenge?

LARSON: As a rule, no. However, I did find that steeping myself in Nazi pathology for four to five years took a toll on my psyche, conjuring in me a kind of low-grade depression. I'm happy to say, however, that once the book was done, the depression lifted completely.

SEAMAN: Does hubris fascinate you?

LARSON: Hubris does fascinate me. Excess confidence can often lead men to do very interesting things, often at great cost to everyone else. Throughout history, hubris and tragedy have been frequent companions.

SEAMAN: Let's talk about research. You've said you want your nonfiction books to read like novels, and they do because you bring every scene and detail to such vivid life. How do you acquire all the requisite information, and how do you utilize it?

LARSON (laughing): Yeah, that's the challenge. First of all, I have the luxury of being able to do this full-time. So I can spend a 40-hour workweek doing nothing but reading books and traveling. I get pretty well-funded, so I can go the distance. To some extent now, you can do a lot of the same if you're not as well-funded because of online resources, although I find online research so tedious I could scream.

SEAMAN: So there's archival research and out-in-the-world research.

LARSON: Right. The way it starts, for me, is you read the broad stuff, the big survey histories and so forth. You kind of circle in, getting closer and closer to the nub of things by going into what I call the intimate histories—the published diaries, documents, letters—and all the while you're looking for the right characters. Then you have an idea of who these characters might be; you come down to a half-dozen characters, one of whom could be central to the story. Then it's time to go to the archives. The Library of Congress is stop one. The manuscript division. It's a bad thing to plan too far and with too much detail about how much you need and where you should go. There's no substitute for parachuting in and flailing. Inertia is a powerful force in my life. I can put off anything for a long time. Just ask my wife.

SEAMAN: There's always something else to read.

LARSON: Absolutely. So then you go to the archives. I love it. I love going through boxes filled with files that are full of stuff. You never know what you're going to find in the next folder. The problem with online research is you always know what's coming. Somebody else has selected what's online. The serendipity effect is crucial, finding things that are potentially really valuable to you. Say, an envelope with nothing in it, nothing associated with it, could be valuable because it might have so-and-so's return address on it. Or it might confirm a contact. Little detective-like things. I just love those. In the case of "In the Garden of Beasts," Martha Dodd, the central character, has 70 linear feet of documents, letters, writings. The first couple of files in the first box, if I remember correctly, were calling cards that she collected. Hundreds of calling cards. They were common currency in that period; they were very important to the ebb and flow of social life. So here they are, and I'm going through them, and here's the calling card for Hermann Göring. I'm holding this calling card that Martha held at one time, that Göring held and gave to her. There's this little electric charge that comes from stuff like that, and that's the fun that keeps you going.

My favorite find for "In the Garden of Beasts" was two locks of Carl Sandburg's hair I came across in one of the files. What the—?! It was very cool. I knew that Martha and he had an affair—later in the files, I found material that definitely supports that fact—but I couldn't get my mind around her having an affair with an older guy. She's 24, and Sandburg's 50-something. But there are the locks of hair; it's true. You need those little discoveries.

With "The Devil in the White City," so much of the stuff I came across I found hard to believe. I'm not even talking about the serial killer part; I'm talking about the World's Columbian Exposition and who participated in it. One thing I didn't know about when I proposed the book was the fact that the mayor, Carter Henry Harrison, was shot and killed the night before the elaborately planned closing ceremony, which was cancelled. What the hell? So you look at these critical moments. The thing that stood out in the files in the Chicago Historical Society was the evidence tag for the gun that was used to kill Harrison. Of course, no one knows where the gun is. That's the missing element. So it's the tactile contact with the materials.

And, of course, you have to go to the places and get a sense of what's there, even though there may not be much left. I didn't know Chicago before I started writing "The Devil in the White City." Suddenly, I'm here doing this research for this book, and one of the things that leapt out at me was the power of the lake in defining the city. Not just how the day looks—the light in summer, say—but the shifting moods of the lake at any one time. That became very important to know and to see. I like to think the lake is a character, a quiet character. I think it would be a different book without my having seen the lake. Subtle, intangible things matter.

When I went to Berlin for "In the Garden of Beasts," I discovered the really attachable thing, which I think somehow infuses the entire book, when I was just walking around, looking for addresses. I found the location, but the Dodds' house is no longer there. Believe it or not, it's an empty lot with a fence around it. How strange is that? It's prime territory; what's going on there? But what I realized, in a miniature epiphany, was that everything was in walking distance from that spot. Walking distance to Gestapo headquarters. Walking distance to Hitler. You could walk across the park to the Reichstag. Suddenly, I realized that all the action took place around the eastern quarter of Tiergarten, the park. The location is very important to know. It played a key role in the ultimate choice of the title: "The garden of beasts" is the literal translation of "Tiergarten." I learned, also, that it was one of the few places you could go and feel safe from surveillance, and that Ambassador Dodd used the park for conversations with diplomats. It became very important to the writing to know that all this was there. Things magically popped up. Then I could see Dodd walking out the door. You've got to have moments like that. If the story doesn't come alive for you, it's not going to come alive for your readers.

SEAMAN: You're a master at conjuring the physical worlds your characters occupy, and you also try to get inside their heads.

LARSON: Hmm. Be careful with that . . .

SEAMAN: Ah, well, I have that impression.

LARSON: Right. You have that impression. I know this is not what you're getting at, but let me preface this by saying I get a kick out of people saying to me, "You must have made this up. Because this is dialogue. How could you know this?" I put this note in every one of my books, and everyone ignores it:

"Anything between quotation marks is from a written document. All dialogue that appears in this book is taken verbatim from the sources in which it initially appeared."

So what I'm getting at is that it is the reader who brings the magic, I am convinced. I'm trying to lay out all those little vivid details that might spark the imagination. The reader comes to this with his or her vast experience of reading novels and everything else, and puts those dots together. It's kind of like removing the noise from a digital photograph, so that instead of pixels, you have this smooth thing. So the reader is providing the sense that it's dialogue when it's not.

I think the same thing happens when you say I go into their states of mind. I will only propose what somebody is thinking or not thinking if I have something concrete in hand that makes that clear. If I have a letter that Dodd wrote to Roosevelt saying, "These people are crazy," I'm totally justified in saying Dodd thought they were crazy. But you absolutely cannot make that stuff up out of whole cloth because then you pass into another realm entirely.

SEAMAN: You have written novels. Are you ever tempted to go back to writing fiction? Perhaps to take a break from all this rigor?

LARSON: You know, when I left San Francisco to go to Baltimore in the devil's bargain—my wife is a physician, and she was offered a great job at Johns Hopkins—I intended to work on novels. And while I enjoyed it, there's something about this sort of writing that I find very satisfying. Part of it is the adventure story that I get involved in by going places. The challenge of finding the best stuff. It suits an element of my personality. I'm very compulsive. Partly, it's easier; you know, you've got to go with what you've got. If you find the story and you get enough details, you can tell a good story. There's a great paradox with fiction. If I tried to write a novel in which I proposed that the daughter of the American ambassador was sleeping with the first chief of the Gestapo, no one would believe it. But because it happened— wow!—this is interesting. I really like that. Also, I don't think I have the sensibility to be a novelist. To be a novelist, you've got to do really rotten things to your characters. You've got to paralyze them; you've got to give them cancer—all these awful things. I don't have it in me. But it's not to say I won't do it sometime in the future. I might try it again.

SEAMAN: What sort of notes do you take in the field and when you're going through library and archival material? And how do you organize and work with all the information you gather?

LARSON: First of all, I don't believe in coming and spending six months in a city in a hotel, reading everything as I go. My M.O. is to read far enough into a document or book to think, "This could be valuable," and then I photocopy it. Or, today, I take a digital photograph. So I make hundreds and hundreds of copies and bring them home. Some will be worthless, but it's still cost-effective. Then I find the highlights in those things, and I index each document, and each collection of documents, with little tabs, so I know that's where the best quotes are. And as I'm doing this, I create a chronology, in which everything is tied to specific times and days. The result, before I start to write, is about 100 single-spaced pages covering everything day-by-day-by-day, with little references to each of the indexes of the copied documents. So it might say "Tiergarten," and then there would be the name of the source and a Roman numeral, and then just a couple of notes about that particular quote, enough to make me remember it. I know exactly where it is; I can go right to it.

This detailed chronology is my secret weapon. Because chronological order is the key to any story. If you simply relate a historical event in chronological order, you have done much more than most historians do. I'm appalled when I read books about things I'm interested in—the Third Reich or whatever—by how many times historians just don't tell it in the order that it happened. By how much they jump around. It's so weird. Chronological order is the most important thing. So I have, essentially, a default outline for my entire project. The major events will declare themselves because that's where the most information is. So when I go through this chronology, there are obvious points where a chapter is going to be, and there are obvious places where I can see that if I end this scene there and jump here, that's good foreshadowing.

SEAMAN: You have created this powerful two-track approach to telling complex stories, in which you do end each chapter with a dramatic pause and a forerunner of what is to come.

LARSON: But they're very natural breaks. I'm not just dicking around. My chronology says, "This happened then," and, "Meanwhile, this is going on here, and it will influence the outcome of that scene." That's very powerful.

SEAMAN: It enables you to present amazing juxtapositions and also a rich sense of simultaneity.

LARSON: And you never know that those things are simultaneous until you do a chronology, and you realize, "Oh, that's the same day." Who knew? That's what I love. Until I do the chronology, I never know where those little serendipitous overlaps are, but they always appear.

SEAMAN: You become fluent in these materials.

LARSON: Well, I do and I don't. I have what I think is a serious flaw. I have a really limited memory. It's always been the case. With each book, it's very hard for me, afterward, to do interviews about it because I've forgotten most of it. So this process, this chronology, is really a way of compensating for my lack of an ability to memorize detail, although I am very good at conceptual recollection. So that's the way the chronology is vital to me, to spark the recollections and to help me make vivid the conceptual things.

The memory problem goes way back. I love to play the piano, but I cannot memorize pieces. I can't. I consider myself to be very musical. I'm very good at improvising. But I can't remember lyrics. I could not sing a single song for you. Except "Row, Row, Row Your Boat." I could do that. So, it's an elaborate system to compensate for my failure.

SEAMAN: Speaking about memory, and about documentation, I wonder what you think about the future of research? If all of us are communicating in emails and Tweets, what will writers interested in excavating the facts about our time have to work with in the future?

LARSON: Well, that is a very interesting question. In a hundred years, when people are writing about now, they will have Tweets. Twitter gave a huge trove of Tweets to the National Archives. This could be of immense value in terms of providing a sense of currency to an event. You know, Tweet, Tweet, Tweet—sort of like telegrams once did. But it will be tougher to conduct deep research, especially because people don't write long, detailed letters anymore. So, we'll see what happens. But I'm glad I've got letters to rely on. And documents.

SEAMAN: Are you at all concerned about the digitization of books? The changes e-books are bringing to publishing, maybe also to writing itself and reading?

LARSON: I don't know what's going to happen, obviously. But I can tell you that with "In the Garden of Beasts," half the sales were e-books. My attitude is that people will always want a good story. They will always consume good stories. And as long as there are people around who will produce them, there will be a market for them. It is interesting that there are such cutthroat battles underway over e-books, with high stakes. A lot of money is being spent to try to capture readers, stories and books; that shows that nobody thinks e-books are going to go away. The question is, who's going to get the profit from that? Things are changing. J.K. Rowling is selling her books now without digital rights. She can do that. She's powerful. You cannot buy an e-book of hers, of Harry Potter, unless it's through her store. But you can use her e-books anywhere, on any device. So things are in flux. I am sorry for bookstores; they're getting hammered by this. But I do think the best bookstores will endure.

SEAMAN: On your website, you have a logo with a pencil and . . .

LARSON: Two Oreo cookies.

SEAMAN: Is that your coat of arms?

LARSON: That is my coat of arms. A young woman suggested that I come up with a logo. So I told my Web designer that I wanted a logo and suggested Oreos and pencils or something. And God bless her, she came up with the perfect logo. I love that logo. What it relates to is the fact that when I'm working—and now it's every day that I'm researching or writing—my day starts very early. I make some coffee, half decaf, half black, and I have one Oreo cookie. A bad day is two Oreo cookies. And the pencil is Ticonderoga Number Two. The best pencil ever made. Ticonderoga Number Two Soft. I use those to write passages that are particularly difficult. Using a computer is great; you can spew and rewrite a paragraph 10 times. But there are passages that are too important, too complex, to do that. I have yellow legal pads; I can even tell you which kind: yellow legal pads with a reinforced back made by Tops. So I sharpen my pencils, and what I find is that it almost invariably comes relatively easily because when you write longhand, you've got to think about it before you write, because the manual effort is significant. It matters. That really helps.

A senior editor for Booklist, Donna Seaman is a recipient of the Studs Terkel Humanities Service Award. She created the anthology "In Our Nature: Stories of Wildness," and her author interviews are collected in "Writers on the Air: Conversations about Books."

CREDITS